George Washington

AN AMERICAN ICON

☆ ☆ ☆

The Eighteenth-Century Graphic Portraits

George Washington
AN AMERICAN ICON
The Eighteenth-Century Graphic Portraits

BY

WENDY C. WICK

Curator of Prints, National Portrait Gallery

with an introductory essay by

LILLIAN B. MILLER

Editor, Charles Willson Peale Papers,
Smithsonian Institution

THE SMITHSONIAN INSTITUTION TRAVELING EXHIBITION SERVICE

AND THE

NATIONAL PORTRAIT GALLERY

SMITHSONIAN INSTITUTION

1982

A BARRA FOUNDATION BOOK

Introduction and illustrations © by The Barra Foundation Inc., 1982

Published by the Smithsonian Institution Traveling Exhibition Service (SITES) and the National Portrait Gallery, Smithsonian Institution, with the generous support of The Barra Foundation. SITES is a program activity of the Smithsonian Institution that organizes and circulates exhibitions on art, history, and science to institutions in the United States and abroad.

Library of Congress Cataloging in Publication Data

Wick, Wendy C., 1950–
   George Washington, an American icon.

   "A Barra Foundation book."
   Bibliography: p. 173
   Includes index.
   1. Washington, George, 1732–1799—Portraits. 2. Portrait prints—United States. I. Smithsonian Institution, Traveling Exhibition Service. II. Smithsonian Institution. National Portrait Gallery. III. Title.
   N7628.W3W5   769′.423′0973   81–607889
   ISBN 0–86528–015–0   AACR2

   ISBN 0–86528–014–2 (pbk.)

Distributed by the University Press of Virginia
Box 3068, University Station, Charlottesville,
Virginia 22903

Cover:
Mezzotint by Charles Willson Peale, 1780. National Portrait Gallery [11].

Title page illustration:
Engraving by Saint-Mémin, 1800.
National Portrait Gallery [74].

Book design by Gerard A. Valerio, Bookmark Studio

Edited by Diana Menkes

Composed in Baskerville Linotype by Service Composition, Baltimore, Maryland

Printed on Mohawk Superfine by Garamond/Pridemark Press, Baltimore, Maryland

Contents

☆　　☆　　☆

Foreword

☆ ☆ ☆

The Smithsonian Institution Traveling Exhibition Service (SITES) is pleased to join the National Portrait Gallery in presenting *George Washington, An American Icon: The Eighteenth-Century Graphic Portraits.* This work focuses for the first time on the eighteenth-century portrait prints of our first President. We are particularly pleased to assist in the dissemination of this scholarly new research which has been so thoroughly conducted by Wendy Wick, curator of prints at the National Portrait Gallery. SITES is indebted to Ms. Wick and her capable assistant, Barbara Bither, for their untiring effort on behalf of this book and the exhibition. Many on the National Portrait Gallery staff have also given much support in all phases of planning

The book and exhibition would not be possible without the support of The Barra Foundation, Inc. Its assistance and enthusiasm for the project are greatly appreciated. Our gratitude also extends to all lenders of material for the book and the exhibition. Many have generously given their time and expertise.

Several members of the staff at SITES have played indispensable roles. The exhibition coordinator, Nancy Davis, greatly facilitated and contributed to the total concept of the project, and Anne Gossett added her expertise in the advanced stages of planning. Andrea Stevens, publications officer, shared her exceptional talent as knowledgeable advisor and manager of the publication. Deborah Lerme, education coordinator; Eileen Harakal, public information officer; Emily Dyer, registrar; Mary Sheridan, assistant registrar; and Lori Dempsey, exhibitions assistant; are to be especially thanked for their assistance.

As this book and exhibition celebrate the 250th anniversary of George Washington's birth, we hope they will heighten appreciation of the eighteenth century and encourage further scholarship in this field.

PEGGY A. LOAR
Director, SITES

Preface

☆   ☆   ☆

George Washington is a familiar face to curators of the National Portrait Gallery. Weekly, it seems, we are presented with portraits of Washington for analysis or authentication. He comes to us in the form of paintings, sculpture, engravings, chromolithographs, tin trays, snuff boxes, even daguerreotypes—a photographic process not invented until a full generation after Washington's death. We spend a great deal of time trying to make sense of these images both to ourselves and to the public.

Many of the inquiries are about prints. Most of the letters come from expectant owners convinced they have an original portrait of incalculable national importance and financial value. They are inevitably disappointed to discover that their pictures are of some historic interest but little monetary worth. The difficulty they have judging which prints are important documents of our culture is understandable. Thousands of printed portraits of Washington in different media were produced between the eighteeth century and the twentieth, and the glut resulted in inevitable repetition and aesthetic degeneration. Sorting through such a quantity of material to make artistic and historical judgments is in itself a monumental task. It is no wonder that the most current catalogue of all the engraved portraits of Washington was published in 1904, and little serious study of any of these images has been attempted.

When an exhibition and catalogue on prints of Washington was suggested, I felt challenged to focus on some small segment of this enormous output to see what these images could tell us about the culture that produced them and what they communicated about this historic figure. Since it had not been done before, it seemed reasonable to concentrate on the prints of Washington published during his own day. In dismissing the colorful, commercial prints of the nineteenth century, I wondered what was left, where these likenesses came from, how prevalent and accurate they were, and how Washington's own contemporaries viewed their Commander in Chief and their President. Without the sentimental lithographs and anecdotal steel engraving of later generations, the eighteenth-century portraits began to seem fresh and exciting: a small mezzotint, a magazine frontispiece, a crudely cut almanac cover, which, perhaps for the first time, presented the image of Washington to one of his countrymen.

My goal, then, was to isolate and document all the printed portraits of Washington made in America through 1800. Inevitably there have been some inadvertent omissions, but I have attempted to be inclusive. In order to get the full picture of what was published, I wanted to include not only separately published engravings, but book and magazine illustrations and relief cuts printed in or on broadsides, almanacs, music sheets, and primers. European prints are not included in the catalogue but are illustrated and discussed generally in the essay for the purpose of comparison.

With so many Washington portraits unsigned and undated, it was not an easy task to isolate the eighteenth-century pieces. In general, a print has not been included unless there is firm evidence that it was published in 1800 or before. In order to locate the illustrations, I went through all the Evans American Bibliography Readex cards, magnified the pages that had pictures rather than text, and then tracked down those imprints with portrait illustrations. (This research was part of a larger study I had started on eighteenth-century American portrait prints.) The omissions inherent in the filming of the Evans bibliography may therefore be reflected in this volume. Lost editions of the ephemeral primers, almanacs, and broadsides turn up with frequency, and some of them undoubtedly have small cuts of Washington. With these exceptions, however, I hope to have included all the American publications through 1800 in which each illustration appears.

Excluded from this study are scenes and cartoons. There is some interesting Washington material in this rejected group, such as the print of *Federal Hall, The Seat of Congress* by Amos Doolittle, showing Washington's first inauguration, and a 1788 almanac illustration, *Representation of the Federal Chariot*, depicting thirteen men pullng Washington and Franklin toward ratification of the constitution. This type of image, however, must be left for others to study. There are many crude prints in the catalogue, and to some extent I found them particularly interesting because they have been so long ignored. However, there was one group of cuts that seemed too crude and insignificant to qualify as Washington portraiture: alphabet cuts in American primers in 1799 and 1800. During these years, instead of the traditional whale illustrating the letter **W,** a miniature stick figure was substituted in a number of primers (such as *The New-England Primmer Improved,* New York: Naphtali Judah, 1799) accompanied by an appropriate verse, such as "By Washington, Great deeds were done." Reproducing several different stick figures of Washington did not seem to serve any purpose. Occasionally, an American imprint will be illustrated by an English engraving that has been imported and bound into the edition. These are not considered American prints and have also been excluded.

Since this volume grew out of a larger project, it is difficult to separate the assistance I received in my research on Washington from the cooperation and advice extended to me on many visits to Americana collections. I can solve this problem only by extending my thanks in a general way to various assistants and volunteers who have worked with me in the past few years and to the competent staffs of the following institutions where I have done research: American Antiquarian Society, Boston Museum of Fine Arts, Massachusetts Historical Society, Essex Institute, Boston Public Library, Houghton Library at Harvard University, Worcester Art Museum, John Carter Brown Library, Rhode Island Historical Society, Connecticut Historical Society, Yale University Art Gallery, New Haven Colony Historical Society, New York Public Library, New-York Historical Society, Metropolitan Museum of Art, Library Company of Philadelphia, Historical Society of Pennsylvania, Free Library of Philadelphia, Independence National Historical Park, Winterthur Museum, Library of Congress, Mount Vernon, Huntington Library. Of particular assistance during my research on this project, I must single out Georgia Bumgardner, Judy Larson, Karen Papineau, Elizabeth Roth, Robert Rainwater, David Kiehl, Peter Parker, Gordon Marshall, Ken Finkel, Christine Meadows, John Cushing, Wendy Shadwell, Peter Van Wingen, Beverly Orlove, and, at the National Portrait Gallery, Ellen Miles, Robert Stewart, Monroe Fabian, Linda Neumaier, Margaret Christman, Lillian Miller, and the staff of our library.

I am extremely grateful to the fine staff of the Smithsonian Institution Traveling Exhibition Service, who has published the catalogue and is organizing the tour of the show. Of the many SITES employees who have participated, Nancy Davis deserves particular thanks. She has been a remarkably efficient, conscientious, and enthusiastic coordinator, overseeing the many details of the project with skill and sensitivity. I am also indebted to Anne Gossett for her assistance in planning for the tour.

The production of the book has been expertly guided by the SITES publications coordinator, Andrea Stevens, who enlisted the considerable talents of editor Diana Menkes and designer Gerard Valerio. On our own staff at the National Portrait Gallery, many people have provided invaluable assistance. I want to mention Harold Pfister, the acting director; Nello Marconi, the designer of the exhibition, and his assistant, Albert Elkins; as well as Suzanne Jenkins, Beverly Cox, Frances Wein, Sandra Westin, and Christine Smith. To Barbara Bither, my assistant, who ordered all the photographs for the book and cheerfully took on many extra tasks, and to Marvin Sadik, the former director of the Gallery, who first approved the idea and read the manuscript, I am especially grateful.

The lenders to the exhibition have been particualry generous and cooperative in making their prints available to us. These institutions and individuals are mentioned in the checklist of the exhibition at the back of this volume. Finally, neither the exhibition nor the book would have been possible without Robert L. McNeil, a Commissioner of the National Portrait Gallery and President of The Barra Foundation, who first suggested a Washington show and who has provided considerable support throughout the project.

WCW

Introduction

☆ ☆ ☆

LILLIAN B. MILLER

The year 1800 found America in deep mourning. Just two weeks before the dawn of the new century, on December 14, 1799, the nation's foremost hero had died. Legendary while still alive, in death George Washington continued to accumulate legendary qualities: the dying hero had recognized the mortal nature of his illness, accepted death without complaint, and died without fear. As he died, so had he lived: stoically, courageously, aware. All the republican values that the country identified with its national mission—selflessness, benevolence, prudence, reason, self-discipline—were embodied in its hero. The saga of Washington, begun while he was still a young and unseasoned military leader, after his death became inextricably bound with the meaning of America.

The transformation of Washington into a national icon took place in literature during the Revolutionary period,[1] when the Congress, seeking a military leader to help achieve a peaceful settlement of the country's controversy with Great Britain, elected the Virginian Commander in Chief of the continental forces gathering in Cambridge, Massachusetts. By this act Washington was placed in the forefront of the developing nation's attention and made the symbol of the unity that was so much desired but still so difficult to achieve. The task facing the revolutionists in America was to make what they wrought significant, to prove that the effort had not been in vain. In the image of Washington created during the war and expanded during the years of peace that followed, American writers found all the properties required for a unique symbol of the national purpose.

Obviously, each age endows its heroes with its own values, hopes, and expectations; and in its unconscious imagination it establishes the symbolism needed for validating its assumptions. What Washington's contemporaries saw in him was an image of virtuous leadership to which all Americans, whatever their region or class, could be rallied. When, for instance, the Supreme Executive Council of Pennsylvania voted in 1779 a resolution requesting Washington to sit for his portrait to Charles Willson Peale, it justified its commission with an expression of the need to "excite others to tread in the same glorious & disinterested Steps which lead to public happiness and private honor." [2]

Although the requirements of revolution defined Washington as a hero, Washington himself, in both his physical and moral presence, provided the basic ingredients for the heroizing process.

The notes for this essay begin on page 168.

Virginia Congressman and later Chief Justice John Marshall wrote, in what became the standard biography of Washington after his death, of Washington's impressive image, dignity, restrained demeanor, noble expression, and distinguished air. He was "tall, upright, and well-made," John Bell wrote in 1800. Other writers noted his towering frame of over six feet, which "straight as an Indian" allowed him dominance over all men. The "solidity" of his physique conveyed an impression of strength and stamina corroborated by "strong, manly and command-ing" features and thoughtful, sometimes "penetrating" blue eyes which "on great occasions [be-came] remarkably lively." Like the Roman heroes whom Washington himself so much admired, his features were classical, and when combined with a natural gravity and a "reserved and serious" temper, they created an impression of dignity, nobility, and "equanimity" that assured "profound respect, and cordial esteem. He seemed born to command his fellow man," Bell concluded.[3]

The impression of Washington's great physical strength and energy extended to his mental and moral condition. He was a man capable of undertaking "everything on a great scale, propor-tioned to his great and comprehensive mind." Just as his body was "robust, his constitution vigorous," so did he possess strong judgments, "a large proportion of common sense and a solid command of himself." His physical gracefulness indicated moral balance, his serious mien ex-pressed "determined resolution," and his entire "exterior suggested to every beholder the idea of strength. . . ." Although Thomas Jefferson found "his colloquial talents . . . not above mediocrity," others considered his reticence a quiet strength. All these characteristics were much admired by eighteenth-century Americans. They promised a leader of balanced judgment, rationality, and prudence—exactly the kind of man capable of leading a middle-class revolution to a successful conclusion and helping the states establish themselves as a viable republic.[4]

Washington's height and vigorous constitution were attributed to the American environment. The physician and historian David Ramsay believed that Washington's physical strength was the result of America's "mountain air, abundant exercise in the open country, the wholesome toils of the chase, and the delightful scenes of rural life." His experiences on the American frontier ac-counted for his military expertise, but Nature accounted for his noble stature. Nature also in-fluenced his noble character, and both stature and character became, as John Adams wrote in 1783, "an exemplification of the American character." [5]

The facts of Washington's life that the eighteenth-century biographer selected as important enough to be emphasized were also designed to invest Washington with special significance. In all his adventures he was favored by the gods. Even Washington believed that "the miraculous care of Providence . . . protected me from beyond all human expectation." [6] Beginning with his mission to the Indians and the French in the Ohio Valley in 1753, the eighteenth-century narra-tive of Washington's rise to greatness took him through the disastrous battle of Fort Necessity in 1754 and the death of General Edward Braddock following his defeat at Monongahela. An aide-de-camp to the British general at this time, Washington had two horses shot from under him and four bullets tear through his clothing, but under "the miraculous care of Providence," he emerged unscathed and triumphant, capable, despite illness and fatigue, of leading the disarrayed army in an orderly retreat. In 1758, during the French and Indian War, Washington rode between two Virginia columns panicked into firing at each other instead of the enemy. Striking up the soldiers' guns with his sword to prevent a wholesale massacre, he again emerged untouched. During the

Revolution, Washington would continue to ride through battles uninjured by flying bullets. His invulnerability seemed to make him an object of divine attention, expanding the myth, as he himself believed, that "a kind of destiny . . . has thrown me upon this service."[7]

The accounts of these episodes are reminiscent of the rites of passage imposed upon the young hero of classical mythology—Jason, for example, who retrieved the golden fleece and returned to claim his throne; or Aeneas, who descended into the underworld in order to learn from the shade of his dead father before returning to found Rome and take up his worldly burden; or Ulysses, whose encounters with a succession of dangers preceded his return to family, throne, and power. Like these and countless other mythological adventurers, Washington undertook his odyssey into the dangerous unknown of the American wilderness, encountered and conquered "fabulous forces," and returned to his community knowledgeable and aware, "with the power to bestow boons on his fellow-man."[8] Thus, in 1775 the poet Philip Freneau acclaimed him as the coming savior of "New Albion's freedom," who like "A Roman Hero or a Grecian God"—"a second Diomede"—proved his mettle

> . . . at wild Ohio's flood,
> When savage thousands issu'd from the wood
> When Braddock's fall disgrac'd the mighty day,
> And death himself stood weeping o'er his prey,
> When doubting vict'ry chang'd from side to side,
> And Indian sod of Indian blood was dyed.[9]

Succeeding events expanded the Washington legend, to be repeated as the earlier episodes were by biographers, eulogists, and poet laureates seeking to embalm their names along with Washington's in the nation's history. From Washington's efforts to restore "tranquillity on the frontiers," the biographer quickly moved to his success as a farmer and his cultivation of the "arts of peace" up to 1775, emphasizing Washington's attachment to the land, the virtues of the rural life, and the fact that agriculture provided sufficient outlet for his ambition. The cycle of Washington's career from war to peace recalled the Roman general Cincinnatus, the military genius who was happy to forego power and return to the simple agrarian life when his services were no longer required. This was an unusually attractive image to Americans, who were convinced of the purity of agrarian pursuits and the preeminence of the civilian over the military in government. Even during the Revolution the term "citizen" frequently preceded that of "soldier" in descriptions of Washington, and most biographers interspersed such nonmilitary epithets as "sage" and "gentleman" in their descriptions of the Commander in Chief. Washington's refusal of a salary at the time of his appointment to the command of the American army strengthened the conviction that he harbored no ambition beyond that of serving his country; indeed, as suspicious John Adams pointed out, his altruism in this respect created a "dangerous enthusiasm" for the General among the multitude.[10]

The "virtuous simplicity" of Washington's life as Commander in Chief also recommended him to Americans, and even to visiting French dignitaries influenced by Enlightenment conceptions. Both Americans and foreign observers were impressed by Washington's willingness to give up the blue sash of military authority as an "unrepublican distinction," his enjoyment of such simple pastimes as playing ball with his aides-de-camp, and his ability to conduct himself "without pompousness or flattery." [11] Before the end of the Revolution, Americans had already adopted him into their families, naming their children after him and referring to him as "father." As early as 1778, Bailey's Lancaster almanac called him "Des Landes Vater," the father of his country, and thereafter biographers of Washington enjoyed dedicating their pages to the "youth of the country," with the advice that they should follow their "Father's" example.[12]

"The dazzling splendor of [Washington's] military achievements" did not, of course, go unrecognized. Whether Washington was actually the military genius some of his contemporaries claimed is not as important as the fact that after the successful completion of the Revolution his leadership in the war effort placed him on top of Olympus. Whatever political hostilities were directed against him or whatever controversies concerning his policies arose, he never descended from that glorious pinnacle. During the early years of the conflict, when the American Army met frequent defeats and discouragement, Washington remained sturdily in charge, seemingly unflappable, constantly concerned and reassuring. Although modern biographers now recount his moments of great worry and fatigue during the course of the Revolution, that was not the impression he conveyed to contemporaries. For instance, after the loss of New York in 1776—which was mitigated by the victories at Trenton and Princeton—Francis Hopkinson noted Washington's balance: "He is the best and the greatest man the world ever knew, . . . neither depressed by disappointment and difficulties, nor elated with a temporary success. He retreats like a General, and attacks like a Hero." [13]

The most audacious of Washington's efforts during the Revolution—the crossing of the Delaware on Christmas day, 1776, and the devastating attack on the Hessians—clinched Washington's glory as a military genius. Temporarily it resulted in Congress granting him dictatorial powers for six months and in encouraging new recruits into his badly decimated army. Not even Washington's failures later at Brandywine and Germantown could diminish his stature, despite the conspiracy of disaffected politicians and generals to replace him in the so-called Conway Cabal. The ordeal of Valley Forge instead entered into Washington folklore, and during the last years of the Revolution, as Washington's armies continued to harass the British and win victories, Washington's image became even more deeply engraved in the country's consciousness as "the chief instrument in the hand of Providence, for conducting the arms of his country through a tedious and perilous war." Reporting on Washington's behavior during a retreat of the American army at the Battle of Monmouth, the Marquis de Lafayette wrote that he

> seemed to arrest fortune with one glance. . . . His presence stopped the retreat. . . . His graceful bearing on horseback, his calm and deportment which still retained a trace of displeasure . . . were all calculated to inspire the highest degree of enthusiasm. . . . I thought then as now that I had never beheld so superb a man.[14]

Washington's compassion and dignity also entered into his legend. Although some may have thought that his gallantry to ladies should not have been extended to Mrs. Benedict Arnold—Peggy Shippen—on the occasion of her husband's traitorous scheming with Major André, with the coming of peace and the diminution of hostility toward Tories, Americans began to approve of the benevolence he extended to wives and children of Loyalists who had been left behind to face the wrath of patriots. They particularly enjoyed the story of his dignified behavior at Cornwallis' surrender at Yorktown in October 1781, especially his appointment of a substitute to accept Cornwallis' sword when it was offered by Cornwallis' substitute, and of his return of the sword to the defeated general.

Washington's resignation as Commander in Chief and return to agricultural pursuits reinforced the earlier Cincinnatus image that had been associated with him and strengthened the conception of him as an honest, modest, benevolent leader. During the years of his retirement, until he was recalled to public service by the constitutional convention, poets and painters who flocked to Mount Vernon to record the appearance of America's hero continued to portray a retired general "equally industrious with his plough as his sword." He was cited as an example of "diligence, temperance, frugality, and improvement in the noble and most useful science of agriculture; which is now, and must be for ages to come, the great source of riches and glory of the United States of America." The image of Washington the farmer was so powerfully attractive that when the French sculptor Jean Antoine Houdon came to chisel the hero's image in marble he presented him as a country squire overlooking his productive lands.[15]

Given the regional suspicions and rivalries that the constitutional convention was forced to cope with in its efforts to establish a truly national government, it was inevitable that its members should turn to Washington to preside over the proceedings as a symbol of national unity and the embodiment of the effort that had gone into the creation of an independent nation. Washington's response to their call proved his patriotism once again, reflecting, as Washington himself put it, "the principle by which my conduct has been actuated through life." [16]

Certainly Washington's presence at the proceedings of the convention influenced its decisions —especially its necessary compromises—and there is no doubt that his approval of the Constitution encouraged its ratification.[17] Having spurned a military dictatorship more than once, Washington became the logical candidate for first President of the republic, Americans by now being convinced of his disinterestedness and restraint.

Washington's success in creating a government capable of maintaining order at home and in steering the country clear of entangling foreign involvements became the final test of the hero's perfection. Although partisan politics marred his last years in office and brought grumblings of criticism about the conservative President from Jeffersonian radicals, still the force of his image withstood the attacks. The country rallied behind him in 1796 when he refused to submit papers regarding John Jay's treaty with Great Britain to a hostile Congress—a Federalist measure that appeared to the Republicans as a sacrifice of national interests for the benefit of the commercial North. Americans, however, agreed with Washington's claim that the treaty-making power was the prerogative of the Executive and the Senate, and so vociferous was the reaction to Congress' partisan ploy that Jefferson, leader of the Republican majority, was forced to admit that Washington outweighed Congress "in influence over the people, who have supported his judgment against their own and that of their representatives." [18]

Washington's sacrifices to his country's needs and attempts to maintain the nation's liberty and strength were universally recognized and applauded. Especially during the Anglo-French conflict of 1798, which gave rise to the fear of a French invasion, did Washington again prove what was already generally accepted, that he placed country above personal comfort. Asked by President Adams to take command of the American armies, the aging leader accepted and promised to serve "if French lawlessness and contempt of every principle of justice, and violation of solemn compact and of laws which govern all civilized nations" should make it necessary. Once again Washington refused to accept a salary and went about organizing an army even though he believed that an actual invasion was improbable.[19]

Washington's death soon after, "without a struggle, and in the perfect use of his reason," re-emphasized to a grateful nation the extent of his great sacrifice. His will providing for his family and for the eventual freeing of his slaves corroborated characteristics which were already well known: dignity, magnanimity, philosophical calmness and resignation, and the "confidence of a Christian." Quickly apotheosized as a god upon earth and placed among the immortals for all time, he now became a permanent example to the nation, teaching as President Adams said, "wisdom and virtue to magistrates, citizens, and men, not only in our present age, but in future generations, as long as our history shall be read." [20]

☆   ☆   ☆

Both the reality and the image of Washington owed much to classical history which, as Peter Gay has pointed out, provided eighteenth-century statesmen and philosophers "with illustrious models and a respectable ancestry." Thoroughly schooled in Latin and Greek, educated Americans viewed contemporary life through classically tinted glasses, taking what they needed or wanted from that past to explain, inform, or direct their present. Even the uneducated, as Benjamin Franklin pointed out as early as 1721, found "a charm" in a Latin phrase or quotation, responded to allusions to Roman heroes, and made immediate associations between Roman history and their own. If Rome "belonged to every educated man," as Gay has written, in America it also belonged to the semi-educated, who learned from newspapers, cartoons, almanacs, and broadsides, shared the classical associations of their leaders, understood the symbolic references, and drew appropriate conclusions.[21] It was not accidental, for example, that in adopting the Great Seal of the United States in 1782, Congress should have approved symbolism emanating from the classical past: an eagle, emblem of imperial Rome, over whose head shines a "glory" of thirteen stars, in whose talons float an olive branch and a sheaf of arrows, symbolizing peace and war, and whose beak holds a ribbon inscribed "E Pluribus Unum." On the reverse side are two Latin mottoes from Virgil—"Annuit Coeptis" and "Novus Ordo Seculorum"—best known by Shelley's paraphrase, "The World's Great Age begins anew / The Golden Years return." [22]

If the classical past provided the analogues and associations that went into the creation of the image of Washington, it was incipient American nationalism that gave him center stage and promoted the myths that surrounded his exploits. When Washington took command of the straggling American army and militiamen in Cambridge shortly after the rout of the British army by the minutemen at Concord and Lexington, America was still a collection of colonies, each with its own economic interests and social distinctiveness. Despite the fact that most of the colonists were of British descent (except for the Dutch in New York, the Swedes in New Jersey, and the Huguenots scattered throughout), suspicions and hostilities pervaded the relationships of the colonies. Washington the Virginian, for instance, considered the New Englanders "an exceedingly dirty and nasty people," [23] and Bostonians were not happy with the sight of Virginia riflemen under Daniel Morgan's command brawling, drinking, and occasionally swimming nude in the Charles River.

Throughout the war Americans continued to fight with a local pride that seldom transcended their native colony or state. Their localism was best reflected in the Articles of Confederation and in the tariff barriers erected by individual states to the economic disadvantage of the others. Even when the Constitution was finally adopted and Washington elected the first President of the newly united states, localism did not disappear. It erupted in the formation of Federalist and Republican parties and became particularly virulent during Washington's second administration as regional prejudices united with economic interests to separate people and sections. Only Washington, it was felt, could hold the government together. Attempting to persuade the President to accept a second term, Jefferson told him, "North and South will hang together if they have you to hang on." [24] Not until after the War of 1812, in fact, did the country begin to establish a psychological identity as a nation; and throughout the first half of the nineteenth century national unity remained a desired but hardly attained ideal.

In such a situation, symbols to which all Americans could respond became a national necessity. The design of a flag, a seal, or a document, and the organization of parades and ceremonies were all symbolic efforts to crystallize a sense of nationhood, to excite responses and associations of cultural or patriotic significance. A hero who would be identified with national unity and stability, whose presence would act as a national center, was also a requirement. Washington's enormous popularity was of course mostly the result of his own achievements and personality, but it was also derived from this great psychological necessity. Washington's firm patriotism became a model for many Americans. When, for instance, he addressed his mutinous officers at Newburgh in 1783 and urged them to have patience and trust that the injustices they were experiencing would be remedied, he only got through to his audience when, at the end, he inadvertently referred to his own sacrifices for his country. "Gentlemen," he said, "You will permit me to put on my spectacles, for I have not only grown gray, but almost blind in the service of my country." Later, when he reluctantly agreed to attend the convention called to consider the creation of a stronger federal government, his decision to do so dramatized, as Madison wrote to Jefferson, his "zeal for the public interest." [25]

Republicanism as a definition of behavior and character also contributed to the Washington image, even as Washington seemed to be the embodiment of republican ideals. Republicanism emphasized a static energy that during a time of revolutionary change must have promised a desired stability: benevolence, disinterestedness, restraint, rationality, a capacity for compromise, patriotism—in fact, all the virtues recommended by the classical tradition which informed Washington's life and influenced his behavior. The parades and ceremonies planned in Washington's honor publicly glorified these virtues, thus serving didactic as well as symbolic purposes. For instance, an illuminated transparency created by Alexandre-Marie Quesnay, Chevalier de Beaurepaire, to hang at the window of his lodging on Second Street in Philadelphia to celebrate the surrender of Cornwallis, featured thirteen stars each aiming a ray of virtue toward the name of "His Excellency General Washington." The thirteen qualities were wisdom, justice, strength, temperance, faith, charity, hope, courage, religion, love, policy, friendship, and constancy.[26]

This theme was picked up by the Washington eulogists. Elhanan Winchester noted "the virtuous simplicity which distinguishes Washington's private life." [27] David Ramsay wrote:

> Truth and utility were his objects. . . . Neither passion, party spirit, pride, prejudice, ambition, nor interest influenced his deliberations. . . . He sought for information from all quarters, revolved the subject by night and by day, and examined it in every point of view. Guided by these lights and influenced by an honest and good heart, he was imperceptibly led to decisions which were wise and judicious. . . .[28]

"Honesty," Ramsay concluded, was Washington's "best policy." It was this absolutely essential republican quality, picked up and expanded in the nineteenth century by such folk mythologists as Parson Weems, that became permanently incorporated into the Washington image.

☆   ☆   ☆

When we compare the image of Washington developed in the eighteenth century with that of a similar military and civilian hero—Andrew Jackson—in the early nineteenth century, we are struck by the marked differences in heroic values. As John William Ward has pointed out, the Jackson image embodied three major elements: Nature, Providence, and Will.[29] In the nineteenth century Nature was no longer defined as an environment that helped to mold character. Rather, "natural" meant uncultivated or spontaneous, an absence of artificiality and discipline; and, as associated with the western yeoman farmer or the informally educated, it glorified intuition and an experiential understanding of natural processes. Providence in the nineteenth century was no longer a direct intervener in the affairs of men but was a bounteous provider of opportunity for men to act upon. And the exercise of Will was not a social but a personal act, demanding an exertion of the self over inhibitory social obstacles—a grand individualism that bent everything to its command.

To nineteenth-century Americans Jackson was portrayed as Napoleon; in the eighteenth century Washington was identified as the Roman general Fabius, who defeated Hannibal in the second Punic War by avoiding decisive encounters in the field and maintaining a steady harrassment of the enemy with marches and countermarches. Not only was Napoleon a more romantic image in terms of daring and monumental military campaigns as compared with the cautious and conservative Fabius, but he was a democratic hero who had risen, not from an aristocratic and landed position, but by dint of his own genius. Napoleon's achievements lay within recent memory, Fabius' in the legendary past. The differences in the images point up the special nature of the classically oriented era of the American Revolution, with its emphasis on republican rather than democratic virtues and on a heroism which involved social rather than individual values.[30]

The ages also had different psychological requirements. The constant reference to Washington as a father symbol cannot be avoided. Colonial Americans had grown up with the image of a revered king, whom they spoke of, at least up to 1776, in terms of profound respect. Peter Shaw has pointed out that the great outburst of pamphlet attacks on the king just preceding the Declaration of Independence, such as that found in Thomas Paine's *Common Sense,* constituted a "killing of the king—an orgy of symbolic destruction necessary to the establishment of popular sovereignty." Beliefs and attitudes conditioned over a long period of time do not die quickly, however.

If, indeed, George III was destroyed as a symbolic entity in 1776, the need for another symbol of authority to fill the vacuum existed—a need that seems to have been satisfied by the austere and commanding figure of Washington.[31]

It is interesting to note that the pictorial image of Washington that has most satisfied the requirements of the American people is Gilbert Stuart's sober, almost grim, representation of him in the "Athenaeum" likeness of 1796 (see Fig. 38).* This image is so commonly accepted that, as John Neal wrote in 1868, if Washington returned to life and stood side by side with this portrait and did not resemble it, he would have been rejected as an imposter.[32] Aristocratic, elder states-manlike, fatherly, Stuart's painting and later renditions offered assurances to the citizens of the new nation that as heirs to Roman republican virtues they would prosper morally and materially under the benevolent paternity of George Washington.

*Figure numbers refer to those illustrations in the main essay; references to catalogue numbers are enclosed in brackets.

George Washington
AN AMERICAN ICON

☆ ☆ ☆

The Eighteenth-Century Graphic Portraits

WENDY C. WICK

Mezzotint by Charles Willson Peale, 1780. National Portrait Gallery [11].

☆ ☆ ☆

When the delegates to the Continental Congress elected a Commander in Chief for the rebelling American forces in 1775, they chose a man who was already legendary. Years before, when the young Major Washington led an adventurous western expedition into Indian and French-claimed territory, even George II had heard of his reckless statement: "I heard the bullets whistle, and believe me, there is something charming in the sound." [1] By 1775 Washington had lost his love for bullets, but his reputation as a man and a soldier was well known. With his sudden rise to international prominence as leader of the colonial rebellion, curiosity about this impressive man's looks as well as his character flourished everywhere.

Written descriptions of Washington were tantalizing, emphasizing his towering height, his strong physique, and a dignity of expression and bearing that invariably inspired respect in friend and foe alike.[2] In 1760 a fellow lawmaker in the Virginia House of Burgesses had described the young Washington's appearance:

> His head is well shaped, though not large, but is gracefully poised on a superb neck. A large and straight rather than prominent nose; blue-grey penetrating eyes which are widely separated and overhung by a heavy brow. His face is long rather than broad, with high round cheek bones, and terminates in a good firm chin. . . . His mouth is large and generally firmly closed.[3]

Twenty-three years later an Englishman named George Bennet wrote down his impressions after visiting Washington:

> He is a tall genteel figure of a man, rather exceeding 6 foot in height—His countenance is grave, composed, mild and penetrating—his nose is long & of the Roman shape—his eyes a little hollow under the eyebrows but active and lively. . . . His hair is a little gray & combed smoothly back from the forehead & in a small queue—no curlls & but very little Powder to it.[4]

In time, a great number of artists attempted to record Washington's features and to capture those qualities of dignity and leadership that impressed those who met him.[5] Washington's famous statement—"I am so hackneyed to the touches of the Painters pencil, that I am altogether at their beck, and sit like patience on a Monument whilst they are delineating the lines of my face" [6]—was written in 1785 when he was less than half way through his public career. Many more portraits were to follow. Citizens of the larger cities were frequently able to see these images, while universi-

The notes for this essay begin on page 169.

ties, governmental bodies, and wealthy individuals commissioned their own portraits of the General. But many of Washington's countrymen, as well as curious Europeans dazzled by this peculiarly American hero, did not have access to these paintings and sculptures. Printed portraits, for most people, were the only visual resource available to satisfy their curiosity.

From 1775 through the end of the century, images of Washington appeared as "framing" prints, as book and magazine illustrations, as almanac and broadside cuts, and as ornamented music sheet titles. Never before in America had a single subject produced such a quantity of visual material over an extended period of time. Children opening their primers and schoolbooks were confronted by the "American hero" [6]. The ubiquitous yearly almanac, second only to the Bible in its importance in every home, was often crudely ornamented with his recognizable portrait. Broadside verses and engraved music sheets bore the image of Washington whether the words applied to him or not. The monthly magazines, spending a large proportion of their budgets on an engraving for each number, often featured the President. Books of official letters, patriotic poems, Revolutionary War histories, biographies, and eulogies began with the requisite frontispiece of Washington. And engravers of all levels of competence and respect for authenticity issued separate portrait prints for framing. It was the first time in America that the likeness of a public figure was disseminated so broadly to so varied an audience. The incalculable influence of these images was extended even further as they were copied on Liverpool pitchers, printed cotton textiles, Chinese reverse painting on glass, coins, medals, mirror knobs, tavern signs, and other ornamented crafts and manufactures. Thus the prints not only played a critical role in the iconography of the man in his various roles as military leader, statesman, and father of his country, they also became, by 1800, part of the iconography of American visual arts. The printed images of Washington, therefore, warrant the same analysis and discussion that the better-known paintings and sculptures have long received.

The artists who produced Washington prints faced two challenges: the need to present a likeness, and the urge to create a symbolic context for it. The first of these involved the engraver's choice of which portrait to copy. Since only a few printmakers had the opportunity to make portraits of Washington from life, the others either had to invent a fictional likeness or to find a painting, another print, a medal, or some other image to copy. One easy solution to the problem was to reuse an old copperplate or relief-cut block, changing the identity of the face merely by relettering the name. An American cut of the English poet John Dryden, for instance, made in 1773, served as a portrait of patriot Samuel Adams in a primer of 1777 and as George Washington in a primer of 1799 [67]. Using a print of one person to portray another was not uncommon in eighteenth-century American illustration, and if not an admired practice, it was an accepted one. The prints of George Washington, however, introduced a new level of authenticity into graphic portraiture. For even the simplest of illustrations, an inaccurate likeness was the exception rather than the rule; as Washington's face became better known, an authentic portrait was usually expected. Portraits of him in all media were so available that engravers could, with little effort, copy a real image rather than concoct a fictitious one or substitute a false one.

In Europe, fictitious likenesses of Washington proliferated until the 1780s, when they gradually were replaced by authentic portraiture. With fewer original paintings available to copy from, derivative prints grew further and further away from the original source until they were sometimes barely recognizable as Washington. Nevertheless, printmakers generally attempted to present an accurate likeness. Since Washington was a figure of international prominence, the extent to which particular portraits were circulated in Europe, and the replacement of old likenesses by new ones, are important parts of the story of how his contemporaries viewed him.

Occasionally it is difficult to determine exactly which painting served as the engraver's model. Much original portraiture, especially drawings, no longer exists. Even if the life portrait had a known history in one city, the existence and travels of the painter's own replicas or other artists' copies are not always apparent. The name of the Salem artist Benjamin Blyth would never have been associated with John Norman's engraving of Charles Willson Peale's portrait [15] had the inscription not revealed that it was Blyth's drawing of the original painting that the engraver copied. The prints were seldom exact copies of the original paintings. Translated into a less-refined medium by less-skilled artists, the prints are sometimes only crude reflections of the original artist's conception. Frequently the printmaker took liberties, adding or subtracting details, altering the costume, changing the composition. Nevertheless, it is possible to trace or to recognize in many prints the original artist of the portrait. Broken down to its most basic components—the shape of the face, the treatment of the hair, the highlighting of features, or the folds of drapery—the original is often evident, shining through even the thick lines of a simple cut.

Once the likeness had been secured, printmakers searched for an appropriate decorative or symbolic embellishment. The emblematic figures and devices that played an important part in American printmaking of this period were drawn from the allegorical vocabulary of eighteenth-century European art. For centuries, the complex tradition of visual symbolic language had been defined for new generations by emblem books, such as Cesare Ripa's *Iconologia* of 1593 (an English edition of this popular work, George Richardson's *Iconology,* had been issued in London in 1779). American artists and engravers, however, did not necessarily have to read European emblem books. The communication of a popularized visual symbolism happened at a very basic level. A wide variety of imported prints, including book and magazine illustration, maps with decorative cartouches, trade cards, documents, and cartoons, made this allegorical and symbolic language commonly understood.

The English illustrated magazines, for instance, were an important source of allegory for American artists and craftsmen. Periodicals such as the *London Magazine* and the *Universal Magazine* offered an engraved allegorical frontispiece for each yearly volume as well as engraved portraits, landscapes, or maps that were issued with each monthly number. A twenty-year run of the *London Magazine* from 1765 to 1785 included such common allegorical figures as Minerva (Wisdom), Hercules (Valour), Britannia, Fame, Faction (Discord), Harmony (Concord), Father Time, Apollo, Mars, Mercury, the four Continents (with America as an Indian princess), Envy, Plenty, and Peace. Devices like the snake, laurel wreath, liberty pole and cap, and cornucopia abound. Engravers such as John Norman borrowed entire compositions [18] from these magazines. Other printmakers borrowed occasional figures or devices. Thus the embellishments so commonly used for Washington prints—the figure of Fame, the goddesses representing America or Columbia or Liberty, the laurel wreath, the cannon, the snake, the sword—did not have to be newly invented or explained.

The portrait prints of Washington fall logically into three distinct groups. From 1775 through the 1780s Washington was portrayed as Commander in Chief with an emphasis on accurate likeness and military ornamentation. From 1789 to 1797 printmakers attempted to present Washington as a presidential figure. From his retirement in 1797 through 1800 the printed portraits depicted a national symbol, reflections of a leader whose accomplishments had become associated with the whole country. In the beginning each tiny symbolic ornament enriched the portrait image of Washington. By 1800 the portrait itself, with or without allegorical embellishment, had become a symbol of the new nation's identity. In between was a quarter century in which Washington's own contemporaries, reflecting the attitudes and events of their own day, developed an American icon.

Commander in Chief

☆   ☆   ☆

In 1775 George Washington stepped into national public life and international prominence as Commander in Chief of the American forces. Printed portraits followed almost immediately. On both sides of the Atlantic pictures representing the new military leader were in demand. Starting out with crude cuts and fictitious likenesses, the publishers were soon able to issue more accurate images, ornamented with appropriate military symbols. By the time the Revolution was over, portraits of the Commander in Chief were widely available. American patriots, colonial schoolchildren, farmers in rural areas, intellectuals in European cities, all had access to printed images of the famous General who had led American troops to victory.

Camp Songs and Early Cuts

Shortly after the Commander in Chief arrived in the Boston area in July 1775, locally published almanacs and broadside songs began to appear with a double profile cut of George Washington and his Adjutant General, Horatio Gates [1]. The ornamental cuts that appeared on ephemeral material such as this were generally carved out of a block of soft type-metal (in the manner of a woodcut), locked together with the type, and printed in relief. These crudely made, inexpensive images were "illustrations" only in the decorative sense. Rather than a visual interpretation of a text, they were often modest printers' ornaments, designed for quick recognition. Nevertheless, their visual imagery reached a broad local audience at each appearance. The intriguing feature of the double cut of Washington and Gates is the possibility that the profiles could be an attempt at authentic likenesses. When compared with profiles of the two men by Pierre Eugène Du Simitière, made slightly later, there is a vague resemblance which suggests that the straight-nosed profile on the left is Washington and the double-chinned profile on the right is Gates.

Unfortunately, the first publication of this cut is unknown. It was probably made for a broadside illustration in the second half of 1775 or early 1776 when Washington, with his Adjutant General, was setting up his command in Boston. The earliest known appearance of the cut is on a Massachusetts broadside of the Declaration of Independence, issued in 1776, where the identity of the profiles is ambiguous. However, by the time the illustration reappeared in *Bickerstaff's Boston Almanack for 1779* (published in 1778), it was labeled the "Glorious Washington and Gates."

FIGURE 1. Pennsylvania-German almanac, relief cut by unidentified artist, 1778 [3].

Shortly afterward, the cut was used as the heading for a broadside verse entitled "Washington: A Favorite New Song in the American Camp." Addressed to "vain Britons" and promising to "laugh at all your empty puffs," this spirited camp song offered a "huzza for Ward and Washington," implying that the second portrait was intended to be General Artemus Ward rather than Gates. This loss of identity was common for relief-cut portraits of the period as the blocks were passed back and forth between publishers. The profile of the Commander in Chief suffered the same fate. The Washington half of the block survived to be reused in the 1790s, in books, broadsides, and almanacs as an all-purpose illustration suitable for any fictional hero.

The introduction of many of the important iconographic elements associated with Washington prints appeared in another crude but early image, the cover of a Lancaster, Pennsylvania, almanac published in 1778 (Fig. 1; [3]). Hovering above a miscellany of astrological symbols and representations of the Old World and the New was a winged figure of Fame holding a portrait of Washington and trumpeting out the words "Des Landes Vater." It was the first instance of Washington being called the father of his country.[7] The unknown artist of this illustration was also the first to represent him in a medallion portrait, the first to crown him with a laurel wreath, and the first to associate him with the trumpeting figure of Fame. Although the military struggle of the Revolution was far from resolved and the effect of his leadership was still in question, Washington was depicted in this illustration as symbolic of America. Although no attempt at a likeness, his portrait, together with a bejeweled Indian princess, Iroquois longhouses, and leaping deer, was clearly emblematic of the New World in contradistinction to the Old. Despite its crude execution and rather incoherent composition, this important picture is an indication that Washington's symbolic role, complete with its most common iconographic components, had been suggested very early.

First Authentic Likeness

Although any crude cut would have passed as a likeness of "His Excellency" during the early days of the Revolution, it was not long before an authentic image of Washington, based on a portrait painted from life by the Philadelphia artist Charles Willson Peale, began to replace all others. Scientist and inventor as well as artist, Peale was a Renaissance man whose painted portraits of the prominent citizens of his day are a major visual resource of Revolutionary history. Peale's role in introducing the likeness of Washington in both Europe and America becomes, through a study of the early prints, far more significant than previously recognized.

Peale had first painted Washington from life in 1772 in the uniform of his Virginia militia. In 1776 Peale had the opportunity to paint a new likeness of the Commander in Chief, a portrait commissioned by the president of Congress, John Hancock (Fig. 2).[8] This 1776 painting, which was made in Philadelphia and taken to Boston by Hancock, was the first authentic likeness of Washington to appear in American prints. Completely dominating the American images of the General through the 1780s, and having an important influence on European prints as well, it remained a legitimate likeness throughout the century. The basic components of Peale's 1776 portrait were repeated so frequently—in engravings, books, magazines, almanacs, primers, and broadsides—that they were eventually recognized by most of Washington's countrymen and contemporaries.

The first of the prints to spread the influence of Peale's 1776 likeness was a mezzotint now attributed to Major Joseph Hiller, Sr., a soldier and engraver from Salem, Massachusetts [2]. The laborious mezzotint process was an engraving technique that produced a rich, dark tonal image. These prints were extremely popular in England, where skilled printers were available and assistants did the tedious rocking of the plate before the engraver made his design. In America, mezzotints were imported and admired, but few engravers even attempted the technique. Hiller's portrait of Washington, therefore, must have been especially impressive. The engraving was most likely made in 1777 when Hancock—and, presumedly, this Peale painting—returned to Boston from Philadelphia where the Continental Congress had been meeting.[9] Accompanied by a companion print of Martha, Hiller's mezzotint was a lively portrayal of Washington in uniform and leaning on his staff in his role as Commander in Chief. Like the Peale painting, the mezzotint included in the background the smoke and flames of Charlestown, which had been shelled and burned by the British during the battles of Breed's Hill and Bunker Hill in June 1775.[10]

Peale himself made the second print after his 1776 painting. In London in 1768 Peale had learned mezzotint engraving and had produced an allegorical print of William Pitt, depicted in Roman dress. When he returned to America, he was bitterly disappointed that the Pitt mezzotint sold so poorly.[11] His next effort at mezzotint engraving came one decade later when he made his first print of George Washington. Unfortunately, his Washington mezzotint is unknown today, but it was recorded in Peale's notebook diary on October 16, 1778: "Began a drawing in order to make a medzotinto of Gen. Washington. Got a plate of Mr. Brookes and in pay I am to give him 20 of the prints in the first 100 struck off." [12] Peale presented copies of the print to various people, including Washington himself and the "French Ambassidor," Conrad Alexandre Gérard.[13] The following year, he gave one to the Swiss artist and collector Pierre Eugène Du Simitière, who noted it in his accession book: "A small mezzotinto of a head of Gen. Washington done by Mr. Peale, painter, of this city—given by him." [14] Most of the impressions Peale hoped to sell, mainly through booksellers. His records indicate that he distributed dozens of the prints to various agents in the city.[15]

One artist who was inspired by Peale's small mezzotint head was the engraver John Norman, who himself became an enthusiastic purveyor of the image of Washington. "Lately from London," Norman arrived in Philadelphia around 1774, when he advertised himself as an engraver of maps, architectural illustrations, portraits, landscapes, frontispieces, and various shipping documents. In addition, he and his temporary partner, John Ward, offered their services for ornamenting watch cases and silver, printing copperplates, teaching drawing, and selling an "assortment of Pictures" and frames.[16] One of these pictures, which Norman advertised in August 1779 as "an elegant head of General Washington," was undoubtedly Peale's mezzotint.[17]

On June 15, 1779, John Norman advertised in the *Pennsylvania Evening Post* "a Primer adorned with a beautiful head of general Washington." [18] Although no copy of this primer has been found, a small engraving of Washington [4] has been identified as Norman's frontispiece.[19] Apparently Norman based this portrait on Peale's 1778 mezzotint, which he also sold in his shop. The distinctive oval face in the frontispiece, the curl of hair sticking out at one side, and the long straight nose were characteristic features of the Peale likeness that Norman was to repeat in his other prints of Washington.

The use of a Washington portrait as the frontispiece to a primer was significant. Many colonial

FIGURE 2. Oil on canvas by Charles Willson Peale, 1776. Brooklyn Museum.

FIGURE 3. Detail from *Philadelphia Almanack for 1780*, engraving by John Norman, 1779 [5].

children learned their first lessons from these modest but indispensable little schoolbooks. Norman's was the first of a great number of children's primers in which the usual portrait of the English king was replaced by an image of the new hero. Initially Washington's portrait appeared because of his prominence as a military leader. Ultimately the requisite Washington frontispiece served not only as a national symbol but also as a paragon of moral conduct for all children to emulate.

Just a few months after the publication of the *Primer,* Norman repeated his image of Washington by integrating it into an ornamental heading for a broadside almanac (Fig. 3; [5]). Usually almanacs—yearly calendars with astrological calculations, weather predictions, and listings of local events—were published in pamphlet form. However, they were occasionally issued as broadsides and posted for easy reference. Long exposure, hard use, and obsolescence all contributed to the destruction of these ephemeral items, and few survive today. Whereas most broadside almanacs either were unillustrated or were ornamented with very crude cuts, Norman's engraving was a fairly sophisticated pictorial design combining the portrait with decorative, allegorical, and heraldic motifs. It was nevertheless available, affordable, and comprehensible to everyone. A household necessity rather than a luxury, an almanac would be purchased by many who could not afford an expensive print.

Norman's almanac portrait of Washington [5] was enclosed in an oval frame flanked by twin figures of Fame with their trumpets and ornamented with cartouches, palm branches, and banners. On either side of the portrait were oval medallions, each encircled with a coiled serpent, which contained the arms of Pennsylvania on the right and a shield with a snake device on the left. At the bottom, balancing the leafy swags above the portrait, another snake winds gracefully through the border design while supporting the toes of both trumpeting ladies. Though Norman's design was pictorially complex—and perhaps made to appeal to sophisticated tastes—the meaning of its allegory was immediately apparent to any uneducated laborer or farmer. George Washington, surrounded by military banners and cannon, was the central figure in a struggle that was already several years old. The rattlesnake, skillfully introduced throughout the design, was a recognized symbol of the American colonies.[20] The arms of Pennsylvania would have been familiar to many purchasers of the almanac, and the female figure with a trumpet was a widely known allegorical depiction of Fame. No antiquated heraldic motifs, indecipherable Latin mottoes, or obscure symbolic allusions hindered the reading of the design. If the educated gentleman, familiar with heraldic and decorative ornament, appreciated shields, graceful scrolls, and leafy swags, the militia-man could understand the banners and cannon, the colonial rattlesnake, and the picture of his General. For a wide cross-section of the populace the Peale face of Washington was already well launched.

Popularization of a Portrait

Around 1780, John Norman left Philadelphia and moved to Boston. At about the same time, the Norman-Peale face of Washington was introduced to New England. A small relief-cut portrait of Washington, probably made by Paul Revere, first appeared in *Weatherwise's Town and Country Almanack for 1781* [6]. Copied from Norman's almanac engraving [5], the image was radically simplified for the bolder relief cut (probably made from type metal). The essential ingredients of the face are exaggerated: oval-shaped head, almond-shaped eyes, a long straight nose, a curl of hair on one side, and the rosebud mouth all suggest the Norman engraving and, by extension, the Peale painting. Palm branches, banners, and cannon are arranged along the bottom of the picture and around the oval frame. The white holes above and below the portrait are evidence of an attempt to copy Norman's cartouches, just as the leafy branch waving aimlessly at the top of the oval is a remnant of his curving leaf decoration. Curiously enough, despite its shortcomings, the little portrait retains its dignified appearance and its message of military strength. In October 1781 Paul Revere sent a "small engraving" of Washington—probably this cut—to his cousin in France, who in his response described it as "representing a gallant warrior." [21] Within the context of American almanac and primer illustration it was gallant indeed, and very popular. The little block had an extraordinary longevity, appearing over and over again as the frontispiece to almanacs and primers published in Boston, Concord, and Medford, Massachusetts, and Amherst, New Hampshire, throughout the last two decades of the century (see entry [6]).

The strongest evidence of the popularity of the Revere cut is the number of imitations. Clearly it was considered especially suitable for primers, children's books, and almanacs. By 1785 the image had returned to Philadelphia, where a copy of the Revere cut appeared in one of Thomas Dilworth's spelling books [7]. This block was later resurrected as "Farmer Washington," illustrating *The Citizen and Farmer's Almanac*. A third cut appeared in several Boston almanacs and primers of the 1790s [8]. A fourth, an extremely crude Boston imitation with only a token attempt at banners and scrolls, was used for broadsides as well as primers and almanacs [9]. Although the identity of this last portrait was sometimes unclear, it was definitely returned to its original purpose when it appeared on two broadside poems lamenting Washington's death.

FIGURE 4. Relief cut attributed to Paul Revere, 1780 [6] and relief cuts by unidentified artists, 1780–1800 [7–10] showing evolution of the Norman-Peale likeness.

Finally, a fifth version, appearing in Philadelphia in almanacs from the late 1790s, presented Washington with a surly countenance and a pointed head [10]. It was a long way from Peale's 1776 painting, but the oval face with the curl of hair, the requisite banners, cannon, cartouches, and scrolls was by this time familiar (Fig. 4; [6–10]). The readers of Samuel Ivins' *Columbian Almanac* were no doubt perfectly comfortable with this cut. The original Peale image, gradually evolving through the hands of John Norman and Paul Revere, had reached a point where the very crudest of imitations would trigger a response in the national consciousness.

The Legacy of Charles Willson Peale

While his 1776 painting was being disseminated in various types of prints, Charles Willson Peale continued to create more Washington portraiture. During his career he painted Washington from life seven times[22] and made numerous replicas and occasional prints after those life portraits. Peale was apparently conscious, not only of the role his Washington paintings had in satisfying the demand for an appropriate likeness, but also of the importance of engravings in extending the fame—and potential earnings—of his portraits. Having studied in London, he was no doubt aware of the expanding English print industry, quickly becoming lucrative to painters, engravers, series of prints after his own paintings. What Peale lacked, however, along with other American publishers, and printsellers,[23] and he was convinced that he too could make a fortune selling a engravers, was the industry that supported the printmaker in England. Without wealthy publishers, suppliers for plates, ink and paper, skilled printers, experienced printsellers, and enthusiastic clients, making and successfully marketing a series of prints was a significant challenge.

Hoping to overcome some of the difficulties, Peale attempted to import prepared plates, paper, and tools from Europe. In September 1779 he asked the French minister, Conrad Alexandre Gérard, to send him "a Copper plate prepared for metzotinto" and "a few quires of Paper proper for that sort of work (which is only made in France)"; in October he solicited from William Carmichael, on his way to Spain with the American delegation, "paper and copper Plates for me to Etch a set of Heads of the Principal Characters who have distinguished themselves during this Contest"; and the following March he sent another American, who was traveling to France, a long

list of desired supplies, including "1 sett of Grounding Tools for Midtzotinto prints" as well as three copperplates prepared for mezzotint and one ream of paper.[24]

Although his attempts to get imported supplies were apparently unsuccessful, Peale began to engrave another mezzotint of Washington. In 1779, he had painted a new life portrait of the Commander in Chief, commissioned by the Supreme Executive Council of Pennsylvania. A confidant and victorious image of Washington, the painting was instantly popular and the demand for replicas—one foreign emissary ordered five[25]—no doubt convinced Peale that a mezzotint would also be successful. The publication of the print was announced in the *Pennsylvania Packet* on August 26, 1780. It was a dignified, three-quarter-length depiction of Washington (frontispiece; [11]) with the college buildings of Princeton in the background in reference to his victory there. Technically, Peale's mezzotint is beautifully executed. Furthermore, although the print is copied from his painting, Peale was able to transfer into a different medium the feeling of a life portrait, with all the qualities of direct and personal experience between artist and sitter that the term implies. Communicating more about the character of the Commander in Chief than any of the other prints, the 1780 Peale mezzotint remains unexcelled among the early graphic images of George Washington. Nevertheless, evidence suggests that the sales of the mezzotint did not meet Peale's expectations. Although he appeared enthusiastic about printmaking in 1779, after the publication of the 1780 Washington print he did not engrave again for seven years. In 1785 he sent two portraits to England to be engraved instead of making the prints himself.[26] Expecting the same market that printmakers found in England, he was inevitably disappointed.

Finally, by February 1787, Peale had forgotten his disappointment and returned to his long-contemplated scheme of making a series of portrait prints. On February 2, 1787, Peale wrote to a friend that he had begun "one other great work, the making of Mezzotinto prints from my collection of portraits of Illustrious Personages." He complained that the undertaking "will cost me much labour as I am obliged to take the plates from the rough and doing the whole business myself, even the impressing." [27] Nevertheless, he had completed mezzotint portraits of Benjamin Franklin, the Marquis de Lafayette, and a prominent Philadelphia clergyman, Joseph Pilmore, by May 1787. That same month Washington was elected president of the constitutional convention and became the next obvious subject for the series. Not wanting to trouble him, Peale wrote reluctantly to ask for another sitting, explaining his "great desire . . . to make a good mezzotinto print that your numerous friends may be gratified with a faithful likeness." [28] As usual, Washington complied with the request. Peale produced another handsome mezzotint, a bust portrait of Washington in an oval-shaped frame, which he advertised for sale in August of 1787.

Unlike other printmakers, Peale felt no need to ornament his portraits with allegorical figures or symbolic embellishments. He did, however, experiment with color. He printed various states of the Washington mezzotint in brown and red as well as black impressions, and then proceeded to ink his plates with several colors. A single surviving print of Washington in colors (now at the New York Public Library), a pioneer attempt at copperplate color printing in America, is a testament to Peale's extraordinary combination of technical ability and aesthetic sensitivity.

Once again, Peale's 1787 series was not the financial success he expected. Sending some proofs of his prints to his former teacher, the American artist Benjamin West in London, Peale wrote on November 17, 1787, "this is a work which I mean to pursue when I have no other business to do, for the sale is not such as to induce me to pursue it otherwise." [29] Nevertheless, although Peale could not match the distribution of the English printmakers, his contribution to a national concept of Washington cannot be overstated. His own paintings and mezzotints, and the prints and illustrations copied from them, brought to a wide range of people a visual image of the Commander in Chief, an image which became so ingrained it lasted throughout the century even when other likenesses of Washington had begun to predominate. In some of the later, more modest engravings and cuts after Peale, his various life portraits, in themselves quite distinct and different, begin to merge. Only the oval face, almond-shaped eyes, and long straight nose remain to identify Peale's interpretation of Washington. Not only were there many Peale portraits and replicas to copy from, there were also painted copies by other members of his large family, such as those by his nephew Charles Peale Polk.[30] If the influence of specific paintings on specific prints cannot be traced by the end of the century, the general impact of Peale's portrayal of Washington can be clearly recognized as extraordinary.

John Norman's Search for Allegory

The engraver John Norman was not only responsible for popularizing the Peale likeness, he was also the first printmaker to explore, through a series of images, a symbolic and allegorical context for the Washington portrait. Unlike Peale, Norman was not a skilled artist. Uncomfortable with making his own designs, he preferred to copy others whenever possible, and his engravings are generally rather coarse and poorly executed. Nonetheless, he emerges as an important purveyor of the Washington image, concentrating on a recognizable likeness and attempting to elevate the portrait by imposing symbolic ornament and allegorical settings that were both ingenious and naive. Although his allegory was not always entirely appropriate for Washington, his efforts to find an enobling symbolic context can still charm the modern viewer just as they must have intrigued his own contemporaries.

Norman's previous Washington prints had all been illustrations. In 1782, however, he undertook an ambitious pair of framing prints of George and Martha Washington, publishing two versions of each [15, 16]. The inscription on the better portrait of George [15] states that it was "taken from an Original Picture in possession of his Excy Govr. Hancock." This was Peale's 1776 portrait, and the words "B. Blyth del." (*delineavit* = drew) on the left indicate that the Salem artist Benjamin Blyth[31] made a drawing of it from which Norman engraved his plate. Although the expression seems unusually serious, the oval shape of the face, and the nose, eyes, and mouth are the same Peale characteristics which had appeared in Norman's primer frontispiece of Washington [4] and his broadside almanac [5]. Norman added to this likeness appropriate ornamentation. The oval frame is made into a medallion hanging by a ring and resting on a pedestal; graceful leafy swags hang from the corners; and the space at the bottom is filled with such military ornaments as cannon, cannonballs, banners, bayonet, sword, and drum. Norman's skills are stretched to their limits in this print. Despite its weighty inscription—"Temperance, Prudence, Fortitude, Justice"—the tiny pedestal looks completely overwhelmed by the relatively enormous medallion. Nonetheless, combined with the recognizable likeness and an inscription which is almost a sampler of lettering styles, the embellishments created the formality that was expected of the engraved portrait in the eighteenth century.

One of the most intriguing of Norman's Washington portraits is his full-length figure of George Washington in a suit of sixteenth-century field armor [17]. The reference in the inscription to a monument ordered by Congress referred to a congressional resolution of 1783 proposing a bronze equestrian statue of Washington—"represented in a Roman dress, holding a truncheon in his right hand, and his head encircled with a laurel wreath"—to be erected in the nation's capital.[32] Perhaps unwilling to draw such an image without a model to copy, Norman apparently approximated Roman costume by copying an illustration in a book called *Display of Heraldry* by John Guillim, first published in England in 1611. Faithfully copying the full-length figure in armor, as well as the staff, glove, plumed helmet, and background battle in the illustration, Norman engraved on top of the body his oval-shaped face of Washington.

Ridiculous as an armored Washington might seem, especially substituting for an equestrian figure in Roman dress, Norman's print was probably not a satire on the congressional proposal. Not only were cartoons and caricatures engraved in a different pictorial style during this period, but the armored figure also expressed an allegorical message of triumph over an enemy that was perfectly appropriate for a portrait of Washington. Armor occasionally appeared in other American prints with a similar allegorical purpose. An engraving of John Hancock by Paul Revere published in the *Royal American Magazine* of 1774 was flanked by an image of Liberty on one side and a fully armored figure on the other, a design borrowed from an English print.[33] Toward the end of the century, the artist John James Barralet frequently used the helmet as a symbol of military strength in his portraits of Washington [64, 65, 101], and in one memorial print he had the figure of America weeping over Washington's armor [101]. Whether or not Norman's engraving summoned comparisons with historical images such as Saint George, the armored Washington, with its recognizable Peale face, was no doubt perfectly acceptable.

Norman's next attempt to elevate the Washington portrait was another borrowed allegory. Although he may not have actually cut the cover for *Weatherwise's Town and Country Almanack for . . . 1784* [18], he was obviously its designer. Inside the almanac the picture is described as "a plate, representing the Victorious General Washington, survey'd in pleasing attitudes, by Wisdom and Valour, while Britannia deplores her loss of America." If the medallion portrait against an obelisk, the weeping female figure, and the goddess of Fame are reminiscent of mourning imagery, there is good reason. Like other American engravers, Norman borrowed heavily from English magazine illustration. In this case he copied a print published as a memorial to William Duke of Cumberland in the *London Magazine* of 1765. The fact that Washington still lived was not a problem for the imaginative Norman. By suggesting that Britannia was weeping for the loss of her American colonies, he could use a mourning image with the portrait of Washington as a symbol of those colonies. Although the cut itself is very coarse and the use of mourning imagery seems inappropriate, Norman's attempt to depict Washington in the context of national rather than personal glory was significant.

As publisher of the *Boston Magazine* of 1785 Norman again used a Washington portrait as the focus for an allegorical frontispiece. The illustration was explained on the inside cover of the magazine:

> Nature stands ready to strike the Lyre, while the Genius of Liberty presents a medal of the
> illustrious man who hath defended her standard in this new World—Fame blows her trumpet, and
> Astrea finds a part of the earth where she may fix her residence.

This time Norman borrowed the idea and composition for his print from a French portrait engraving of the philosopher Montesquieu.[34] By substituting Washington's portrait, changing a putto in the corner to the ubiquitous figure of Fame, and removing the author's name from the books in the lower left corner, Norman could adapt the French allegory conveniently to his purposes. For the colonists who felt they were on the side of righteousness in the struggle against Great Britain, Justice (Astrea)—familiar as the stately blindfolded female holding the scales— played a logical part in George Washington's victory. Liberty had an obvious connection with the war for independence, even though it was more often embodied by a female rather than by a male "Genius." The multi-breasted Natura was a more unusual allegorical figure for Washington prints. Nevertheless, by extension, Washington's military success had unshackled the prosperity of the new nation, and the fecundity of her natural resources could be celebrated along with his victory. In the center of this grand compositional scheme Norman placed "a medal of the illustrious man" who had defended the standards of liberty. Crude as it was, there was no need to further identify the portrait. The familiar oval face, surrounded by thirteen stars, could only be one man.

John Norman and Charles Willson Peale, along with the relief-cut artists who copied from them, created an American image of the hero of the Revolution that lasted throughout the 1780s. From almanac cover to stylish mezzotint, a recognizable likeness of Washington was established, and the search for symbolic significance and appropriate allegorical ornamentation was underway.

A Formidable Fictitious Figure

Curiosity about the legendary Commander in Chief was not limited to America. In fact, by 1775 the potential market for Washington prints abroad was so tempting that foreign publishers did not wait for accurate portraits of the General to arrive on their shores. Thus the first European prints of Washington were completely fictitious. They were also immensely influential.

Between 1775 and 1778 one or more London publishers, using the names C. Shepherd,

FIGURE 5. Mezzotint by unidentified artist after "Alexander Campbell" (published by C. Shepherd), 1775. Hart 730a. Library of Congress.

FIGURE 6. Mezzotint by unidentified artist after "Alexander Campbell" (published by C. Shepherd), 1775. Hart 721. Private collection.

Thomas Hart, and John Morris, issued a series of mezzotints of the officers of the Revolution.[35] These enterprising publishers, anticipating the demand on both sides of the ocean, had the first of the mezzotints, two different prints of George Washington (Figs. 5 and 6), ready for sale by September 1775. Having no authentic portraits available to be copied from or compared with, they cared little about quality or accuracy. Using the same basic formula, they published prints of Benedict Arnold, Horatio Gates, John Hancock, Esek Hopkins, Sir William Howe, Richard Lord Howe, Charles Lee, Israel Putnam, Robert Rogers, John Sullivan, and David Wooster as well as Washington.[36] Most of the portraits were three-quarter-length figures with fleshy faces and generalized features. The officers, with little variety, wore tricornered hats, broad-lapeled uniforms, gorgets, sashes, and sometimes ribbons across the breast.

If the publishers assumed that priority alone would make these awkward and obviously fictitious likenesses popular, they were right. Bust-length variants were engraved in London; whole sets were produced in Augsburg inscribed with the names "Ioh Martin Will" or "Joh. Lorenz Rugendas"; copies appeared with French and German inscriptions; and the images were imitated for book illustrations throughout Europe. Of particular interest is a set of engraved portraits which was published in Paris by Esnauts and Rapilly (Fig. 7). Probably engraved by Jean-Victor

FIGURE 7. Engraving attributed to Jean-Victor Dupin (published by Esnauts and Rapilly), no date. Hart 743. National Portrait Gallery.

FIGURE 8. Mezzotint by unidentified artist after "Alexander Campbell," no date. Hart 737a. Private collection.

Dupin, they are distinctive not so much for the derivative portraits as for the format and ornamentation. The cannon, banners, liberty cap and pole, and palm and laurel branches that appear on the Esnauts and Rapilly engravings became common elements in American portrait prints of the Revolution.

The two mezzotints of George Washington (Figs. 5 and 6) bore little resemblance to each other, yet on both of them the same bit of fraud was introduced to give a sense of authenticity: "Done from an original Drawn from the Life by Alexr. Campbell of Williamsburgh in Virginia." No such painter is known to exist; and Washington himself, with good humor and resignation, denied having sat for the portrait. Washington's aide Joseph Reed sent a copy of one of the prints to Martha Washington, a gift which the General acknowledged in a letter of January 31, 1776: "Mrs. Washington desires I will thank you for the picture sent her. Mr. Campbell, whom I never saw to my knowledge, has made a very formidable figure of the Commander-in-Chief, giving him a sufficient portion of terror in his countenance." [37]

All of Europe was soon exposed to the "Campbell" likenesses of Washington. The plate for the three-quarter-length portrait was sent to Augsburg, where the print was reissued by Johann Martin Will.[38] A bewildering variety of copies followed (for example, Fig. 8). Since the original Shepherd-Hart-Morris mezzotints were all fictitious and quite similar to each other, copyists some-

20

His Excellency George Washington Esq.
Captain General of all the American Forces

FIGURE 9. Engraving by unidentified artist, 1780. Published in *An Impartial History of the War in America* (London, 1780). Hart 760. Library of Congress.

times used them interchangeably, borrowing poses and details indiscriminately. Their influence was reflected in the telltale gorgets, tricornered hats, and thick waist sashes of many book illustrations. The full-length portraits of the officers in *An Impartial History of the War in America* (London, 1780), for instance, are similar in many details to the mezzotints. Although the Washington plate from this volume (Fig. 9) is not very close to the "Campbell" prints, it shares some of the features of the series.[39]

The equestrian portrait of Washington produced its own set of imitations, issued by Johann Martin Will[40] and others. The illustration of Washington in Christoph Heinrich Korn's *Geschichte der Kriege* (Nurnberg, 1777–1778),[41] although a bust portrait, is one example of the influence of this other "Campbell" likeness. The engravings of Washington on horseback also inspired textile design, such as a printed handkerchief, probably produced in America, entitled "George Washington Esq. Foundator and Protector of America's Liberty, and Independency."[42] The influence of the "Campbell" print on two variant equestrian engravings of Washington with his arm outstretched [99, 100] was more indirect. Their direct source was another printed handkerchief (Fig. 10) entitled "Gen. Washington directing to return to Justice the Sword which gained Independence to America."[43] The striped saddlecloth of the central equestrian image of this fabric, the outstretched arm, and the curled edge of the coat are similar to the two engravings. The central portion of the handkerchief, with its troops of soldiers and waving flags, may have been influenced not only by the "Campbell" print but also by the medal honoring the Revolutionary general Daniel Morgan which was designed by Augustin Dupré in Paris in 1785 or 1786 (Fig. 11).[44] Hovering above the image of Washington on the handkerchief is the figure of Fame, and profiles of American patriots surround the central design. In the prints only the equestrian figure in a circular frame is represented.

The "Campbell" engravings proved to be formidable indeed. Within only a few years these fictitious images of Washington had spread throughout Europe.

Du Simitière's Collection of Generals, Ministers, and Magistrates

Eventually replacing the fictitious "Campbell" portraits in Europe were three authentic likenesses of Washington—by Charles Willson Peale, John Trumbull, and Pierre Eugène Du Simitière—which were introduced almost simultaneously in the 1780s. Du Simitière, a Swiss artist who was working in America, drew a profile portrait of Washington which, he noted in his commonplace book on February 1, 1779, was

> a drawing in black lead of a likeness in profil of his execellency general Washington, form of a medal, for my collection. N.B. the general at the request of the Hon Mr. Jay President of Congress, came with him to my house this morning & condescended with great good nature to Sit about ¾ of an hour for the above likeness having little time to Spare, being the last day of his stay in town.[45]

Du Simitière was a self-appointed antiquarian and historian of contemporary events. Conscious of the historical importance of the American struggle, he collected contemporary books and

FIGURE 10. English handkerchief, 1783. Reproduced from John Jay Ide, *The Portraits of John Jay* (New York: New-York Historical Society, 1938), Plate 1m.

FIGURE 11. Commemorative medal to Daniel Morgan by Augustin Dupré, c. 1789. Reproduced from Joseph F. Loubat, *The Medallic History of the United States of America* (1898; reprint, New Milford, Conn.: Flayderman, 1967), Plate VIII.

pamphlets relating to the Revolution and, in the same spirit, made a series of profile portraits "in black lead" of prominent officers and statesmen. These drawings he intended to have engraved in Europe. According to his notebook, on September 16, 1779, he delivered fourteen drawings to the French minister, Conrad Alexandre Gérard, who was leaving for France. The following day he sent Gérard "a memoir [on] how I Should wish the Subscription might be set on foot, . . . also instructions drawn up in french for the engravers." Gérard was to add his own portrait to the group, bringing the number to fifteen.[46] The next week Du Simitière noted that he had "sent to Mons. Gérard a new picture of Gen. [Thomas] Mifflin requesting him to return the first which is not fit to be engraven." [47] Two more drawings, portraits of Samuel Huntington and Gouverneur Morris, were delivered October 18, 1779.[48]

Fourteen of Du Simitière's drawings finally did reach France, where they were engraved by Bénoit Louis Prévost (Fig. 12). Issued first without, and then with, inscribed names beneath the portraits,[49] the prints were published in two parts[50] under the title *Collection des portraits des généreaux, ministres, & magistrats qui se sont rendus célèbres dans la révolution des treize Etats-Unis de l'Amerique-Septentrionale.* They were advertised in the *Mercure de France* on February 24, 1781. A few months later Du Simitière finally saw a single engraving of John Jay. Although he questioned how a separate print had been sent when his instructions specified they should only be sold as sets, he wrote Gérard, on August 28, 1781, that he did admire the style of engraving:

> It added greatly to my satisfaction to see how masterly the engraving has been performed, and I am under great obligations to Mr. Prevost for the Justice he has done to my drawings, the elegant neatness of the ground to which the medallion is suspended pleases me much as well as the size of the print which will answer very well to insert in a quarto or large Octavo Edition of a history of the revolution when a good one comes to be wrote.[51]

Transatlantic shipping of portraits of American heroes was a risky business during the war. According to Du Simitière's letters, a number of the prints were captured by the enemy, some sets arrived incomplete, and others came water-soaked and stained. He was able to present one set to Washington, he wrote Gérard; and some of the gentlemen of Philadelphia, including the Chevalier de la Luzerne, Robert Morris, and Chancellor Livingston, did purchase the prints. However, Du Simitière complained that he did not have enough complete sets to advertise them and had to dispose of them privately.[52] Finally, on September 25, 1782, he placed a notice in the *Pennsylvania Journal:*

> A Few complete setts of the prints of his Excellency General Washington, and other General Officers, Presidents, and Members of Congress, Ministers Plenipotentiary, Governors, &c. engraved in Paris, from the original likenesses drawn from the life, by M. duSimitiere, are to be had at his Museum . . . N.B. Those Gentlemen who have purchased the first six prints, have now an opportunity of compleating their setts.

The subjects of the portraits were not all equally popular. Few patriots would have wanted a portrait of Benedict Arnold by 1782, and as the war dragged on, other figures lost some of their public appeal. The print of Washington, however, was always in demand. Du Simitière admitted that it was the Washington portrait published in the first set of six prints that encouraged sales. "I disposed of ten pretty readily of the second setts," he wrote,

FIGURE 13. Engraving by B. B. E[llis?] after Pierre Eugène Du Simitière, 1781. Hart 75. National Portrait Gallery.

FIGURE 12. Engraving by Bénoit Louis Prévost after Pierre Eugène Du Simitière, 1781. Hart 68. National Portrait Gallery.

... but they did not go of[f] so well as the first owing to the likeness of our general being with the first and not in the second. . . . I could have sold many prints of our commander in chief, but I would not have done it had it been in my power as it would not have [been] an object of sufficient value and that I believe some purchased a whole sett principal[ly] on account of that likeness.[53]

After the Revolution the author William Gordon wrote to Washington inquiring about portraits, no doubt to illustrate his history of the war. In response Washington wrote him on March 8, 1785, recommending Du Simitière's engravings:

If Mr. Du' Simitire is living, and at Philada., it is possible he may have miniature engravings of most, if not all the military characters you want, and in their proper dresses: he drew many good likenesses from the life, and got them engraved at Paris for sale; among these I have seen Genl. Gates, Baron de Steuben, &c., as also that of your hble. servt.[54]

Gordon did not use Du Simitière's engravings. In fact, the difficulties of shipping during the war combined with Du Simitière's refusal to sell any separate prints probably resulted in a relatively small circulation of his profile of Washington in America. With the exception of one small wood-cut for a primer [47], the Du Simitière image was not copied for American prints.

In Europe, however, the Du Simitière profiles flourished. A close copy of the Washington

25

engraving was made in Madrid by Mariano Brandi in 1781. Du Simitière noted that the Spanish print had been sent to America, but he had not yet seen it.[55] In 1783 the whole set was published in London in two different versions. The first, published May 10, 1783, by W. Richardson, was a group of thirteen engravings—omitting Gérard—by Burnet Reading, entitled *American Legislators, Patriots, and Soldiers, Who Have Distinguished Themselves in Rendering their Country Independent.* The other set (Fig. 13), published by R. Wilkinson on May 15, 1783, included twelve engravings—omitting Gérard and Arnold—by "B.B.E.," possibly an engraver named Ellis. Bound together with a title page, they were issued as *Portraits of the Generals, Ministers, Magistrates, Members of Congress, and Others, Who Have Rendered Themselves Illustrious in the Revolution of the United States of North America.* As a result of these publications, American profiles began to appear everywhere in England, in magazines, on transfer-printed ceramics, on enamel mirror knobs, and on printed cotton textiles (Fig. 10).[56] As in America, the Washington profile was the most popular and was used for book and magazine illustration in Leipzig, Berlin, and Göttingen as well as in London before the end of the century.

European Prints after Trumbull and Peale

The second likeness of Washington to be introduced into Europe in the early 1780s was painted by the Connecticut artist John Trumbull, who had served as aide-de-camp to the General. Soon after Trumbull arrived in London, in July 1780, he painted the picture from memory, aided perhaps by his own copy of a portrait by Charles Willson Peale.[57] Trumbull's painting was sold to an Amsterdam banker named De Neufville, but before it left London it was engraved by the fashionable printmaker Valentine Green, "Mezzotinto Engraver to his Majesty, & to the Elector Palatine." The print, published on January 15, 1781, was impressive and sophisticated (Fig. 14). Executed in a smooth, refined mezzotint style, it was a full-length image of Washington standing on the bank of the Hudson River. A bust-length version of the portrait was engraved by Green in 1783.[58]

It was not long before the Green mezzotints were copied for book illustration. One engraver, Jacques Le Roy, copied the full-length print as an illustration for Michel René Hilliard D'Auberteuil's *Essais historiques et politiques sur les Anglo-Americains,* published in Brussels in 1781.[59] In another, creative adaption an Irish engraver used the Trumbull figure of Washington in his frontispiece for *The Gentleman's and London Magazine,* published in Dublin by John Exshaw in June 1783 (Fig. 15). Instead of standing on the cliffs of the Hudson, Washington rests his foot on British flags and books and documents labeled "Brit. Stat.," "Acts of Parl.," "Stamp Act," and "Boston Port Bill." He holds a scroll reading "American Freedom established by Valour and Perseverance." Hovering above him, the figure of Fame blows her trumpet and holds a laurel wreath over his head.[60] This latter image was becoming a familiar iconographic element of Washington prints both in America and in Europe.

The full-length Green mezzotint also seems to be the source for a whole series of European illustrations of Washington which feature a black stock with the uniform. Most of these prints were descendants of William Sharp's frontispiece (Fig. 16) for *A Poetical Epistle to His Excellency*

FIGURE 14. Mezzotint by Valentine Green after John Trumbull, 1781. Hart 84. National Portrait Gallery.

George Washington, written by Charles Wharton and published in London in 1780. The inscription on the Sharp engraving indicates a publication date of February 22, 1780, before Trumbull even arrived in London. However, details of the face and uniform and the arm crossed over the chest are so reminiscent of Trumbull's Washington, it seems likely that the inscription date is wrong and that Sharp copied an early proof of the Green engraving later in the year. The Sharp illustration, with its distinctive black stock, was copied in Paris by Noël Pruneau and was the basis for several imitations in England.[61] The image also appeared in an American edition of Wharton's book, in which the Sharp frontispiece was copied by Richard Brunton [13].

Both the Brunton engraving and the French copy by Pruneau repeated the allegorical embellishments of the Sharp print, which included cannon, cannonballs, banners, liberty cap, snake, and the motto "Dont Tread on Me." Originally the author and an unidentified friend, both Americans living in England, had ambitious plans for the frontispiece to the poem. In letters to Wharton, the friend had described his efforts to persuade Benjamin West to make a full-length drawing of Washington for the frontispiece. West was too busy to comply, and the friend wrote that he had finally gotten a print of Washington from Paris. He described it as a "tolerably good likeness, . . . a front face and only of bust size." [62] Probably it was the print published by Esnauts and Rapilly (Fig. 8) in which appear several symbols from the Sharp illustration—the cannon, cannonballs, banners, branches, and liberty cap. The motto and the snake device in the Sharp engraving, both emblems on the first official flag raised on the ship *Alfred* in 1775, were featured on the fictitious mezzotint of naval hero Esek Hopkins, published in London by Thomas Hart the following year.[63] Although Sharp thus used a variety of prints as sources for his allegorical embellishment, he chose the authentic likeness after Trumbull for his portrait of Washington.

In addition to these engravings, the full-length Trumbull figure of Washington, combined with the Du Simitière profiles, was included in an English cotton fabric printed with scenes of "America Presenting at the Altar of Liberty Medallions of her famous sons." [64] While the full-length image of Washington on this fabric was crowned with laurel by a figure of Fame, various allegorical goddesses holding profiles of American patriots approached a goddess of Liberty. Another printed textile of the period that helped to popularize Trumbull's image featured scenes of the "Apotheosis of Benjamin Frankin and George Washington." [65] Surely Trumbull would never have expected that the influence of his Washington painting would reach the extent of Irish magazine illustration and allegorical bed hangings. The appearance of Trumbull's and Du Simitière's images in magazines and on printed textiles confirms the broad influence the printed portraits could have. Arriving in Europe at just the right moment, these likenesses were quickly incorporated into the popular imagery of the American scene.

The Trumbull and Du Simitière portraits did have competition, however, from the third authentic likeness to arrive in the 1780s, that painted by Charles Willson Peale. Actually the influence of Peale on European prints was based not on one painting but on several. Unfortunately the knotty problem of which Peale paintings reached Europe, and when, has never been unraveled. Tracing the exact source of individual prints is thus greatly complicated. References in Peale's papers suggest that various Washington portraits were sent abroad,[66] but it is often difficult to know what images actually reached the printmakers.

It seems likely, however, that the first of Peale's Washington paintings to reach Europe was

FIGURE 15. Engraving by unidentified artist after John Trumbull, 1783. Published in the *Gentleman's and London Magazine*, Dublin, June 1783. Hart 88. Print Collection, New York Public Library.

FIGURE 16. Engraving by William Sharp after John Trumbull, 1780. Published in Charles Wharton's *A Poetical Epistle to His Excellency George Washington* (London, 1780). Hart 92. Library of Congress.

a replica of the portrait he painted for John Hancock in 1776 (Fig. 2). It was owned by, or at least in the possession of, the Marquis de Lafayette.[67] In 1780 the French engraver Noël Le Mire produced a Washington print after a painting by Jean Baptiste Le Paon (Fig. 17), which, according to the inscription, was based on "le Tableau Original appartenant a Mr. Marquis de la Fayette." Although the French painter created a much more elaborate picture by the addition of a military encampment, tent, horse, attendant, and a large number of labeled documents pertaining to the Revolution, the face and figure of Washington, with his left hand tucked into his vest, are essentially the same as Peale's 1776 painting. Significantly, a companion piece of Lafayette was issued by the same artists. The Marquis, who arrived in America in 1777, had returned to France temporarily from January 1779 to April 1780 and could have taken a painting back with him at that time. Another French print, engraved by Justus Chevillet (Fig. 18) and published in the 1780s, also bears an inscription that it was designed "d'apres un Tableau fourni par M. le Marquis de la Fayette." Although it is a bust-length portrait and is a distinctly French interpretation, the face is basically similar to the Peale image.

FIGURE 17. Engraving by Noël Le Mire after Jean Baptiste Le Paon after Charles Willson Peale, 1780. Hart 31. National Portrait Gallery.

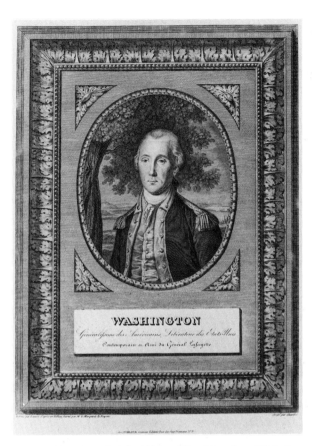

FIGURE 18. Engraving by Justus Chevillet after Michel Honoré Bonnieu after Charles Willson Peale, c. 1780–1785. Hart 29d. National Portrait Gallery.

FIGURE 19. Engraving by Thomas Cook after Charles Willson Peale, 1783. Hart 40. Private collection.

In 1785 the Washington engraving by Le Mire was copied in mezzotint in England and published by Carington Bowles.[68] The Le Mire print may also have been the basis for small bust-length engravings of Washington such as the portrait by Thomas Cook on a broadside entitled "A Circular Letter from his Excellency George Washington," published in London in 1783 (Fig. 19), or the portrait by William Angus in John Andrews' *History of the War* (Vol. 1, London, 1785).[69]

By 1785 another Peale image was also available in London (Fig. 20). Peale himself, perhaps frustrated by the poor sales of his own mezzotint engravings, sent two paintings to London to be copied as prints. On December 10, 1783, he wrote to Benjamin West: "Genl. Reed carries over with him a portrait of Genl. Washington & one of Genl. Greene to get plates engraved for me. I have left it to his discretion to do the best he can for me. Your advice will oblige me." [70] Peale's bust-length portraits [71] were sold to the publisher Joseph Brown, who organized the production of the engravings. Valentine Green, after his success with prints after Trumbull, was chosen to engrave the mezzotints after Peale. The English artist Thomas Stothard made drawings based on the paintings, transforming the portraits into full-length figures and adding background details. The painting of Washington that Peale had sent over was probably based on his life portrait of 1779. Stothard added a horse and cannon and gave Washington a relaxed and elegant pose. Like Green's mezzotints after Trumbull, the print after Peale was smoothly executed and sophisticated.

GENERAL WASHINGTON.

It lacked, however, the direct and personal characterization of Washington that is evident in Peale's own prints after his paintings. Nevertheless, it was undoubtedly well received in London, where it served as a model for other printmakers.

From these French and English engravings, as well as from other Peale paintings that were sent abroad, the Peale face of Washington was widely disseminated throughout Europe. In the process, most of the subtlety of Peale's different characterizations of Washington at various points during and after the war was lost. Prints derived from other prints moved further away from the original sources, with inevitable degeneration. Washington scholar William S. Baker, writing about these foreign engravings, noted that the Peale image of Washington

> seems to have been at once taken hold of and either copied or used as a groundwork, for the production of pictures calculated to please the popular taste. From these copies and pictures, engravings were made and repeated again and again, losing naturally in every step, the force and character of the original. This is proved by Lavater, who in his remarks upon the one published in the French edition of his Essay on Physiognomy (afterwards copied by Holloway for the English edition and also by Zerlamsler), says, "If Washington is the author of the revolution, we have seen him undertake and accomplish with so much success, it is positive that the designer must have lost some of the most striking features of the original." [72]

Nevertheless, the degree to which European artists used some derivative of the Peale image of Washington was extraordinary.

The Revolution and its outcome had astonished European observers. From 1775 through the 1780s portraits of American patriots enjoyed a vogue in the print markets. Most desirable of all were images of the famous American Commander in Chief, the one outstanding hero of the war. Publishers eagerly supplied a remarkable variety of Washington prints, which, when not fictitious, were based on authentic portraits by Du Simitière, Trumbull, and Peale. But news of the Grand Convention meeting in Philadelphia in 1787 and the Constitution resulting from it suggested that George Washington had a new role to play in the American drama. All reports indicated that the Commander in Chief was soon to be elected President of the United States.

FIGURE 20. Mezzotint by Valentine Green after Thomas Stothard after Charles Willson Peale, 1785. Hart 18. National Portrait Gallery.

FIGURE 21. Engraving by Amos Doolittle after James Trenchard, 1788–1789, first state of [25]. Hart 840. John Carter Brown Library, Brown University.

The Presidential Image

☆   ☆   ☆

After serving in 1787 as head of the Grand Convention and campaigning on behalf of the new Constitution it produced, George Washington was the inevitable choice for the nation's first President. In April 1789 he journeyed to New York for his inauguration. Parades, songs, orations, and fireworks greeted him at every stop. The cover of *Bickerstaff's Boston Almanack* published that year featured two portrait medallions hung from an arch ornamented with stars and a federal eagle [24]. Although there was no attempt at likenesses, this image of the new President and Vice-President recalled the triumphal arches and decorations that had greeted Washington as he journeyed toward New York.

America's military hero had become a statesman. Depicting this transformation was not an easy task for printmakers. References to Washington's political career were not as obvious as indications of his military glory. With the exception of Amos Doolittle, most printmakers did not attempt to suggest a political presence. Like Charles Willson Peale's 1787 mezzotint portrait [21], made while Washington was president of the convention, the presidential prints made in America were generally straight portraits with little symbolic embellishment. Washington was still the hero of the Revolution and was often depicted in uniform, but there was less emphasis on military ornamentation.

The ubiquitous cuts after Peale were still appearing in almanacs and primers during Washington's two terms in office. More expensive engravings, however, began to feature new portraits. The delicate profile by Joseph Wright and the unidealized likenesses by Edward Savage became the presidential images. Predominant in American prints, they were also exported to Europe, where they were copied, modified, sent back to America, and copied again. When the Commander in Chief became President, the young oval-faced Peale image began to give way to these older, more serious depictions.

A Political Portrait

The one print that did represent Washington's new career was Amos Doolittle's *Display of the United States of America* [25]. This large, ambitious engraving, depicting Washington's new role in the nation's history, was unsurpassed as a visual political statement. The theme of the print was the recently adopted Constitution and the newly strengthened federal government that resulted from it. The portrait of Washington was surrounded by a heraldic ring of state seals each inscribed with population statistics and congressional representation. These interlocking circles were not only an elaborate framing device for the portrait, they were also a symbol of the indissoluble unity to which the states had pledged themselves. It was a dramatic change from a loose confederation of colonies to a nation with a strong federal government, and the central focus of that change—and of the print—was the new President, George Washington.

Unfortunately, in the first state of the print (Fig. 21), Doolittle had copied for his portrait an engraving of Washington from the *Columbian Magazine* of 1787 [20], an awkward portrayal by James Trenchard that looked little like its subject. Doolittle's copy of it was the principal weakness of his design. Apparently Doolittle was aware of its drawbacks and changed the portrait in the second state of the print to resemble the profile by Joseph Wright [26]. Although he made consistent changes in the plate, the portrait remained basically the same.

Doolittle's attempt to record territories and new states on the print and adjust the population statistics necessitated constant changes in the plate. Nevertheless, despite its impracticality, it was a brilliant design, and Doolittle had high hopes for its success. His dedication "To the Patrons of Arts and Sciences in all parts of the World" suggests that he planned to export his engraving. He also reused the basic symbolic scheme for a print of John Adams, and supposedly again for a print of Thomas Jefferson.[73]

The Presidential Profile

The profile image which Doolittle had used for the second state of his print and which quickly became a favorite was produced by Joseph Wright in 1790 (Fig. 22; [26]). Although the story that Wright had sketched Washington as he sat in a pew in Saint Paul's Chapel in New York is probably apocryphal, the artist had painted and modeled his subject from life several years earlier.[74] The etching he produced in 1790 was a bust-length portrait in uniform with a distinctive vertical profile and tightly compressed lips that gave an air of resolute determination. Small, and printed on heavy card stock, the etching could be sent easily through the mails, which helped to broaden its influence. Thomas Jefferson purchased Wright's print and sent it to his daughter Martha Jefferson Randolph.[75] Salem minister and diarist William Bentley was sent one as a gift by his friend Benjamin Goodhue.[76]

Wright's etching was immediately and widely copied for prints and illustrations as well as coins and medals both in America and abroad. Small as it was, it seemed to have an inspirational quality that motivated a number of artists to make their first attempts at printmaking. In Philadelphia James Manly designed a medal of Washington [27] based on Wright's profile and then made an engraving after it. He had advertised the medal, available in gold, silver, and white metal, on March 3, 1790.[77] Included in the notice was an endorsement signed by four prominent men who testified that the medal was a "strong and expressive likeness and worthy the attention of the citizens of the United States of America." The words featured on the reverse of the medal—"General of the American Armies 1775. Resigned 1783. President of the United States 1789"—were repeated, along with Washington's birthdate, in the inscription of the print.

William Rollinson's "first attempt at copperplate engraving," according to William Dunlap in 1834, was his 1791 copy of the Wright etching [29].[78] The etching also inspired, in 1793, the initial printmaking effort of the young Joseph Hiller, Jr. [36]. Hiller made a second attempt at engraving a profile of Washington the following year [37], and this 1794 portrait was much closer to Wright's original. Like its model, it was printed on heavy card stock. In fact, most of the copies known are on the backs of playing cards.[79] The existence of a seal with a similar profile suggests that Hiller might have made the print to send to a seal-cutter in London.[80]

The unsigned engraving in the *Massachusetts Magazine* for March 1791 [28] was a version of the Wright profile that was distinctive for the figure-eight design of the epaulet. Both the Wright etching and the *Massachusetts Magazine* engraving made their way to Europe, where they were copied and modified. The former was the model for an accurate adaptation engraved by Gottfried Arnold Lehman in Amsterdam in 1791 (Fig. 23) and for a less successful copy by John Chapman in London in 1793.[81] The *Massachusetts Magazine* portrait was the basis for Thomas Holloway's engraving for the London *Literary Magazine and British Review* of July 1792 (Fig. 24). Holloway made substantial changes in the uniform, buttoning up the coat for an entirely different effect. His version was copied by Hendrik Roosing of Rotterdam in 1793 and by George Murray in London for the *Pocket Magazine* of 1795.[82]

Holloway's engraving was also the portrait source for an allegorical frontispiece published in Dublin in the *Sentimental and Masonic Magazine* of June 1795 (Fig. 25). The blindfolded figure of Justice wearing a Masonic apron and holding a sword and a pair of scales leans against a medallion portrait of Washington. As explained in the verse beneath, a female representing Freedom embraces the portrait, and the figure of Honor, wearing Minerva's helmet, kneels next to it. The adoring attention of these ladies, the pyramid in the background, and the winged cupid hovering above are images usually reserved for a deceased hero's memorial, but for this artist Freedom's "darling son" warranted such treatment while still alive. Allegorical presentations of Washington were to increase significantly after his retirement; during the presidency, however, the unembellished portrait was still more common. Ultimately the Holloway version of Wright's profile returned to America as well, where a copy by H. Houston, without symbolic embellishment, appeared in the *American Universal Magazine* for February 1797 [49]. Representing Holloway's reinterpretation of Wright's original portrait, it completed a transatlantic circle of borrowed visual imagery that was characteristic of the period.

One other adaptation of Wright's profile spawned a progeny of print copies. These engravings can be related to Wright's painting, now at the Cleveland Museum of Art,[83] in which the face is a profile similar to the etching, but the body has been turned to a three-quarter pose. This profile type was engraved by John Scoles in 1795 for Charles Smith's *The Gentleman's Political Pocket-Almanac* [42]. It was copied for a 1795 London edition of Hume's *History of England* and again in 1800 as the heading to a London broadside of Washington's Farewell Address.[84]

Clearly, Wright's modest profile had captured the imagination. In the opinion of one recent critic, "Wright's profile heads of Washington, with their wide currency in engravings, must be accounted among the most influential of his portraits, sharing with Stuart's three-quarter views and Houdon's bust the creation of the President's likeness as it exists in the mind of the public."[85] The Wright etching is, in fact, beautifully executed as well with feathery drypoint lines and sensitive modeling of the face. Although it was probably not the first artist's etching in America, as some have claimed,[86] it deserves consideration not only for its popularity but for its artistic merit.

FIGURE 22. Etching with drypoint by Joseph Wright, c. 1790 [26].

FIGURE 23. Engraving by Gottfried Arnold Lehman after Joseph Wright, 1791. Hart 139. Print Collection, New York Public Library.

GENERAL WASHINGTON.

Published as the Act directs 1 Aug 1792 by C.Forster Poultry.

FIGURE 24. Engraving by Thomas Holloway after Joseph Wright, 1792. Published in the *Literary Magazine and British Review*, London, July 1792. Hart 167. Private collection.

FIGURE 25. Engraving by unidentified artist after Joseph Wright, 1795. Published in the *Sentimental and Masonic Magazine*, Dublin, June 1795. Hart 154. Print Collection, New York Public Library.

Engrav'd for the Masonic Magazine

When FREEDOM, first her glorious Day had won,
She smil'd on WASHINGTON, her darling Son.
Mild JUSTICE claims him as his Virtues rise,

Edward Savage's Success

Joseph Wright's major competition for a presidential image of George Washington was the work of Edward Savage. In 1789 the Massachusetts-born artist had painted a portrait of Washington for Harvard University (Fig. 26), probably making at the same time a replica for himself.[87] Savage was acutely conscious of the commercial potential of such an image during the year of Washington's inauguration. He began at the same time a large painting of the entire Washington family and a copperplate of the same subject. Perhaps Savage knew of the expanding market in England for prints after portraits and history paintings, or had heard that William Woollett's 1776 engraving from Benjamin West's *The Death of General Wolfe* had earned about 15,000 pounds.[88] Like Charles Willson Peale, Savage was convinced that he would make a fortune reproducing his own paintings in print form. Although his expectations were perhaps exaggerated, he was far more succeful than most American painters at selling his engravings.

Probably realizing his lack of engraving skills, Savage abandoned work on his large copper-plate of the Washington family when he went to England in 1791. Once in London, he revived his ambition to make prints. In December 1791 he published a print of Henry Knox,[89] and on February 7, 1792, he issued his stipple engraving of George Washington [31] after the Harvard portrait. Savage must have had ample assistance from a skilled London engraver, for the Washington print, like the portrait of Knox, is well executed with minute stippling that creates a soft tonal effect, particularly in the face. Washington had turned sixty the month the engraving was issued, and although the face in the print is more serene and dignified than careworn, Savage obviously had not tried to disguise the President's age. The small stipple engraving was soon copied for illustrations by both American and European printmakers. In London one unsigned print was issued on August 10, 1793.[90] Another variant, which according to the inscription was "from an Original Miniature in the Possession of Benjamin Smith of Philadelphia," was published in London on June 19, 1794 (Fig. 27). Savage's likeness must have seemed far more current than many of the prints then in circulation.

Having conquered the stipple technique, Savage attempted the laborious mezzotint process. His first subject was again George Washington, in a print published in London on June 15, 1793 [33]. A companion print of Benjamin Franklin after a portrait by David Martin followed a few months later.[91] Like the stipple engravings, Savage's mezzotints are, as first attempts in the medium, exceptionally well executed. They are quite large, have a very fine, smooth grain, and are modeled with subtlety and softness. Undoubtedly Savage had a technician to prepare the plate, a skilled printer to print it, and a guiding hand more experienced than his own throughout the engraving process. The inscription of the Washington print, "Savage pinx. et sculp.," indicating that he was both painter and engraver, does not reflect the assistance that he most certainly had.

Nevertheless, the print was an impressive production. Its source was a small oil portrait on a panel, now at the Chicago Art Institute, which depicted a three-quarter-length figure seated at a table, holding a document (Fig. 28). The painting was signed and dated 1793, and the face was based on Savage's Harvard portrait. In the print, the document on the table is clearly a plan of the City of Washington bordered by a section of the Potomac river labeled "Eastern Branch." It was

FIGURE 26. Oil on canvas by Edward Savage, 1789. **Fogg Art Museum, Harvard University.**

FIGURE 27. Engraving by unidentified artist after Edward Savage, 1794. Hart 226. Print Collection, New York Public Library.

a new type of Washington engraving. Dressed in black velvet rather than the usual uniform, Washington contemplates the new federal city and the future of the government it was built to accommodate. Here was a statesman rather than a soldier, a man with age, wisdom, and dignity in his face. It was truly a presidential image.

Savage sent copies of his two mezzotints to George Washington along with a letter dated October 6, 1793:

> I have taken the liberty to send two prints. The one done from the portrait I first sketched in black velvet, labours under some disadvantages as the Likeness never was quite finished. I hope it will meet with the approbation of yourself and Mrs. Washington as it is the first I ever published in that method of Engraving. The portrait of Doctor Franklin which is published as the companion, is done from a picture in the possession of Mr. West.[92]

Another version of the Savage mezzotint [34] has a slightly coarser grain but is otherwise similar in all details. Few copies of this engraving are in existence today, suggesting that it was not published. Probably executed at the same time, it can be attributed to Savage with the assumption that he undoubtedly had assistance in engraving his plates. The published version of the mezzotint had, in contrast, wide circulation. Although it was too elaborate a composition to be frequently imitated for book illustrations, it probably found a healthy market for framing both in America

41

FIGURE 28. Oil on panel by Edward Savage, 1793. Art Institute of Chicago.

and in Europe. Judging from the number of impressions still in existence today, Savage's Washington print was as popular as most English mezzotints.

After his return to America, Savage finally published his large engraving of the Washington family [55]. Having painted the portraits of George and Martha Washington and her two grandchildren in 1789–1790 and having obtained new sittings from the President and his wife in 1795,[93] Savage finished the *Washington Family* canvas, now at the National Gallery, in 1796.[94] The engraving was not published until March 10, 1798, after Savage had hired the skilled English stipple engraver David Edwin, who had arrived in Philadelphia the previous December. Having heard favorable comments about the engraving, George Washington ordered four impressions, requesting that they be put in "handsome, but not costly, gilt frames with glasses." [95] In response Savage wrote to Washington on June 3, 1798, explaining the history of the print and his hopes for its success:

> Agreeable to Col. Biddle's order I delivered four of the best impressions of your Family Print. They are choose out of the first that was printed. Perhaps you may think that they are two dark, but they will change lighter after hanging two or three months. The frames are good sound work. . . . The likenesses of the young people are not much like what they are at present. The Copper-plate was begun and half-finished from the likenesses which I painted in New York in the year 1789. I could not make the alterations in the copper to make it like the painting which I finished in Philadelphia in 1796. The portraits of yourself and Mrs. Washington are generally thought to be likenesses. As soon as I got one of the prints ready to be seen I advertised in two of the papers that a subscription would be open for about twenty days. Within that time there was 331 subscribers to the print and about 100 had subscribed previously, all of them the most respectable people in the city. In consequence of its success and being generally approved of I have continued the Subscription. There is every probability at present of its producing me at least $10,000 in one twelve month. As soon as I have one printed in colours I shall take the liberty to send it to Mrs Washington for her acceptance. I think she will like it better than a plain print.[96]

Much controversy has ensued over whether Savage actually engraved his own plates or merely marketed, under his own name, prints engraved by his assistants and apprentices. His detractors, starting with his disgruntled apprentice John Wesley Jarvis, claimed that Savage's London prints were too good to be engraved by someone new to the techniques; that he had hired another English engraver before David Edwin; and that Edwin produced all of Savage's prints from 1798 to 1801, assisted by other apprentices.[97] Later defenders of Savage's printmaking countered every charge.[98] From the evidence given by Jarvis, Edwin, and Dunlap, it is safe to assume that many of Savage's plates were group efforts. His print of the *Washington Family*, for instance, although started by him, was finished by Edwin. Savage also undoubtedly had assistance for his London plates. On the other hand, Savage surely knew something about engraving and was intimately involved with the production of his prints. He conceived the idea, provided the original painting, probably put the design initially on copper,[99] supervised any assistants, and published the final product. Assistance notwithstanding, they are as much his engravings as anyone else's.

Like the mezzotint engraving, a large number of *Washington Family* prints are still in existence, which would suggest that Savage's optimistic predictions for its success, if exaggerated, were not altogether unreasonable. There was good reason for its popularity. The presidential image of Washington contemplating the plan of the federal city is repeated in this print. But Washington's personal virtues as a family man were suggested as well by depicting him surrounded by his wife, his black servant Billy Lee, and two of Martha's grandchildren, Eleanor Parke Custis and George Washington Parke Custis. Washington's military accomplishments were also alluded to, for he is shown in his uniform rather than in black velvet.

Advertised in the *Pennsylvania Gazette* on March 21, 1798, the *Washington Family* was described as "an elegant Engraving, . . . The whole is executed in a style evincive of the rapid progress of an elegant art, which has hitherto been in a very crude state in this country." In all three of his Washington engravings Savage made an impact, not only on the financial and artistic progress of graphic arts, but on the image of the nation's first President.

Embellished with a Portrait

The years of Washington's presidency were a prosperous era for the book arts in America. Newspapers were filled with advertisements for volumes of literature, history, biography, and collected writings. New magazines were started in many major cities with ambitious promises for literary entertainment and cultural education.[100] Whenever possible, engraved illustrations were included in these publications, or at least an engraved frontispiece. A growing number of monthly magazines, for instance, spent a large proportion of their budgets to issue an engraving with each number. On those occasions when publishers tried to exclude the plates, complaining about their cost, the readers resisted. The preface of the 1791 volume of the *Massachusetts Magazine* suggested that "eight pages extra would at times be more gratifying, than the . . . trivial decoration of a plate, which only amuses the eye, without informing the mind, or meliorating the heart." The reader's response was duly noted by the contrite publishers in the preface to the next year's volume: "Three month's experience was decisive: The admirers of this polite art earnestly called for their resumption: They were instantly gratified." Portraits were a favorite subject for both magazine engravings and book frontispieces. "Embellished with an elegant portrait" was a frequent advertisement. When no other image seemed appropriate, an engraving of Washington almost always was. Thus, in a wide range of publications from almanacs and magazines to histories and poems, a portrait of the President was often featured at the front.

Relief cuts of Washington after Charles Willson Peale had not disappeared. In many inexpensively adorned primers [51], almanacs [30], and schoolbooks [32], tiny oval-shaped faces peered forth, reminding new generations of Washington's virtues. The *South Carolina Weekly Museum,* the only magazine published south of Baltimore in the eighteenth century,[101] reprinted the same cut of Washington on the wrapper cover of each number as well as on the frontispiece to the yearly volume [50]. Even the relief-cut illustrations, however, were beginning to show some experimentation with different likenesses of Washington. The little cut that illustrates a 1794 Philadelphia volume, *The Life of General Washington* [38], appears to be based on a portrait by John Trumbull. The frontispiece cut of a 1796 Germantown edition of the *New England Primer* [47] was copied from the Washington profile drawn by Du Simitière. The ubiquitous Peale face clearly was being challenged.

The same was true for engraved illustration. It is difficult to tell which Washington portrait inspired Elkanah Tisdale, who made a frontispiece for the *Monthly Military Repository* in 1796 [43], but it bore no resemblance to Peale's. The same year William Rollinson made an engraving of Washington [44] after a miniature by Walter Robertson. It was included in William Winter-botham's four-volume commentary on the United States, which was illustrated with portraits by various engravers. Although most of the portraits were copied from plates in the English edition, Rollinson took his likeness of Washington from an engraving by Robert Field published in Philadelphia in 1795 [39].

The most popular likenesses for book illustrations were those by Savage and Wright which dominated the separate prints during these years. As previously mentioned, the unsigned profile after Wright published in the *Massachusetts Magazine* for March 1791 [28] had, with its distinctive figure-eight epaulet, an influence on European prints of Washington.[102] Variations of Wright's image also appeared as frontispieces to the *American Universal Magazine* of February 1797 [49] and *The Gentleman's Political Pocket-Almanac for . . . 1796* [42].

John Scoles was one of the many engravers who copied Edward Savage's prints of Washington [40]. Scoles' plate of the President, based on Savage's three-quarter-length mezzotint of Washington seated at a table [33], was published in another volume of Winterbotham's commentary on the United States. Savage's stipple engraving [31] was an even more popular source than his mezzotint. The frontispiece of a volume of Washington's *Official Letters to the Honorable American Congress* [46], published in 1796, was "ornamented with a striking likeness" after Savage.[103] Another volume of letters published that year under the title *Epistles Domestic, Confidential, and Official from General Washington* proved to be entirely fraudulent. Washington wrote to Secretary of State Timothy Pickering that the letters were "a base forgery, . . . I never saw or heard of them until they appeared in print."[104] However, the frontispiece, an aquatint by William Rollinson after the familiar Savage stipple, was certainly authentic [45]. Perhaps the author hoped to make his volume more convincing by including a widely recognized frontispiece portrait of Washington.

The engraver H. Houston made his version of the Savage portrait for a January 1798 issue of the *Philadelphia Monthly Magazine* [73]. In the frontispiece to the yearly volume the publisher claimed that the engravings were "finished in a stile calculated to please even connoisseurs" and were "equal, if not superior, to the engravings that generally accompany Magazines, whether foreign or domestick." Shortly after the publication of this print, the Houston plate was reengraved and used for a German-language magazine published in Philadelphia. In 1800 the worn plate was reused again for the frontispiece to *Mount Vernon*, a long poem by John Searson. Judging from the title page, the poet had hoped to illustrate the volume with "a copper-plate likeness of the General . . . taken from an actual view on the spot by the author, 15th May, 1799." However, the view of Washington at Mount Vernon was never made into a print, and Houston's badly re-engraved plate was pulled out once again to serve as a frontispiece.

European Prints of the President

In Europe interest in the first President of the United States was almost as keen as curiosity about the Commander in Chief had been, and portrait prints of Washington continued to circulate throughout the 1790s. The European prints were more diverse during these years than the

FIGURE 29. Engraving by unidentified artist after Charles Willson Peale, 1794. Published in Johann Kaspar Lavater's *Essays on Physiognomy* (London, 1789–1798), Volume 3, Part 2 (1798). Hart 21. National Portrait Gallery.

FIGURE 31. Engraving by Louis Charles Ruotte after François Bonneville after Pierre Eugène Du Simitière, 1796. Published in *Portraits des personnages célèbres de la Revolution*, Volume 1 (Paris, 1796). Hart 172. Print Collection, New York Public Library.

American publications, with older portrait types appearing along with more recent ones. Accuracy varied widely as the print copies grew further away from their original sources. The Peale image was still generating descendants, some of them now almost unrecognizable. One example was an engraving from the London edition of Johann Kaspar Lavater's *Essays on Physiognomy* (Fig. 29), published in several volumes during 1789–1798. "The English artist," noted the inscription, "has followed the lines of the Print in the French original, after a picture by Piehle, on account of the remarks of Mr. Lavater." Another favorite image of the 1790s, ultimately derived from Peale, was the full length of Washington standing in front of a camp tent. The first engraving of this subject was by Noël Le Mire after Jean Baptiste Le Paon (Fig. 17) with a Peale face of Washington. Published in 1780, it was copied in an English mezzotint published by Carington Bowles in 1785,[105] which in turn was the source of several mezzotints published in the 1790s (for example, Fig. 30).[106]

The Savage and Wright images that dominated American prints of the presidential years enjoyed a vogue in Europe as well. Savage's stipple bust of Washington [31] and his three-quarter-

46

GENERAL   WASHINGTON.

Late President of the United States of America, —— From a fine Original Engraved at Paris.

Published 15th May 1797. by LAURIE & WHITTLE, 53 Fleet Street, London

FIGURE 30. Engraving by unidentified artist after Jean Baptiste Le Paon (published by Laurie and Whittle), 1797. Hart 34. Print Collection, New York Public Library.

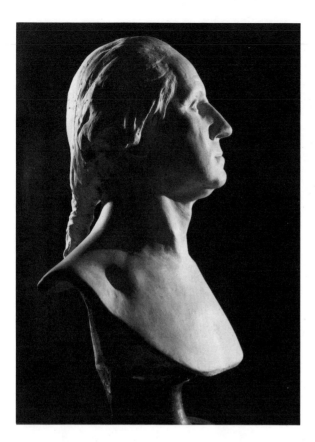

FIGURE 32. Clay bust by Jean Antoine Houdon, 1785. Mount Vernon Ladies' Association.

FIGURE 33. Engraving by Alexandre Tardieu after Jean Antoine Houdon, c. 1790. Hart 193. Print Collection, New York Public Library.

length mezzotint [33] were both published in London, so they did not need to be exported to have a wide circulation abroad. Wright's etching [26], easily sent through the mail, also reached Europe and was extensively copied. Wright's image, however, did have competition from other profile portraits of Washington during the 1790s. Even the Du Simitière profile, engraved by Prévost in 1781 (Fig. 12), still had validity. One derivation of it, supposedly after a drawing by François Bonneville, was engraved by Louis Charles Ruotte for a work entitled *Portraits des personnages célèbres de la Révolution,* published in Paris in 1796 (Fig. 31).[107]

The sculptor Jean Antoine Houdon was also influencing profile prints of Washington in Europe. Having modeled Washington's face from life and taken a life mask at Mount Vernon in October 1785, Houdon returned to France early in 1786.[108] Not only were there exhibitions of his work in Paris, but Houdon's sculpted likeness of Washington (Fig. 32) also inspired a commemorative medal.[109] The medal, originally commissioned by the American Congress, was designed in Paris by Pierre Simon Duvivier, who produced a profile of Washington related to the Houdon portrait.[110] A similar profile image, which according to the inscription was designed and engraved after Houdon, appeared in a print by the French engraver Alexandre Tardieu (Fig. 33).

Also inspired by the work of Houdon was a miniature by the Marchioness de Bréhan, a sister-in-law of the French minister in America, Comte de Moustier. Bréhan's portrait of

FIGURE 34. Engraving by Antoine Louis François
Sérgent after the Marchioness de Bréhan and Jean
Antoine Houdon, 1790, Hart 206. Print Collection,
New York Public Library.

Washington was engraved in France in 1790 by Antoine Louis François Sérgent (Fig. 34). The
miniature, which resembled the Houdon image, was probably begun in Paris and then
finished after the Marchioness and her brother-in-law had visited the President at Mount
Vernon.[111] On October 3, 1789, Washington noted in his diary: "sat about two o'clock for Madame
de Brienne, to complete a miniature profile of me, which she had begun from memory and
which she had made exceedingly like the original."[112] The portrait was not actually done from
memory, as it is clearly a sculpted bust profile related to Houdon's. The addition of the laurel
wreath to the sculpted bust also suggests that the Marchioness was aware of the medallion portraits
of Washington by Joseph Wright who used this same motif.[113]

Through her brother-in-law, the French minister, Bréhan sent a number of the Sérgent
engravings to the President,[114] who presented them to his friends. One of the little profile portraits
bore the notation on the reverse: "The President's compliments accompany the enclosed to Mrs.
Morris." [115] Mrs. Walter Stewart also received the print, along with a note from Washington, dated
March 16, 1796, which read: "Not for the representation or the value, but because it is the
production of a fair lady, the President takes the liberty of presenting the enclosed with his best
regards, to Mrs. Stewart, praying her acceptance of it." [116]

Providing a contrasting alternative to the small profile prints was Thomas Cheesman's

General Washington.

enormous full-length stipple engraving of Washington, published in London in 1796 (Fig. 35). It was the first print to reproduce John Trumbull's heroic portrait *General Washington at Trenton,* now at Yale University. This painting, sometimes considered the best portrait of Washington as a general,[117] was commissioned by the city of Charleston, South Carolina, in 1792. Although the city rejected the portrait, preferring a more peaceful and "matter-of-fact" likeness,[118] Trumbull considered it the "best certainly of those which I painted, and the best, in my estimation, which exists, in his heroic military character." Choosing to depict Washington in a dramatic moment of decision the evening before the surprise attack, Trumbull wrote that he intended "to give his military character, in the most sublime moment of its exertion."[119]

Sent to London in 1794 with John Jay, who was negotiating the treaty with Great Britain, Trumbull took the opportunity to arrange for an engraving of his painting. He had painted several replicas,[120] one of which he left with his publisher, Antonio di Poggi.[121] Engraved by the London artist Thomas Cheesman, the print was a faithful copy, depicting Washington as calm and resolute despite the rearing horse and frantic figures behind him. Although published long after the event, the engraving as a heroic portrayal of the leader of the Revolution was unequaled among the prints of Washington. Not only was it undoubtedly admired in Europe, it was also exported to America. In 1800 a New York newspaper, advertising another Washington print, recalled that an earlier one "engraved by Cheeseman from a picture by Trumbull, has considerable merit."[122] Despite this approval, the Cheesman engraving was not copied by American printmakers until a later generation. Particularly appealing to the nineteenth-century heroic conception of Washington, Cheesman's print was to inspire many engravings in the future. In Washington's own day, however, many people may have preferred, along with the city fathers of Charleston, calm and peaceful images of their President in his civic role.

If historical portraits of Washington as a general were no longer quite appropriate, mere likenesses were also beginning to seem insufficient to portray all that this aging leader now represented. By the time of his retirement in 1797, after two terms in office, the Washington image depicted in prints and illustrations was becoming more than just a recognizable face.

FIGURE 35. Engraving by Thomas Cheesman after John Trumbull, 1796. Hart 104. National Portrait Gallery.

FIGURE 36. Oil on canvas by Gilbert Stuart, 1796. Jointly owned by the National Portrait Gallery and the Museum of Fine Arts, Boston.

National Symbol

☆   ☆   ☆

Washington's second term in office had been a period of wrenching political division. Opposition to John Jay's controversial treaty with Great Britain in 1795 brought the pro-English Federalists and the pro-French opposition to the brink of violence. Bitter partisan attacks, including vicious personal criticism of the President, appeared in the newspapers. The prints of Washington, however, do not reflect animosity or even doubts about the beloved General or the policies of his administration. Despite vituperative anti-Federalist sentiment in Philadelphia, Washington was still thought of as the father of his country. By the time he retired in 1797, the prints reflect this sentiment, raising him above partisan quarrels to suggest the accomplishments and leadership of his entire career.

Washington had been a military hero; he had served as politician and statesman. The earlier prints and illustrations had depicted the Commander in Chief or the President. But there was still one role left for him, at least in the visual images. Washington was to become, in his retirement, a national symbol. His accomplishments were no longer seen as the work of a single human being but as the destiny of a new nation. His likeness came to represent the whole country; his career became its history. No longer was a print of Washington simply a portrait.

Washington's symbolic role was established both through repetition of likenesses and through allegorical embellishment. Portraits by Charles Willson Peale, Joseph Wright, and Edward Savage were already widely popularized. They were joined, in this later period, by the image that would in the future dominate them all—the likeness of Gilbert Stuart (Fig. 36). The cumulative effect of these repeated, familiar portraits was the development of a symbolic meaning. The tiny head of Washington appearing on a patriotic songsheet, on a broadside poem, or on a banknote was no longer simply a likeness or an ornamentation. Each familiar face was a reminder of its last appearance. The development of allegorical embellishment could only add to the symbolic content of the likeness. John Norman's ingenuous attempts to depict Washington within a symbolic context had launched the search for appropriate emblematic and allegorical ornamentation. Now another artist had arrived to take up the task. While Washington was still serving his second term in office, John James Barralet, shunning conventional presidential images, was beginning to suggest a new type of portrait print.

John James Barralet and Washington Iconography

By all accounts the Irish-born artist John James Barralet, who arrived in Philadelphia in 1795, was eccentric and irascible. Nevertheless, he was a skilled and energetic artist who had worked in London as a painter and a designer of stained glass, book illustration, and theatrical scenery. As a result of this experience, Barralet had an understanding of the judicious and dramatic use of symbolic embellishment that was to be influential in the elevation of Washington prints from dignified presidential portraits to inspiring national symbols.

Barralet's involvement with images of Washington started in 1795, as controversy over John Jay's unpopular treaty was swirling around the President and his administration. On the first of August, no doubt to counter this passionate public reaction, the artist Walter Robertson published Robert Field's engraving of Washingon [39]. Although the portrait was based on a miniature by Robertson (Fig. 37), the symbolic design was conceived by Barralet. Framed with an oak leaf border, the oval portrait was cradled in the wings of a handsome federal eagle. Gracefully draped over its back was the "E Pluribus Unum" banner, a military baton, and the scales of Justice. Palm branches and banners were skillfully placed around the portrait, which was crowned with a sword and liberty cap and the word "libertas" within a laurel wreath. The whole image was suspended in clouds, and a sunburst emanated from the crowning motif. It was apotheosis imagery that presented Washington as nearly godlike. Whether or not the engraving served to remind the opponents of the treaty of the President's overall role in the country's progress is undocumented, but it set a precedent for the developmnt of a new type of Washington print. Although Robertson's miniature never became a standard likeness, the Field engraving influenced a book illustration by William Rollinson [44] and plates in the *Dublin Magazine* of November 1798 and the *Microscope and Minute Observer,* published in Belfast in February 1800.[123] A close copy of the Field print, with the allegorical embellishment, was engraved by E. Walker in London in 1797.[124] Since it was copied from a first state of the Philadelphia print, it was lacking the sword and liberty cap device at the top of the portrait, but the rest of Barralet's allegorical setting was recorded for European circulation.

Barralet's next association with Washington portraiture was the production of a print engraved by the Irish-born artist H. Houston [48], who worked in Philadelphia from 1796 to 1798. The use of a black stock with the uniform indicated that Barralet had remembered Robertson's miniature. The face of Washington, however, was broader in this print, with a squarer chin and upward-glancing eyes. A more idealized and classical image than Robertson's, the portrait may have been influenced by a Houdon bust. Barralet's urge for allegorical embellishment was compressed into the title vignette. The liberty cap on a sword, the cloud, and the eagle from Field's engraving were all represented. In a somewhat awkward partial embrace, the eagle is joined by a goddess of Liberty, with a cornucopia and a shield bearing the arms of Washington at her feet. Despite its small size, the vignette states Barralet's symbolic theme in one unified and easily understood design: that the military strength, liberty, and federal union of the United States was achieved through Washington's leadership.

The association of a Washington portrait with an allegorical female figure representing

FIGURE 37. Miniature on ivory by Walter Robertson,
1794. R. W. Norton Art Gallery, Shreveport. Louisiana.

Liberty or America was to increase steadily after Washington's retirement. Before the Revolution, indeed since the sixteenth century, the most common allegorical representation of America or the new continent had been an Indian princess.[125] The Indian maiden on the Lancaster almanac for 1779 [3] descended from this long-standing tradition. However, after the Revolution a Greek goddess wearing flowing neoclassical garments became a popular personification of America.[126] This figure often combined the attributes and appearance of Minerva, the goddess of Wisdom with her helmet and shield; of Liberty, carrying on a pole a Phrygian cap (similar to one worn by freed Roman slaves); of Britannia,[127] a neoclassical goddess, often seated, with a shield; or of Columbia,[128] a bare-headed or helmeted goddess representing America. Appearing in cartoons, prints and paintings, and on textiles, silver, ceramics, medals, and other decorative arts and manufactures, this goddess was recognized in any of her varied forms as a representation of the new nation. The female figure in Barralet's vignette, wearing a plumed helmet and neoclassical dress and holding a sword with a liberty cap, was typical. A similar allegorical figure had appeared in the frontispiece to a 1793 history [35], copied directly from the plate in the English edition. The goddess America had already appeared with the image of Washington in European prints and textiles,[129] and she was soon to become his frequent companion in American allegories.

Barralet was particularly skilled at producing symbolic ornaments that were effective and meaningful without being complex. In 1798 he designed a modest little portrait of Washington to be engraved by his partner Alexander Lawson as an illustration for Smollett's *History of England* [64]. Beneath the portrait on a stone entablature Barralet placed a helmet, sword, and baton flanked by olive and oak branches. These symbols of military strength and the peace acquired through strength were motifs that Barralet was to use consistently in his Washington imagery. Like the title vignette in the previous print, it was a simple, unobtrusive ornament, but its meaning would not have been overlooked.

In a frontispiece for the *Philadelphia Magazine and Review* of January 1799, Barralet went beyond symbolic ornamentation to design a full allegory, entitled *General Washington's Resignation* [65]. The print was described in the explanation of the frontispiece as an "emblem of the American Cincinnatus retiring from public office." Relating Washington's resignation as Commander in Chief in 1783 to his retirement in 1797 after his second term in office, it depicted him appearing before a goddess of Peace who represented America. Submitting his resignation, Washington relinquishes with a gesture of one hand the helmet, sword, and baton lying at his feet, while with the other he points to Mount Vernon behind him. In the foreground of the print are Barralet's usual federal symbols—the eagle, olive branch, and cornucopia. The allegory was a logical expansion of the symbolic themes Barralet had been developing around the Washington image. Starting with his primary subject, the resignation, he created a lucid allegorical statement about Washington's whole career, integrating his representations of military victory, peace, prosperity, federal union, and fame into a handsome, balanced composition.

The influence of theater design on Barralet's work becomes clear in his resignation allegory. According to the explanation of the frontispiece, the print was based on a transparency painting created in Philadelphia in March 1797 for a celebration in honor of Washington's retirement.[130] By the 1770s transparency paintings had become a popular part of public celebrations in England and America. These pictures, which were frequently allegorical, were made with translucent paints on oiled paper or a thin material and lighted from behind.[131] Sometimes combined with architectural constructions in the manner of a stage set, they were in themselves a featured entertainment whether or not actors or speakers were involved. The transparency of Washington's resignation, undoubtedly made by Barralet, was this sort of entertainment display, set up in a public place behind a curtain and revealed to an assembled crowd. Thus the frontispiece engraved by Lawson was a reflection of this other more ephemeral type of visual communication and an indication of the interconnection between these prints and other popular art forms.

The influence of Barralet's theatrical design can also be seen in 1800 in a memorial print published after Washington's death by the engravers Akin and Harrison [70]. The basic design of the engraving was apparently inspired by the staging of a monody on the death of Washington described in a Philadelphia newspaper. The monody was presented by actor Thomas Wignell with "appropriate scenery and decorations, designed and executed by Mr. Milbourne, Mr. Holland and Mr. Barralet."[132] The scenery included a tomb with a portrait of Washington "incircled by a wreath of oaken leaves." Under the portrait was "a sword, shield and helmet and the colours of the United States," and in front was "the American Eagle, weeping tears of Blood for the loss of her General."[133] Whatever the contributions of his collaborators, the Barralet motifs are easily recognized.

Barralet had two other Washington projects during that year of mourning. One of his tasks was to redesign David Edwin's 1798 military portrait of Washington [61] as a memorial (Fig. 38). Barralet enclosed the entire image in a handsome framing device of ruled lines which gave the

FIGURE 38. Engraving by David Edwin after Gilbert Stuart and John James Barralet, 1800. Third state of [61]. Hart 788b. Collection of Stanley D. Scott.

portrait an appropriate formality and dignity. Above the portrait he added the title, "Washington Sacred to Memory," and beneath it he changed an eagle vignette in the inscription to an urn flanked by two mourning figures and military armaments. The alterations were slight, but the print had an entirely new look and meaning and could now compete with the other memorials filling the printsellers' shops.

Meanwhile, a much more complex scheme was preoccupying Barralet's energetic imagination. Drawing upon his years of developing a symbolic iconography of Washington, he was planning a memorial print himself [101]. He seems to have had some sort of collaboration with Simon Chaudron, copublisher of the print, who gave a Masonic funeral oration in January 1800 employing images of apotheosis and the mourning Indian.[134] Drawing from this imagery Barralet created a detailed allegorical scheme.[135] The print was advertised by Chaudron and Barralet on December 19, 1800:

> Apotheosis of Washington. Proof print on view. The subject General Washington raised from the tomb, by the spiritual and temporal Genius . . . assisted by Immortality. At his feet America weeping over his Armour, holding the staff surmounted by the cap of Liberty, emblematical of his mild administration, on the opposite side, an Indian crouched in surly sorrow. In the third ground the mental virtues, Faith, Hope, and Charity.[136]

Although Barralet reused the clouds and emanating light from the Field engraving, the apotheosis image is much more literal, with allegorical figures of Time and Immortality lifting Washington from the tomb toward the heavens in an obvious image of resurrection. Figures of the Christian virtues Faith, Hope, and Charity reinforce this theme. America is personified by both the mourning Indian and the neoclassical female with the liberty cap and pole. The latter is weeping over Washington's armor, including Barralet's favorite image of military strength, the helmet in profile. References to the hero's earthly associations are made in the emblems of the Masonic order and the Society of the Cincinnati which hang over the edge of the tomb. And finally, anchoring the strong diagonal composition in the lower left corner, is Barralet's federal eagle with its shield and banner. On view for subscribers by December 19, 1800, the engraving was the culmination of all Barralet's allegorical statements on the theme of Washington and a tour de force of the memorial genre of portraiture.

The Birth of Gilbert Stuart's Washington

Some of the portraits in the Barralet prints were based on a new likeness of Washington painted by Gilbert Stuart. Stuart's enduring, patriarchal image was to have an extraordinary influence, eventually dominating the visual conception of Washington almost to the exclusion of any other likeness. Through the prints, the beginning of this influence can be traced to the last two years of Washington's life.

Stuart painted three famous portrait types of the President. In 1795 he made his first life portrait, showing the right side of Washington's face, which is generally called the "Vaughan" portrait after an early owner. The other two portrait types were painted the following year when

FIGURE 39. Engraving by Thomas Holloway after Gilbert
Stuart, 1796. Published in Johann Kaspar Lavater's
Essays on Physiognomy (London, 1789–1798), Volume
3, Part 2 (1798). Hart 259. National Portrait Gallery.

Washington agreed to sit to Stuart again. The full-length version is known as the "Lansdowne"
because this type was sent to the Marquis of Lansdowne by a wealthy Philadelphian, William Bing-
ham. The other, an unfinished bust portrait showing the left side of the face, is called the
"Athenaeum" type because it was owned for over a century by the Boston Athenaeum (Fig. 36).
All three paintings spawned replicas by Stuart and copies by other artists, but it was the
"Athenaeum" likeness that established an inexorable hold on the public consciousness.

Stuart's "Vaughan" portrait never had the same prominence as a source for prints as the
other two paintings. It did, however, have some currency in London, where it was engraved in
1796 as an illustration in the third volume of Johann Kaspar Lavater's *Essays on Physiognomy*
(Fig. 39).[137] The engraving was made by Thomas Holloway after the Stuart painting owned by
Samuel Vaughan. The owner's name, featured in the inscription on the print, thus became
associated with this portrait type. It was probably Holloway's print that inspired engraved copies
in London by Ridley, Walker, and Roberts in 1800 after Washington's death.[138] That, however,
was the extent of its influence.

The "Lansdowne" likeness was first engraved in London by James Heath and published on

Detail from Figure 36, oil on canvas by Gilbert Stuart, 1796.

FIGURE 41. Engraving by William Nutter after Gilbert Stuart, 1789. Hart 428. Private collection.

January 1, 1800 (Fig. 40). A large and elegant full-length engraving, Heath's portrait was quite popular. The engraving was exported to and widely advertised in America. One New York newspaper advertisement quoted the reviewer from a monthly magazine:

> Much as we have heard of Gen. Washington, there has not until very lately, been any Portrait of him that deserved much notice. One, sometime since published engraved by Cheeseman, from a picture by Trumbull, has considerable merit, but the leading Portrait is one copied from Stuart by Heath, and which in point of resemblance, is said by those who have seen the General, to be uncommonly faithful.[139]

The Heath engraving received additional publicity from Gilbert Stuart. Planning to publish a print himself, Stuart was outraged that the English publication preceded his. Notices in the newspapers, either advertisements or complaints by Stuart, appeared in New York, Philadelphia, Baltimore, Charleston, Albany, New London, and elsewhere in 1800,[140] establishing the Heath engraving as one of the important Washington prints of that year. Nevertheless, it never had the influence of Stuart's third portrait type; and, like Cheeseman's engraving after Trumbull, it was copied more by nineteenth-century engravers than those of Washington's own era.

The printmakers' fascination with the "Athenaeum" likeness, however, began to develop in the last two years of Washington's life. The London engraver William Nutter published his version in January 1798 (Fig. 41) and issued a variant of it in February. Although the Nutter engravings were undoubtedly exported, the major credit for introducing the "Athenaeum" like-

FIGURE 40. Engraving by James Heath after Gilbert Stuart, 1800. Hart 285. National Portrait Gallery.

ness in America must be given to David Edwin. Edwin was an English engraver who arrived in Philadelphia in December 1797 and found employment with the print publisher T. B. Freeman. By February 12, 1798, Freeman had published Edwin's engraving of Washington based on Stuart's "Vaughan" portrait [54]. It was advertised as "printed in colours on white Sattin." [141] The rarity of the print today and its awkwardness suggest that the engraving was not a great success, and Edwin engraved a new portrait, an "Athenaeum" type, which was published on the first of May. When the original Edwin copperplate was found, it was discovered that Edwin had defaced his first attempted portrait of Washington and engraved the second on the reverse.[142] The "Athenaeum" version was apparently more successful, for it was reengraved and reissued by John Scoles in New York.[143]

In 1798, the year Edwin's prints were published, the threat of war with France had brought Washington briefly back into public life. In July President John Adams appointed Washington Commander in Chief and asked him to start organizing a military command. It was an ideal opportunity for printmakers. An unknown artist named Bartoli designed a portrait of Washington in uniform with a military camp in the background [61]. The picture was engraved by David Edwin, who repeated the "Athenaeum" head of Washington. This Stuart likeness was well suited for the message of strength and leadership that the print was meant to convey. With its handsomely engraved title, embellished with a federal eagle, Edwin's print was an impressive military portrait.

The same stippled head, much reduced in size but still attributable to Edwin, appeared again in the summer's edition of "Hail Columbia" [57]. This popular patriotic song, written by Joseph Hopkinson, was originally issued with a portrait of John Adams mounted onto the music sheet.[144] After Washington's appointment, the music appeared with the "Athenaeum" portrait as the central ornament. It was Edwin's third print of this likeness published within a few months. Clearly his skill in engraving the portrait—even the miniature version is exquisite—and his opportunity to repeat it on different types of prints for broader exposure contributed to the dawning awareness of Stuart's image in the public mind.

A large, full-length print of Washington, engraved in 1798 by Cornelius Tiebout after a design by Charles Buxton [62], followed Edwin's lead. Entitled *George Washington Sacred to Patriotism*, Buxton's complex design featured a figure of Washington (with an "Athenaeum" head) standing on a pedestal in front of a view of Bowling Green, New York. Buxton explained in a letter to Washington that he created the design "to perpetuate the idea of the American Revolution." [145] He did so both literally and symbolically. The view of Bowling Green was the scene of the evacuation of the British from New York on November 25, 1783, and the empty pedestal on the green referred to a statue of George III which had once dominated the square. Washington, on his pedestal, therefore, was an enlightened leader of the independent colonies and a symbolic replacement for the toppled tyrant. Reinforcing the theme was a federal arch with an eagle holding together tablets representing sixteen states. Surrounding the pedestal were symbols of the military might and the prosperity of the new nation. A print of this size and sophistication could only have furthered the reputation of Stuart's likeness as exemplary, among all other images, of Washington's strength and leadership.

The "Athenaeum" likeness had become the favorite portrait of 1798. Other printmakers followed Edwin's and Tiebout's example. Alexander Lawson's engraving of Washington in Smollett's *History of England,* published that year in Philadelphia, was based on a copy of the Stuart likeness by Jeremiah Paul [64]. John Roberts, the following year, used for his engraving a miniature by Benjamin Trott from the Stuart portrait [66]. Roberts presented the print to his pupil Alexander Anderson, who treasured it and engraved his own copies on wood.[146] Together these prints advertised the "Athenaeum" likeness repeatedly to an appreciative audience. In the contest for a predominant image of Washington in his last years, the field was crowded, but the Stuart portrait was off to a running start.

The Nightingale of Liberty

One indication of the new symbolic role of the Washington image was its association with patriotic songs. This began during the Revolution when the relief cuts of the head of the General appeared on broadside verses circulating around the American camps [1]. After Washington's retirement, a more sophisticated combination of song and portrait became popular—the illustrated, engraved music sheet. With the notes and words printed together, new compositions and new lyrics could become, very quickly, a part of popular culture. A number of the important patriotic songs during these years were ornamented with a portrait of Washington. By this time the tiny heads had become more than just mere embellishment. The presence of the familiar Washington face was supposed to add to the stirring content of the words, to be an inspiration to the singer, and, of course, to sell the song to every patriotic browser in the music store.

James Hewitt's song "The Battle of Trenton," advertised in August 1797, was "dedicated to General Washington" (Fig. 42; [53]). The elaborate engraved cover of the music sheet must have attracted attention. A large and elegant goddess of Liberty, wearing Minerva's plumed helmet and holding a pole and cap, dominated the print. She rested her hand on an oval shield which bore the title and the dedication. Surrounding the oval were cannon, cannonballs, drum, spears, and banners, the familiar embellishments of Washington portraiture. But the portrait itself, a direct copy of the Wright etching even down to the ribbon beneath the bust, had been forced out of its usual frame. Having used the large oval for the title, the engraver had to find a way to integrate the portrait into his scheme. Undaunted by this compositional difficulty, he perched the profile between two spears above the oval. Then, to give it appropriate significance (since the portrait was even smaller than the drum), he added in the remaining space a miniature winged female crowning Washington with a laurel wreath and pointing skyward in a gesture of immortality.

The "Battle of Trenton" began a vogue for ornamenting music sheets with a portrait of Washington. The little profile on the cover eventually triumphed over the gigantic Liberty goddess when it was cut out of the engraving and mounted onto issues of the patriotic tunes "New Yankee Doodle" and "The Favorite New Federal Song." [147] Even in its trimmed state a spear or two are generally discernible in the portrait, a vestige of its former role.

The frontispiece for a book of songs, entitled *The Nightingale of Liberty: Delights of Harmony: A Choice Collection of Patriotic, Masonic & Entertaining Songs,* makes use of similar

FIGURE 42. Music sheet of "The Battle of Trenton," engraving by unidentified artist, c. 1797 [53].

imagery with a portrait of Washington. A casual figure of Liberty wearing a Masonic apron lounges against the oval portrait medallion, a pole and cap resting in the crook of her arm. Minerva, in her plumed helmet, peers around at the portrait from the other side, and a scrawny bird teeters precariously up above. The inspiration for this design came from a plate in the *Sentimental and Masonic Magazine* published in Dublin in 1795 (Fig. 25). The lounging figure in the Irish engraving was Justice, wearing a blindfold and carrying a sword and scales. Minerva was kneeling at one side, and the allusion to Liberty was divided between a third maiden called Freedom in the verse beneath the plate and a putto hovering above with the liberty pole and cap. The American engraver simplified this design, removing Freedom and the putto altogether and transforming Justice into Liberty. The bird, clearly, was his own invention. He entitled his engraving, rather unimaginatively, "Frontispiece," with no further identification of the portrait. The medallion in the Irish magazine contained an image of Washington derived from Joseph Wright through an engraving by Thomas Holloway.[148] In *The Nightingale of Liberty* the crude profile had become entirely unrecognizable. However, there was no need to identify the portrait. Everyone would know whose praises the nightingale was singing.

By far the most popular patriotic song of the era was "The Favorite New Federal Song," better known as "Hail Columbia." Set to a well-known tune called "The President's March," the words were written by Joseph Hopkinson in 1798 during the threat of war with France. With mounting tension between the supporters and opponents of the administration, the verses were meant to arouse "an American spirit which should be independent of, and above the interests, passion, and policy of both belligerents." [149] Performed on April 25, 1798, by the actor Gilbert Fox, who had asked Hopkinson to write the song, "Hail Columbia" became an overnight sensation. Abigail Adams, who had attended the performance, wrote that her head ached from the thunderous applause that greeted each chorus.[150] The song became an unofficial national anthem, either scheduled for every musical performance or loudly demanded by the audience. Hopkinson wrote Washington, with some surprise, that the theaters in Philadelphia and New York "have resounded with it night after night; and men and boys in the streets sing it as they go." [151]

The miniature engraving of John Adams on the first issue of the song was mounted in the center of the title above the words "Behold the Chief who now commands!" Washington's portrait was substituted when he was appointed Commander in Chief in July 1798 [57]. Since all the portraits were mounted onto the music sheet rather than engraved on the original plate, a variety of Washington prints, including the one from "The Battle of Trenton," have appeared on different copies of the song. The publisher, Benjamin Carr, may have had extra copies of "The Battle of Trenton" in his shop, and when "Hail Columbia" became the rage, merely cut the Washington profile from the larger engraved cover. Other copies of the song bear the miniature "Athenaeum" likeness attributable to David Edwin [57] or a cruder copy of it [58].

Having discovered this way of ornamenting a music sheet, Benjamin Carr affixed the same miniature Edwin engraving to another patriotic song, "Brother Soldiers All Hail." After Washington's death, Carr composed a "Dead March and Monody," which was played for the funeral on December 26, 1799. Five days later the music sheet was published. Once again, Carr had mounted Edwin's tiny version of the Stuart portrait in the center of the title. Following Carr's example, G. Gilbert's music store issued "The Ladies Patriotic Song" in 1798 with a Washington likeness engraved on the plate in the center of the title [60]. Although a poor copy, the engraving was recognizable as a Stuart likeness.

The patriotic songs of this era were well loved. The popular music sheets were studied over and over by all classes of people until the songs were memorized. Those miniature engraved heads were so often associated with familiar tunes and stirring verses that the image of Washington and the inspiring, patriotic sentiment the songs aroused began to merge together.

Portraits of a Lost Leader

George Washington's death on December 14, 1799, threw not only the songwriters, but poets, essayists, orators, ministers, and printmakers into a frenzy of activity. If the patriotic grief of some was overcome by commercial zeal, it might be excused: there was money to be made from the national tragedy, and the competition was intense. For printmakers, the choice of which Washington portrait to use was an important consideration, whether they were planning a small book illustration or an elaborate allegorical memorial.

A number of publishers and engravers chose to issue unembellished portraits, counting on the impulse to own a remembered likeness of Washington rather than a complex symbolic image. The use of Stuart's "Athenaeum" likeness began immediately, starting with Edwin's miniature engraving on "The Dead March and Monody" [57], published on December 31, 1799. The first portrait print of the year 1800, advertised on January 1, was after the same portrait [68]. Cornelius Tiebout's engraving was described as "a Portrait natural as life, from a painting . . . [by] the masterly Stewart." The notice was addressed to "those who revere the memory of the Great and Good Washington." [152] It may have been hastily produced, for it was not one of Tiebout's best engravings. However, since it was available so soon after Washington's death, it was copied extensively for book illustrations and symbolic memorials. In the mourning print published by Pember and Luzarder in Philadelphia [72], for instance, the Joseph Wright likeness of the first state was changed to a Gilbert Stuart image, possibly based on the Tiebout engraving.

Also advertised on January 1, and issued several days later, was a Philadelphia edition of Washington's Farewell Address with one of David Edwin's versions of the "Athenaeum" likeness as a frontispiece [69].[153] Obviously Edwin had not lavished as much time on this inexpensive illustration as on his larger Washington prints. Nevertheless, it was something to supply the demand, and the publisher attempted to sell it separately for one dollar, advertising it grandiosely as the "best Likeness of the Celebrated Washington which has ever been published." [154] Boston booksellers, who were selling this edition of the Farewell Address, had also been sent extra copies of the little illustration which they advertised in their newspaper notices.[155] Along with this frontispiece and the "Dead March and Monody," Edwin's 1798 military portrait of Washington was reissued in 1800 as a memorial [61], so his interpretation of the "Athenaeum" likeness was well represented.

The Stuart likeness did, of course, meet with competition. Jewelers in New York and Philadelphia in January were advertising mourning rings with miniature Washington engravings by the French emigré artist Charles Balthazar Julien Févret de Saint-Mémin [74, 75].[156] There were two versions of Saint-Mémin's distinctive Washington profile. One was a bust-length portrait in uniform; the other resembled a sculpted head "à l'antique" crowned with a laurel wreath. The tiny engravings were placed under glass in gold rings (Fig. 43) that sometimes had a black enamel border.[157] Despite their size, the Washington rings gave the impression of a strong and distinctive likeness, and Saint-Mémin was already developing a reputation as a physiognotrace portraitist whose images had an unfailing mechanical accuracy.[158] Saint-Mémin's head of Washington "à l'antique" revealed an interest in sculpted bust images that was shared by other printmakers. Many, however, were unable to make a successful transition from three dimensions to two. The portrait in a memorial print by Akin and Harrison had changed in successive states from a Wright-type portrait to one reminiscent of James Sharples [70] to a sculpted bust profile. An anonymous cut in a German-language almanac, featuring an obelisk design and weeping eagle, which was influenced by the Akin and Harrison engraving, also represented a sculpted bust portrait, this time in a three-quarter rather than profile pose [71]. While some of these likenesses may have been influenced by the work of Jean Antoine Houdon, their exact sources are difficult to determine.

Along with occasional relief cuts after Peale, the Savage and Wright likenesses from the presidential years were still quite acceptable in 1800. Like the Akin and Harrison engraving, the first state of the memorial published by Pember and Luzarder [72] featured a Wright-type likeness which was changed eventually to a Stuart image. The engraver William Hamlin, of Providence, Rhode Island, preferred to copy Savage's large mezzotint likeness of 1793 [33]. Hamlin was so inspired by engraving prints of Washington that he created a whole series and was still producing these portraits at the end of his long life.[159] He had started in 1800 when his mezzotint was advertised for sale on March 12 [76]. Although his technique was rather curious and experimental, his image was a straightforward copy of Savage's Washington "in black velvet." Hamlin then attempted an enlarged version [77], made into a memorial by the addition of an urn on a pedestal. A smaller and cruder example of this last image was probably engraved about the same time [78].

Edward Savage's brother John, in 1800, was the publisher of a print after a portrait by Rembrandt Peale [86]. The engraver was David Edwin, who had done so much to promote the Stuart likeness. Although the background of his print was a dense, heavy stippling that did little to set forth the image, the engraving was impressively large for a bust portrait and sufficiently dignified and imposing. Nevertheless, the Rembrandt Peale likeness did not become a favored source for prints. This may have been due in part to David Edwin's memory of Stuart's portrait.

FIGURE 43. Mourning ring with engraving by Charles Balthazar Julien Févret de Saint-Mémin, 1800 [74].

Having engraved the "Athenaeum" likeness so many times, Edwin must have had it in his mind as he worked on Rembrandt Peale's portrait. Comparison of this engraving with an earlier Edwin print [56] suggests that although there are significant differences, the hair, the shape of the eyebrows and chin, and the relative size of the eyes in the face are similar. With the vision of Stuart's Washington dancing before him, Edwin really could not do justice to Rembrandt Peale's life portrait, which had an entirely different feeling.[160] The engraving after Peale was too close to Edwin's prints after Stuart to leave a distinctive impression.

The Stuart "Athenaeum" likeness was clearly in the ascendancy in 1800. William Woolley, an English artist working briefly in America, painted a lugubrious copy of the Stuart face and produced a pair of mezzotints of George and Martha [80]. He used the same portrait in a symbolic memorial [79]. Even John James Barralet, who had worked with a number of different Washington portraits, chose the Gilbert Stuart image for his elaborate allegorical engraving [101]. Although Barralet seemed to prefer a more idealized and youthful image of Washington in his other prints [48, 65], he must have recognized the growing popularity of the Stuart face. Despite the numerous examples of the "Athenaeum" likeness in 1800, however, it was only one of several acceptable portraits. Astounding as its popularity was from 1798 through 1800, the complete domination of the Stuart image was, after all, a later development.

Eulogies, Biographies, and Banknotes

Every author had something to say on the subject of Washington in 1800, and the public was anxious to buy whatever was published. Many poems, orations, and sermons were rushed into print too quickly to wait for the engravers' slow work. But illustrations of Washington were in great demand.

The Peale relief cuts were pulled out once again to illustrate almanac covers [7] and broadside poems with titles like "Columbia's Lamentation" and "The Death of Washington: Or, Columbia in Mourning for her Son" [9]. The same artists that had engraved large framing prints and symbolic memorials in 1800 were called upon to produce smaller, inexpensive portraits for illustration. Just as David Edwin had engraved a Washington frontispiece for an edition of the Farewell Address, Cornelius Tiebout made a small version of his large Washington portrait to illustrate a book of discourses by Uzal Ogden [98], and William Hamlin interrupted the work on his large Washington mezzotints to make a frontispiece for a eulogy [96].

Many of the volumes illustrated with portraits of Washington were eulogies. There seemed to be an unquenchable desire for published elegies and orations. Many were illustrated with later states of earlier plates, and new portraits were often produced quickly with little care taken. Amos Doolittle's engraving for Benjamin Trumbull's elegy to Washington [94], however, seemed to benefit from the small size and simplicity of the design. Using a Joseph Wright profile of Washington, Doolittle added an eagle holding a laurel wreath. Simple and unpretentious, the design was neverthless pleasing and effective. Just as sincere but less successful was the anonymous profile cut on the first page of Michael Houdin's eulogy [97]. The ornamentation of this portrait includes a prominent black coffin. Cannon, banners, and bayonets are grouped appropriately around the oval frame; but because of unfortunate positioning all appear to be hanging upside down.

Along with the eulogies came the publication in 1800 of the first four editions of the most influential biography of Washington ever published. It was written by an imaginative and energetic parson-turned-traveling-booksalesman named Mason Locke Weems. Weems knew his market. Several months before Washington died, the parson was planning a biography, which he described in a letter to the Philadelphia publisher Mathew Carey:

> tis artfully drawn up, enliven'd with anecdotes, and in my humble opinion, marvelously fitted "ad captandum gustum populi Americani!!!["] What say you to printing it for me and ordering a copper plate Frontispiece of that Hero, something in this way [sketch of head with inscription:] George Washington Esqr. The Guardian Angel of his Country. "Go thy way old George. Die when thou wilt we shall never look upon thy like again." [161]

By the time Washington died in December, Weems had been "collecting Anecdotes" about him for six months. He wrote again to Carey in January 1800 about a Washington biography. "Millions are gaping to read something about him," he reminded the publisher; "I am very nearly primed & cockd for 'em." [162]

Weems was far more interested in anecdotes than in facts. Many of his episodes about Washington were figments of his own fertile imagination.[163] No one cared. The book was sentimental, entertaining, and enormously popular. Whether or not his stories were true, they became enduring fragments of American lore. Of the four editions published in 1800, three had frontispieces, as the author had suggested. The first edition,[164] published in Baltimore by George Keatinge, had a small relief-cut frontispiece of an eagle holding a medallion portrait with the inscription "Immortal Washington" [91]. Although perhaps more appropriate for a eulogy than a biography, the image was nevertheless effective despite its coarseness. The Philadelphia publisher Mathew Carey finally printed Weems' work as well. Two of his editions from 1800 had frontispiece engrav-

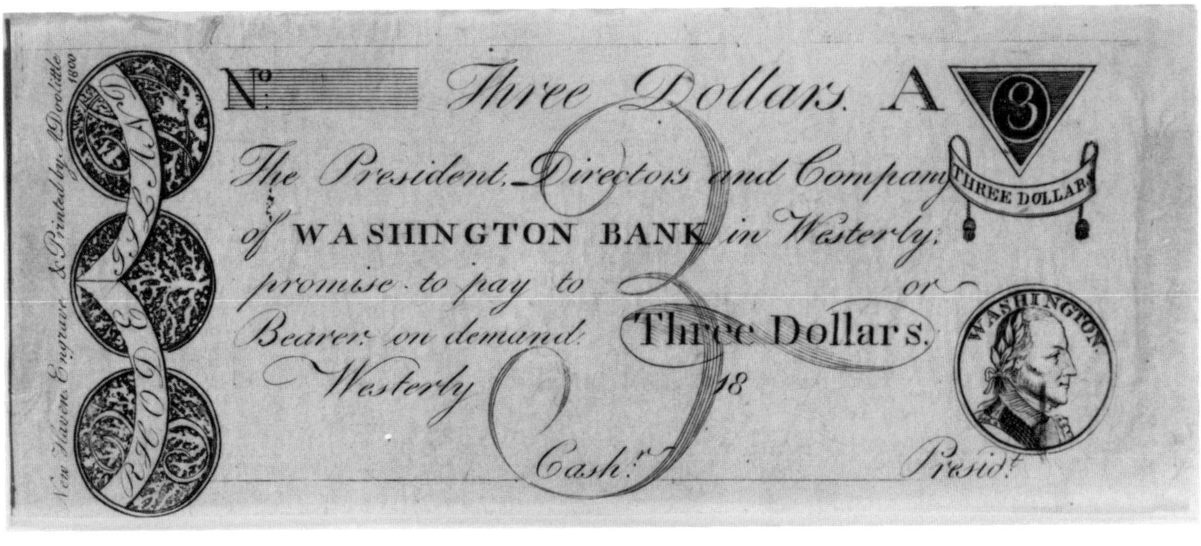

FIGURE 44. Three-dollar banknote engraved by Amos Doolittle, 1800; see [82–85]. Connecticut Historical Society.

ings by Benjamin Tanner after Stuart [92, 93]. Modest as all the Weems frontispieces are, they are significant in that they accompanied a legend that completely eclipsed Washington's actual mortal accomplishments.

Other ephemeral publications of the Washington image did not even need the written word to prove a symbolic point. The first banknotes bearing the face of Washington were engraved in 1800. The directors of the newly established Washington Bank of Westerly, Rhode Island, sent their cashier to New Haven to commission a set of engraved banknotes from Amos Doolittle.[165] Doolittle made three plates of notes which are still owned by the Washington Trust Company in Westerly [82, 83].[166] On each of the notes he engraved a tiny profile bust crowned with a laurel wreath (Fig. 44). It was basically the same image, after Joseph Wright's etching, that had so preoccupied him in successive states of his large print, the *Display of the United States* [25]. Doolittle's banknote profiles of Washington vary considerably from one note to the next, probably because of his inability to make perfect copies. Nevertheless, the tiny heads are instantly recognizable. The directors had not chosen the name of their bank lightly; they were fully conscious of the image of stability and prosperity the name would invoke. The little profile image of Washington, in uniform and crowned with laurel, was intended to have the same subconscious effect.

Symbolic Memorials

Washington had played such a central role in the extraordinary events of a quarter century that his death was an event of great emotional consequence in America, affecting the very identity of the nation. The year 1800 thus became an opportunity to reflect on the significance of the past decades. In honoring Washington the nation was honoring its own history. Along with the illustrations, ephemera, and unembellished portraits published in 1800 were a group of memorial prints that attempted to represent, in symbolic terms, what Washington's death—and life— meant to America. Each one incorporated emblematic and allegorical elements into the design of a Washington portrait in order to express a meaning beyond the familiar likeness.

The memorial prints were the culmination of an iconography of George Washington that had been developing over the past twenty-five years. Recent studies of these memorials have traced their relationship to mourning art, European allegorical traditions, and resurrection and apotheosis themes.[167] Actually few of the allegorical themes, figures, and emblems were new; almost all of them had been suggested in earlier Washington images. But Washington's death brought to full fruition the search for symbolic references appropriate to the significance of the man.

The engraving published by Akin and Harrison on January 20, 1800 [70], influenced by the theatrical set designed by Barralet and his collaborators, was the first memorial of the year.[168] The design was rich with imagery of mourning art: the obelisk, urn, weeping female in neoclassical garb, and drooping willow tree set a precedent for an art form that was to flourish in the nineteenth century. Mourning imagery was not new to America. As an element of neoclassical ornamentation it was prevalent in the English decorative arts that were imported during the last quarter of the century. The Washington memorials, however, helped to popularize the use of this imagery for private mourning pictures. Akin and Harrison advertised that their print was "admirably calculated to ornament the parlour, or hang as a centrepiece between any two other prints." They also offered to print the plate on white satin for embroidering.[169] Obviously their engraving was not made for a rarefied elite. This symbolic imagery, appearing in theatrical design, as a parlor framing print, and in needlework pictures, was truly a reflection of popular art.

On the market in Philadelphia along with the Akin and Harrison print was another image of mourning, published by Pember and Luzarder [72]. Much more crudely drawn, and unsigned by the artist, it offered similar design elements grouped around a Washington portrait. The two fleshy female mourners of the print and the colossal urn between them dominate the picture, relegating the obelisk, the miniature portrait, and the figure of Fame to less prominent positions. Although far less sophisticated than the Akin and Harrison engraving, it had the advantage of being sold with a companion piece entitled "G. Washington in his last Illness" [73]. In contrast to the memorial, this was a narrative deathbed scene complete with a weeping figure of Martha Washington and two of the doctors, who are carefully identified in the inscription. Although the likenesses are fictitious, the details, such as the medicine bottle on the table and the taking of the pulse with the aid of a watch, give an effect of authenticity. The shield and stars within an oval (assumedly part of the bed hangings), are the only suggestion of a significance beyond the sick bed. Together the two prints depict the transition between the mortal and immortal aspects of Washington's life. The symbolic memorial receives an additional significance when compared with a vivid reminder of the man's human frailty.

William Woolley's allegorical engraving of Washington [79], based on his own painting, was commissioned by New York publisher David Longworth and his partner. Woolley's mournful-looking interpretation of the "Athenaeum" likeness was surrounded by a grieving American Indian and identical sad-faced maidens representing Liberty, Virtue, Justice, Poetry, and History. Most of the allegorical prints, despite their theme of mourning, were a celebration of Washington's accomplishments in life and his immortality in death. By the use of federal symbols, the suggestion of sadness was tempered with a note of patriotic pride. Woolley's engraving, in contrast, seems to reflect only the national grief. The newspaper advertisement spoke of the "general gloom which pervades the whole surrounding group" which proves "the universal sensibility created by his death."[170] Threatened by dark clouds of heavy mezzotint tone, which the rays of light can hardly penetrate, even the portrait of Washington seems to mourn. The Indian is the only figure who has a distinct American meaning, and she is lost in grief. With no symbols of federal unity, military victory, peace, or prosperity, the note of patriotism and celebration is lost. One author has suggested that the engraver never came to America, and the publishers simply commissioned and imported the painting and plate from London.[171] While the early dates of the advertisements confirm that the artist was indeed working in New York, Woolley seems to have misunderstood the reaction to Washington's death in America.

The memorial engraved by Enoch Gridley after John Coles, Jr. [81] was, in contrast, exuberant despite its crude execution and mourning theme. Festooned like a Christmas tree with emblems and putti, the obelisk was a monument to the greatness of both Washington and the country. The likeness, despite its crude drawing, was a strong, recognizable military image based on Edward Savage's stipple engraving [31]. The plaque on the base of the monument, incribed

"Renowned in War," "Great in the Senate," and "Worthy the Title of a Great and Good Man," suggested Washington's personal virtue, statesmanship, and wartime accomplishments. The allegorical ornamentation, however, concentrated particularly on Washington's—and America's—military might and past victories. The weeping soldier, cannon and cannonballs, Minerva, Mars, and an unidentified putto, or "genius," carrying a helmet half his height, all underscore the military side of Washington's career. The figure of Fame trumpets out the words "Trenton, Princeton, Monmouth, Yorktown," all sites of American victories during the Revolution.[172] Directly above the portrait Fame holds a laurel wreath containing the words "pater Patriae." As described by a broadside issued with the picture, genii of Truth and Liberty hover at the top of the monument, which is crowned with an urn "blazing with the incense of Memory and Love." Although the "War-worn Veteran" throws down his rifle to take up his handkerchief, the message is not one of gloom. Washington's greatness, his victories, and his immortality are America's. The allegorical figures and chubby putti are not distant, borrowed goddesses as in the Woolley print. Each refers to some aspect of America's proud history.

There were no military references in David Edwin's engraving after Rembrandt Peale [87]. Instead of incorporating diverse emblems and allegorical genii, it was a focused and dramatic apotheosis image that was borrowed from an engraving after Benjamin West.[173] Although the apotheosis theme had been suggested in the Field-Barralet engraving [39], Washington has departed in this print from any earthly reality. The uniform is gone, the sword is nowhere in sight, and he floats serenely on a heavenly cloud, crowned with laurel and light from above. Two friends —Generals Warren and Montgomery according to the newspaper advertisements [174]—welcome him from an ethereal perch. Instead of symbols of military victory or federal union, the view of Mount Vernon beneath serves as a symbol of his earthly existence. Based on a transparency by Rembrandt Peale, the theme of light was repeated in the print in the rays of sun breaking through the clouds and shining down upon Washington's head as an indication of immortality. It is an image of Washington transferred to a spiritual realm.

Rembrandt Peale's design was not the only apotheosis print of the year. Proofs of John James Barralet's symbolic memorial (Fig. 45; [101]) were on view for potential subscribers by December 19, 1800.[175] The last major print of the year, it integrated into a single design the allegorical references, federal symbols, elements of mourning art, and apotheosis and resurrection themes that had gradually entered the iconography of the Washington image. In many ways this engraving was the culmination of the eighteenth-century image of Washington. The figure of Liberty, the American Indian, the federal eagle and shield, the helmet and sword, the "Athenaeum" likeness, mourning images, and various allegorical beings are all represented. Viewers could recognize references to the victories of a military hero and the strong government that had developed under a wise and cautious statesman. But Barralet had elevated Washington, literally and figuratively, into a nonearthly realm. The central symbol of America in this crowded allegorical design was Washington himself. His virtues and accomplishments, his immortality, indeed, his spiritual attainment, were those of America. If Barralet's engraving, with its religious and sentimental overtones, is an introduction to the nineteenth-century myth of Washington, it is also a summary of how his own contemporaries saw him, and depicted him, as their Commander in Chief, as their President, and ultimately as a symbol of the greatness of their nation.

FIGURE 45. Engraving by John James Barralet, 1800–1802 [101].

The Catalogue

☆   ☆   ☆

GUIDE TO THE CATALOGUE

The catalogue is organized chronologically with the exception of a series of related relief cuts [6–10] which are grouped together for comparison. For each print that is an illustration, a chronological list is included of all the publications through 1800 in which that illustration appeared. A ❧ indicates the catalogued image and is followed by the location. Figure numbers refer to those illustrations in the main essay (e.g., Fig. 5). Catalogue numbers cross-referenced in the entries are enclosed in brackets (e.g., [6]).

ARTISTS: The first line of each entry contains the engraver's name and dates and the name of the original painter of the likeness (following the word *after*). Intermediary artists are not included here but are mentioned in the entry text.

MEDIUM: Many intaglio prints of the eighteenth century were made with a combination of processes, employing both etching and engraving. However, the terms mezzotint, aquatint, and stipple are used for prints made primarily by these techniques. The term relief cut includes both prints made from wood and those from type metal.

DIMENSIONS: Measurements are given in centimeters, height preceding width. The actual printed images have been measured as opposed to plate or paper size. The measurements include any printed border but generally exclude the inscription.

INSCRIPTION: Inscriptions are given in italics. Because of the frequent use of different sizes and styles of upper-case letters in one inscription, capitalization is generally restricted to initial letters.

In the eighteenth century Latin words were often used in the inscription to indicate the role of artist or publisher. The most common ones are *pinxit* (or *pinx.*) = painted; *sculpsit* (*sc., sculp.*) = engraved; *delineavit* (*del.*) = drew; *fecit* = made or engraved; *invenit* (*invt.*) = invented or designed; *direxit* = directed or organized; *excudit* = published.

LOCATION/LIST OF PUBLICATIONS: The location of each catalogued object (either separate print or publication in which an illustration appears) is indicated by a ❧. Where possible, an effort has been made to catalogue an early state with complete inscription. When the print has changed dramatically between states (particularly when the portrait image has changed), the state that has been reproduced is noted. Generally, however, there has been no attempt to determine state since this is still an inexact procedure for American prints, with many minor changes in state unrecorded. Information about various states is included in the entry text where appropriate; further information on state changes can be found in the Hart or Stauffer-Fielding catalogues.

The publication list includes all the publications through 1800—broadsides, books, and magazines—in which a catalogued illustration appeared. Titles and imprints are given in shortened form. Following the imprint is an Evans bibliography number. Another bibliography number is occasionally substituted for objects unrecorded in Evans (see bibliographical comments below).

REFERENCES: References are given in abbreviated form with full citations listed in the back of the volume. An effort has been made to limit the references to those which specifically mention the print or the book that it illustrates. General historical references, biographical citations about the artists, and newspaper advertisements given in the entry text are not repeated in the reference section. Exhibition or sales catalogues which merely list the print without providing further information have been excluded. References without page numbers are catalogue numbers (e.g., Hart 675).

BIBLIOGRAPHICAL COMMENTS

Several authors, bibliographers, or compilers are mentioned frequently throughout the catalogue entries. David McNeely Stauffer is the author of the standard reference work for American prints, the two-volume *American Engravers on Copper and Steel* (1907), which includes both biographical information on engravers and a catalogue of prints. A supplement was compiled in 1917 by Mantle Fielding. Relief cuts are not included in the Stauffer-Fielding volumes.

The pioneer scholar of the prints of Washington was William S. Baker, who wrote *The Engraved Portraits of Washington* in 1880. Baker's work was based primarily on his own superb collection of Washington prints now intact at the Historical Society of Pennsylvania. While there are many omissions in Baker's catalogue, he continued to collect and he compiled a manuscript supplement (also at the Historical Society of Pennsylvania) which was never published.

Charles Henry Hart continued Baker's work. His 1904 *Catalogue of the Engraved Portraits of Washington* is still the most current and complete catalogue of Washington prints (although it also excludes relief cuts). Hart borrowed heavily from Baker's manuscript supplement and also tracked down many additional European illustrations and nineteenth-century engravings. Hart published extensively on Washington and on American portraiture. While he discovered and recorded much valuable information, his conclusions must be considered in the light of more recent studies.

An artist, a playwright, and a theatrical manager, William Dunlap was also one of the first historians of American art. His *History of the Rise and Progress of the Arts of Design in the United States,* published in 1834, is an important source of biographical material about American painters and engravers.

Charles Evans was a bibliographer whose massive twelve-volume work on American imprints was published from 1903 to 1934. (The thirteenth volume—completing the Evans bibliography through 1800—was compiled by Clifford K. Shipton in 1955.) A one-volume supplement was produced by Roger P. Bristol in 1970, and in 1969 a two-volume index, *The Short-Title Evans,* was compiled by Clifford K. Shipton and James E. Mooney. Including all the nonserial Evans and Bristol entries in one single alphabetical list, the *Short-Title Evans* was accompanied by a Readex Microprint publication which reproduced all available American imprints through 1800. The *Short-Title Evans* continued the numbering system started by Evans, and these numbers have been used for easy access to the microcard publication.

BICKERSTAFF's
BOSTON
ALMANACK,
For the Year of our REDEMPTION,
1 7 7 8.
Being the Second Year of AMERICAN INDEPENDENCE
And the Second after LEAP-Year,
Calculated for the Meredian of BOSTON, Lat. 42' 25° N.
CONTAINING, besides what is necessary in an Almanack, a
Variety of useful and instructing Pieces.
The GLORIOUS WASHINGTON and GATES.

Calculated by BENJAMIN WEST, a Student in Astronomy, at
Providence, and Author of this Almanack for twelve Years past,
except those false Editions printed by Mycall, of Newbury,
for 76, and by Boyle and Draper and Phillips, of Boston, for 77:
The Author of this genuine Copy never had any Connexions
with those Printers.
DANVERS: Printed by E. RUSSELL, at his Printing-Office
late the Bell-Tavern. (Pr. 12/. per Dozen and 1/. 6d. single.)

1.

Unidentified artist

Relief cut, c. 1775

6.9 × 4.3 cm

The Glorious Washington and Gates

In Congress, July 4, 1776. A Declaration (Salem: Russell, [1776]).

⚓ Benjamin West, *Bickerstaff's Boston Almanack, for . . . 1778* (Danvers: Russell, [1777]). Evans 15705; National Portrait Gallery.

[Jonathan Mitchell Sewall], *Washington: A Favorite New Song in the American Camp* (Danvers: [c. 1778]).

Bickerstaff's Genuine Boston Almanack or Federal Calendar, for 1793 ([Boston]: Russell, [1792]). Evans 25016.

Bickerstaff's Genuine Boston Almanack or Federal Calendar for 1793 (3rd ed., [Boston]: Russell, [1792]). Evans 46388.

Granye, an Excellent Patriotic Irish Song (Boston: Lee, 1793). Evans 46765.

A Worthy Example of a Virtuous Wife (Boston: Russell for Hallowell, 1794). Evans 28136.

Josiah Clark, *The Parent's Monitor* (Boston: Russell, [1794]). Evans 26771.

The first known American print of George Washington, like many other relief cuts of the period, had a long life illustrating a variety of broadsides, books, and almanacs. Because of the scarcity of visual material, any illustration, no matter how small or crude, was valued by printers and publishers, and a portrait was frequently reused without concern for its former identity. This double profile cut was identified in an edition of *Bickerstaff's Almanack for 1778* as "The Glorious Washington and Gates." There is a good chance that it was first made in 1775 or early 1776, when Washington with his Adjutant General, Horatio Gates, arrived in Boston to take command of the colonial army. It probably first appeared on one of the ephemeral broadsides of the time. In the earliest known use of the cut—on a 1776 Salem, Massachusetts, issue of the Declaration of Independence (now at the Massachusetts Historical Society)—the identities of the portraits are unexplained and ambiguous, indicating that it had appeared previously. Comparison with later profile prints after drawings by Pierre Eugène Du Simitière suggests that the cut was indeed intended to represent Washington and Gates, with the straight-nosed image on the left as Washington and the double-chinned portrait on the right as Gates. The illustration was soon reused on a broadside version of "Washington: A Favorite New Song in the American Camp" (also at the Massachusetts Historical Society, where librarian John Cushing is preparing an article on this broadside for the *Proceedings* of the Society). Addressed to "vain Britons" and promising to "laugh at all your empty puffs," this spirited camp song offered a "huzza for Ward and Washington," implying a new identity for the second portrait.

The Washington half of the cut survived and was reused for a variety of purposes in the 1790s. Along with its other appearances, it illustrated a patriotic Irish song and a broadside entitled "A Worthy Example of a Virtuous Wife," where it assumedly depicted the young man whose wife was so exemplary.

Hamilton 82.

HIS EXCELLENCY
GEORGE WASHINGTON ESQ.ʳ

2.

Attributed to Joseph Hiller, Sr. (1748–1814), after Charles Willson Peale

Mezzotint, c. 1777

29.8 × 24.3 cm

His Excellency | George Washington Esqr.

⚜ Private Collection

Accompanied by a companion piece of "Lady Washington," this lively mezzotint was an authentic likeness and the earliest American print depicting Washington in his role as Commander in Chief. The somewhat crude but vivid military scene in the background includes the smoke and flames of Charlestown (Sellers, *Portraits,* p. 225), which had been burned by the British in June 1775, a few months before Washington arrived in Boston. Based on the portrait Charles Willson Peale painted for John Hancock in 1776, the print was originally attributed to Peale by Charles Henry Hart, who assumed it was the lost 1778 mezzotint recorded in Peale's notebook diary (Hart 1). It does not, however, correspond to a contemporary description of that print—"a small mezzotinto of a head of Gen. Washington"—nor is it similar to Peale's quite refined mezzotint style (Sellers, *Portraits,* p. 225). It has since been re-attributed to Joseph Hiller, Sr., a goldsmith and silversmith of Salem, Massachusetts, who was a major in the Revolutionary Army (Shadwell, "An Attribution," pp. 240–241). Since Hiller also produced a mezzotint of Hancock which is very similar in style, he may have been commissioned by Hancock to do all three prints. The Washington engraving was probably made shortly after the portrait was painted, possibly in 1777, when Hancock returned to Boston from Philadelphia.

Joseph Hiller's pair of mezzotints of George and Martha Washington have always been greatly treasured by collectors of Americana (Goodspeed, pp. 40–44; Thorpe, p. 30).

Hart 1 // Stauffer 2427 // Shadwell, *American Printmaking,* 63 // Shadwell, "An Attribution," pp. 240–241 // Sellers, *Portraits,* pp. 220, 225, 242 // Goodspeed, pp. 40–44 // Thorpe, p. 30.

3.

Unidentified artist

Relief cut, 1778

17.4 × 15.2 cm

Des Landes Vater. | Waschington. | 1779.

⚜ David Rittenhouse, *Der gantz neue verbesserte nordamericanische Calender auf das 1779ste Jahr* (Lancaster: Bailey, [1778]). Evans 16053; National Portrait Gallery.

The earliest known instance of Washington being called the father of his country occurs on the cover of a Pennsylvania German almanac published in Lancaster in 1778 (Baker, *Washingtoniana,* p. 6). The design of the relief cut is a miscellany of symbolic references to the Old World and the New, combined with astrological images. The sun, the moon, the zodiac, the figure of the astronomer in the foreground, and the rider on horseback carrying a "Calender" (meaning almanac) are all standard allusions to the calculation of the almanac. The vaguely medieval town and the classical ruin evoke the Old World. The New World is represented by an Indian princess on the far right, who, bejeweled and bare-breasted, is descended from earlier representations of America rather than the more common image with a feathered headdress and skirt from Anglo-American cartoons and illustrations (Honour, passim; Fleming, "1765–1783," pp. 65–69). Another native, on the far left, flourishes a bow and arrow outside a group of longhouses, the Indian dwellings familiar to Europeans ever since the drawings of John White (Honour, p. 74). These symbols are assembled in a seemingly random fashion with the ships of commerce connecting, metaphorically if not actually, the various representations of the two continents. Hovering overhead is the winged figure of Fame, holding a medallion portrait of "Waschington" crowned with a laurel wreath and blasting forth with her trumpet the words "Des Landes Vater."

Baker, *Washingtoniana,* p. 6.

His Excellency General
WASHINGTON

4.

Attributed to John Norman (c. 1748–1817), after Charles Willson Peale

Etching and engraving, c. 1779

14.5 × 8.1 cm

His Excellency General / Washington

❧ [*A Primer* (Philadelphia: Walters and Norman, 1779)]. Evans 16480. Historical Society of Pennsylvania.

John Norman's "chief claim to fame," according to David McNeely Stauffer's biographical note, "is the fact that he was probably the first engraver in America to attempt a portrait of Washington, about 1779" (Stauffer 1:193). Although it now seems that Joseph Hiller's mezzotint [2] took precedence, Norman's engravings of Washington were quite influential in disseminating the image of the Commander in Chief. As early as June 15, 1779, Norman advertised in the *Pennsylvania Evening Post* "a Primer adorned with a beautiful

head of general Washington" (Prime 1:29). No copy of this primer has been located, but William S. Baker found this apparently unique engraved frontispiece, which he attributed to Norman (see Baker's manuscript supplement to his *Engraved Portraits of Washington*, No. 448, Historical Society of Pennsylvania). Charles Henry Hart agreed that it was "much like" Norman's work and could have been the frontispiece for the primer (Hart 41). Not only is the style similar to Norman's other engravings, but the distinctive oval shape of the face, derived from Charles Willson Peale's painting of 1776, was used repeatedly in Norman's portraits of Washington. This primer was the first of many published during Washington's lifetime in which the ubiquitous frontispiece of George III of earlier editions was replaced by a portrait of the new American hero.

Hart 41 // Stauffer 1:193.

5.

John Norman (c. 1748–1817), after Charles Willson Peale

Engraving and etching, 1779

6.6 × 12.8 cm

Within oval frame: *His Excellency / Genl. Washington.*

❧ *Philadelphia Almanack for the Year of our Lord 1780* (Philadelphia: Norman and Bedwell, [1779]). Evans 16415; Special Collections Department, Rutgers University.

In the *Pennsylvania Packet* for September 16, 1779, John Norman and Thomas Bedwell offered for sale, along with children's books, paper hangings, and coffin furniture, the "Pocket and Sheet almanacks for the year 1780 . . . elegantly engraved on copper, having a curious likeness of His Excellency General Washington" (Weiss, p. 7). The broadside almanac, engraved by Norman, was ornamented by a bust of Washington surrounded by twin figures of Fame, the seal of Pennsylvania, a shield and rattlesnake device, garlands, cartouches, and miscellaneous military armaments. The face of the portrait was derived from Charles Willson Peale's 1776 painting of Washington, an image Norman frequently returned to in other engravings of the Commander in Chief. Peale's oval-shaped face of Washington had further circulation when Norman's almanac portrait was copied, probably by Paul Revere, as a relief cut [6].

Military banners and ordnance appear frequently in prints of Revolutionary heroes, particularly George Washington. A French series of portraits of American officers, issued by the French publishers Esnauts and Rapilly around 1778, may have inspired the arrangement of cannon, furled banners, and other military devices at the base of the oval portrait frame.

Hart 42 // Stauffer 2350 // Weiss, p. 7.

The ALMANACK EXPLAINED.

Note that under the Title of every Month is the change of the Moon, every Month contains four columns.

1 Days of the Month
2 o's Rise, Days &c.
3 Moons place
4 Moons Age

COMMON NOTES
AD CLXXX

Dominical Letters BA
Golden Number   14
Epact   23
... of the year   33

Intrepid virtue
triumphs o'er fate
The good can never
be unfortunate.
And is this maxim
graven in the mind
The height of virtue
is to serve mankind.

INDEPENDENCE
July 4th '77
LEWIS XVI KING
of France born
August 24th 1754

JANUARY XXXI	FEBRUARY XXIX	MARCH XXXI	APRIL XXX	MAY XXXI	JUNE XXX
New 6 day at Noon	New 5 day 7 morning	New 6 day 7 morning	New 4 day 6 morning	New 4 day 6 morning	New 2 day 6 afternoon
First 14 day 4 afternoon	First 13 day 7 morning	First 13 day 7 afternoon	First 11 day 3 afternoon	First 11 day 3 morning	First 9 day 1 afternoon
Full 21 day 4 afternoon	Full 19 day at midnight	Full 20 day 9 morning	Full 18 day 7 afternoon	Full 18 day 8 morning	Full 16 day 8 night
Last 28 day 6 Morn	Last 26 day 11 at night	Last 28 day 7 afternoon	Last 26 day 5 morning	Last 26 day 5 morning	Last 24 day 7 afternoon

JULY XXXI	AUGUST XXXI	SEPTEMBER XXX	OCTOBER XXXI	NOVEMBER XXX	DECEMBER XXXI
New 1 day 5 morning	First 7 day 1 morning	First 5 day at noon	First 5 day 5 morning	First 3 day 6 afternoon	First 3 day 5 afternoon
First 8 day 3 afternoon	Full 14 day 8 afternoon	Full 12 day 2 afternoon	Full 11 day 7 morning	Full 11 day 11 at night	Full 11 day 5 morning
Full 16 day 4 morning	Last 21 day midnight	Last 18 day 1 morning	Last 18 day 5 morning	Last 16 day 3 afternoon	Last 18 day morning
Last 22 day 3 afternoon	New 30 day 9 morning	New 26 day 4 morning	New 26 day at noon	New 26 day 12 morning	New 25 day 5 afternoon

A TABLE	A TABLE of Interest at 6 per cent	A TABLE of Interest at 7 per cent	A TIDE-TABLE	ECLIPSES for the Year — 1780	Public Offices

ECLIPSES for the Year — 1780

The first is of the Sun May 4th in the morning at 45 minutes past, invisible here.

The Second is of the Moon May 18th in the morning and partly visible, beginning at 20 minutes after 4.

The Third is a great Eclipse of the Sun Oct. 17th at Noon visible here. Beginning at 24 minutes after 10.

The fourth is a visible Eclipse of the Moon Nov. 11th beginning at 44 minutes after 9 P.M.

Public Offices

Treasury, third street between Arch & Market Street.
Treasurer Second Street between East & Arch Street.
Loan office fourth Street between Market & Chestnut Street.
Lottery office Front Street between Arch & Market Street.
Board of War Walnut Street between Second & Third Street.
Qr. Master General Office Chestnut Street between fourth & fifth Street.
Com. Gen. Mil. Stores Carpenters Hall Chestnut Street.

ENGRAVED Printed and Sold by NORMAN and BEDWELL in Front Street between Arch and Market Streets

THE AMERICAN HERO.

6.

Attributed to Paul Revere (1735–1818), after Charles Willson Peale

Relief cut, 1780

7.6 × 6.2 cm

The American Hero.

[David Rittenhouse], *Weatherwise's Town and Country Almanack, for . . . 1781*, by Abraham Weatherwise (Boston: M'Dougall, [1780]). Evans 16979.

[David Rittenhouse], *Weatherwise's Town and Country Almanack, for . . . 1781*, by Abraham Weatherwise (2nd ed., Boston: M'Dougall, [1780]). Evans 16980.

❧ *The New-England Primer Improved* (Boston: Edes and Son, 1784). Evans 44562; Beinecke Rare Book and Manuscript Library, Yale University Library.

The New-England Primer Improved (Boston: Booksellers, 1784). Evans 18620.

The New-England Primer Improved (Plymouth, 1786). Evans 19816.

The New-England Primer Enlarged (Boston: Draper for Larkin, [1781–1787]).

The New-England Primer Enlarged (Boston: Draper for Booksellers, [1781–1787]). Evans 20542.

The New-England Primer Improved (Boston: Booksellers, 1787). Evans 45106.

The New-England Primer (Boston: White and Cambridge, [1789]). Evans 21986.

The New-England Primer (Boston: White and Cambridge, 1789). Evans 45525.

The New-England Primer Improved (Boston: Bumstead, 1790). Evans 22695.

The New-England Primer Improved (Boston: Coverly, 1791). Evans 23596.

Weatherwise's Genuine Massachusetts, New-Hampshire, Vermont, Rhode-Island, and Connecticut Almanack, for . . . 1792 (Boston: Coverly, [1791]). Evans 23963.

The New England Primer Improved (Concord: Coverly, 1794). Evans 47121.

The New-England Primer, Improved (Amherst: Coverly and Son, 1795). Evans 29146.

The New-England Primer Improved (Boston: Bumstead for Boyle, [1795]). Evans 29147.

The American Primer Improved (Medford: Coverly for Cambridge, 1798). Evans 35107.

Small as it is, this image of George Washington had a remarkable circulation. The cut, which initially appeared in a *Weatherwise's Almanack for 1781*, was first attributed to Paul Revere by Charles Henry Hart. In October 1781 Revere had sent a "small engraving" of the General to his cousin in France. "It is said to be a good likeness," Revere wrote; and his cousin, in response, described it as "representing a gallant warrior." (Hart, "Revere," p. 83.) Although that appears extravagant praise for such a seemingly insignificant item, the little cut did have a considerable effect on its audience. The face of Washington, based on John Norman's almanac engraving after Charles Willson Peale (see [5]; Brigham, p. 108), communicates strength and dignity even in the bold medium of the relief cut. The cannon, cartouches, banners, and oval frame ornamented with palm leaves—all borrowed from the Norman engraving—are creditably depicted; in fact, for a general audience the ornamentation was perhaps more effective in the relief cut than in the tightly composed, complex design of the Norman engraving.

That this combination of "gallant warrior" and national symbol was considered an appropriate influence on children is evident from its great demand as a frontispiece for the *New-England Primer*. The inscriptions in the primers varied from "General Washington" (Evans 20542) and "President of the United States" (Evans 21986) to "the American Hero" (Evans 44562), while there was one attempt, in 1798, to pretend the portrait was "John Adams, President" (Evans 35107). But for two decades this image, which spawned several copies, circulated in primers and almanacs until even the crudest of its imitations must have struck a symbolic note in the national consciousness.

Rosenbach 97, 122 // Hart, "Revere," pp. 83–85 // Brigham, pp. 108–109.

7.

Unidentified artist, after Charles Willson Peale

Relief cut, 1785

7.1 × 6.2 cm

Farmer Washington.

Thomas Dilworth, *A New Guide to the English Tongue* (Philadelphia: Young, Stewart, and M'Culloch, 1785). Evans 44676.

The Citizen and Farmer's Almanac for . . . 1799 (Philadelphia: M'Culloch, [1798]). Bristol 10263.

❧ *The Citizen and Farmer's Almanac for . . . 1799*, by Farmer Washington (Philadelphia, [1798]). Drake 10487; Boston Public Library.

Joshua Sharp, *Citizens and Farmer's Almanac for . . . 1800* (Philadelphia: M'Culloch, [1799]). Evans 36296.

Joshua Sharp, *Citizen's and Farmer's Almanac for . . . 1801* (Philadelphia: M'Culloch, [1800]). Evans 38491.

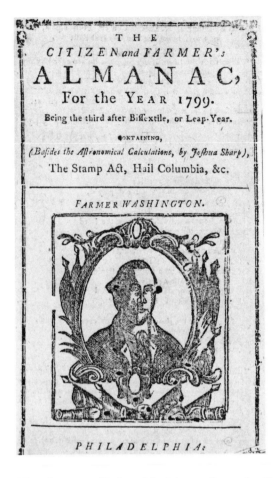

Two features distinguish this cut from the Revere portrait [6] from which it was copied: the entire image is reversed and the right half of the forehead is blank. In Dilworth's spelling book the portrait illustrated a short description of Washington's military career and subsequent retirement to private life along with a single stanza quotation from a poem by Philip Freneau. Thirteen years later it was reused with the title "Farmer Washington," which was not a reference to agricultural accomplishments but an invocation of the image of the Roman farmer-general Cincinnatus. Another example of this familiar association was a toast given on the Fourth of July, 1788, in Wilmington, Delaware, to "Farmer Washington—may he like a second Cincinnatus, be called from the plow to rule a great people" (Freeman 6:146).

After Washington's death the almanac cut was accompanied by an essay which included a physical description:

> He was in his 68th year. The height of his person was about five feet eleven; his chest full; and his limbs, though rather slender, well shaped and muscular. His head was small, in which respect he resembled the make of a great number of his countrymen. His eyes were of a light grey colour; and in proportion to the length of his face, his nose was long.

8.
Unidentified artist, after Charles Willson Peale
Relief cut, 1790
7 × 6.2 cm

The Federal Almanack, for . . . 1791 (Boston: [Bumstead, 1790]). Evans 22498.
The Federal Almanack, for . . . 1792 (Boston: Printed for and Sold by the Booksellers, [1791]). Evans 23981; National Portrait Gallery.
The New-England Primer Improved (Boston: Bumstead for West, 1791). Evans 23595.
The New-England Primer Improved (Boston: Bumstead for West, [1795]). Evans 29148.

The relief cut on the cover of the *Federal Almanack*, copied in reverse from the preceding portrait [7], required no title to identify the image of Washington.

The President of the United / States.

in "The Death of the Brave General Wolf," but it definitely returned to its original identity in 1800 when it appeared on two broadside poems lamenting Washington's death.

Rosenbach 139.

10.

Unidentified artist, after Charles Willson Peale

Relief cut, 1797

7 × 6.3 cm

  ❧ Samuel Ivins, *The Columbian Almanac, for . . . 1798* (Philadelphia: Stewart and Cochran, [1797]). Evans 32309; National Portrait Gallery.

[Samuel Ivins], *Father Abraham's Almanac, for . . . 1798* (Philadelphia: H. and P. Rice, [1797]). Evans 32310.

[Samuel Ivins], *The Pennsylvania, New-Jersey, Delaware, Maryland and Virginia Almanac, for . . . 1798* (Philadelphia: Stewart and Cochran, [1797]). Evans 32311.

A crude copy of the Revere print [6] or one of its successors, this cut looks little like Washington but retains the required cannon, banners, and ornamentation. In the three almanacs it illustrated a short, frequently reprinted essay on Washington.

9.

Unidentified artist, after Charles Willson Peale

Relief cut, c. 1789

7.2 × 5.7 cm

The President of the United / States.

  ❧ *The New-England Primer, Or, an Easy and Pleasant Guide* (Boston: J. White [1789]). Rosenbach 139; Rare Book Department, Free Library of Philadelphia.

The New-England Primer, Or, an Easy and Pleasant Guide (Boston: White and Cambridge, 1790). Evans 45918.

The Federal Almanack, for . . . 1791, by Abraham Weatherwise (Boston: White and Cambridge, [1790]). Evans 23043.

The New-England Primer, Or, an Easy and Pleasant Guide (Boston: White, [1795?]). Evans 29152.

[Robert Treat Paine], *Adams and Liberty. The Boston Patriotic Song* (Boston: White, [1798]). Evans 34296.

The Death of Washington: Or, Columbia in Mourning for her Son [1800]. Evans 37300.

Columbia's Lamentation [1800].

The Death of the Brave General Wolf [and] *The Death of General Wolf. A Song* [1790s]. Ford 1160.

This radically simplified version of the Revere cut [6], with only a token attempt at banners, scrolls, and cartouches, first appeared as "The President of the United States" in editions of the *New-England Primer.* In the *Federal Almanack ·for 1791* the little portrait on the cover was bordered by four lines of verse: "Behold 'tis he! Columbia's Pride, / And Nature's boast—her fav'rite Son— / Of Value—Wisdom—Truth—well try'd— / Hail matchless Washington—."

It could have portrayed either Adams or Washington in the broadside song "Adams and Liberty," and it assumedly represented James Wolfe

HIS excellency general WASHINGTON was born in Virginia on the 11th day of Feb. 1732. Early in life he applied himself to the military profession; and his gallant conduct in the western country, placed his character in a respectable point of view.

When Britain stretched forth her hand to oppress his country, he stept forth to defend her rights. In June, 1775, he was appointed commander in chief of the American army: He was the chief instrument, in the hand of Providence, for conducting the arms of his country through a tedious and perilous war. He served without pay: and in the whole of his command, manifested the most consummate prudence, valour and integrity. In December, 1783, on the concluding of the peace, he resign'd his commission into the hands of the President of Congress; and retired to private life, amidst the deserved congratulations of his countrymen.

In 1789 he was unanimously elected President of the United States, under the new constitution, which the people had formed for themselves, and continued to hold that high office, until the 4th of March, 1797, when he declined any longer accepting the honors thereof, and again retired to private life.—May he long enjoy the well earned applauses of his country.

Chas. Willson Peale pinxt. et fecit | His Excellency George Washington Esquire, Commander in | Chief of the Federal Army— | This Plate is humbly Inscribed to the Honorable the Congress of the United States of America, | By their Obedient Servant, | Chas: Willson Peale.

11.

Charles Willson Peale (1741–1827)

Mezzotint, 1780

30.4 × 25.1 cm

Chas. Willson Peale pinxt. et fecit | His Excellency George Washington Esquire, Commander in | Chief of the Federal Army— | This Plate is humbly Inscribed to the Honorable the Congress of the United States of America, | By their Obedient Servant, | Chas: Willson Peale.

☙ National Portrait Gallery

Charles Willson Peale learned mezzotint engraving in London when he produced, in 1768 or 1769, an engraving of William Pitt. Almost a decade later Peale made his second print, an image of George Washington. Unfortunately, no impressions are known today, but it is documented in Peale's diary entry for October 16, 1778: "Began a drawing in order to make a medzotinto of Gen. Washington. Got a plate of Mr. Brookes and in pay I am to give him 20 of the prints in the first 100 struck off" (Sellers, *Portraits,* p. 224; Sellers, *Peale,* p. 166). One of the engravings, described as "a small mezzotinto of a head of Gen. Washington," was given to the Swiss-born artist and collector Pierre Eugène Du Simitière. The popularity of Peale's 1779 painting of Washington for the Supreme Executive Council of Pennsylvania

probably induced him to try another mezzotint. A dignified, confidant, and victorious image of the Commander in Chief, the painting was instantly popular, and the many requests for replicas—one foreign emissary ordered five—no doubt convinced Peale that a print after it would have a brisk sale (Sellers, *Portraits,* p. 225). The publication of the engraving was announced on August 26, 1780, in the *Pennsylvania Packet:*

> The subscriber takes this method of informing the Public, That he has just finished a Mezzotinto Print, in poster size of his Excellency General Washington, from the original picture belonging to the state of Pennsylvania. Shopkeepers and persons going to the West Indies may be supplied at such a price as will afford a considerable profit to them, by applying at the South-west corner of Lombard and Third-streets, Philadelphia.

> N.B. As the first impression of this sort of prints are the most valuable, those who are anxious to possess a likeness of our worthy General are desired to apply immediately. (Quoted in Sellers, *Portraits,* p. 225.)

Another advertisement in the *Pennsylvania Journal* for December 20, 1780, gave the price of the print as "Two Dollars, . . . or Six Pounds per Dozen to Shop Keepers, or any persons going abroad" (quoted in Prime 1:6).

Peale's print shows Washington leaning against a cannon with the college buildings of Princeton behind him on the right, in reference to his victory there, and a soldier holding his horse on the left beneath a flag of thirteen stars. Peale made some changes from the painting, including updating the uniform by taking off the blue ribbon across the breast and adding three stars to the epaulets (Sellers, *Portraits,* p. 231). A second state of the print includes the date, 1780, after the artist's name. Technically, the Washington mezzotint is a masterful production. Furthermore, because of Peale's ability to translate from his own painting into a different medium, this engraving can be considered—as few prints from this period are—a portrait from life, with all the qualities of direct and personal experience between artist and sitter that the term implies. As a print and as a portrait Peale's mezzotint was unexcelled among the early graphic images of George Washington.

Hart 2 // Stauffer 2428 // Shadwell, *American Printmaking,* 66 // Shadwell, "Peale," pp. 130–131 // Sellers, *Portraits,* p. 231 // Weitenkampf, p. 109 // Thorpe, p. 29 // Baker, "Rare Washington Print," pp. 257–264.

His Excellency Gen.ˡ Washington &c.&c.&c.
Done from an Original Picture of His Excellency at Mount-Vernon.
Painted by M.ʳ Peale 1770

12.

Robert Scot (active 1781–1820), after Charles Willson Peale

Engraving, c. 1780

27.6 × 19.5 cm

R. Scot Del. & Sc. | His Excellency Genl. Washington &c.
&c. &c. | Done from an Original Picture of His Excellency
at Mount Vernon, | Painted by Mr. Peale 1770

❧ Private Collection

In this engraving Robert Scot created a visual amalgamation of Washington's two military careers, as colonel in the Virginia militia, and as General and Commander in Chief of the American forces. The image is based primarily on Peale's painting of Washington in his militia uniform which dates from 1772 (not 1770 as stated on the print). This is the only contemporary print after the 1772 painting of Washington. However, Scot attempted to update the picture to reflect the appointment as Commander in Chief. The "&c. &c. &c." following "Genl. Washington" in the title no doubt refers to his new military designation. The changes in the colonial uniform, however, are relatively minor: the gorget was removed, a

smaller sash was substituted, and the hat was slightly altered.

William Dunlap stated that Scot came from England around 1788 and that he "engraved a whole length of Washington, after C. W. Peale, certainly not flattering to so handsome a man" (Dunlap, *History,* 2:470). However, Scot was in Philadelphia as early as May 29, 1781, when he advertised in the *Pennsylvania Packet,* calling himself "Late Engraver to the State of Virginia" (Prime 1:27). The engraving may predate his arrival in Philadelphia, where he could have copied other paintings and prints of Washington that were more recent than the outdated Mount Vernon portrait with its militia uniform. Competition from more accurate portrayals may explain the rarity of this print today.

Hart 9 // Dunlap, *History,* 2:470.

13.

Richard Brunton (?–1832), probably after John Trumbull

Engraving, 1781

15.9 × 11 cm

Dont Tread on Me | George Washington | Commander in
Chief of ye Armies of ye | United States of America. |
Brunton Scupt,

❧ Charles Henry Wharton, *A Poetical Epistle to His*
Excellency George Washington (Providence: Wheeler,
1781). Evans 17436; American Antiquarian Society.

The *Poetical Epistle to His Excellency George Washington* was written by an "Inhabitant of the State of Maryland," Charles Henry Wharton. Although he later became a leading Episcopal clergyman, Wharton was a Roman Catholic priest living in England when he wrote his poem. First published in Annapolis in 1779, it was reprinted in London in 1780 "for the charitable purpose of raising a few guineas to relieve in a small measure the distresses of some hundreds of American prisoners, now suffering confinement in the gaols of England" (*DAB*—Wharton). Perhaps even more interesting than the poem for English audiences was the appended "Short Sketch of George Washington's Life and Character," written by John Bell, which was the first biographical sketch of the Commander in Chief to be written by an American (Baker, *Washingtoniana,* p. 2).

On March 17, 1781, a Providence, Rhode Island, edition of the *Poetical Epistle* was advertised in

the newspaper (*American Journal and Daily Advertiser*). The frontispiece for the edition was engraved by Richard Brunton, said to be a deserter from the British army (Warren, p. 83). Thus by some twist of fate, a poem written by an American living in London was illustrated by an Englishman living in America. His engraving, a portrait of Washington with a liberty cap and rattlesnake ornamenting the top of the frame, banners, cannon, and cannonballs at the bottom, and the rebellious motto "Dont Tread on Me" printed above the picture, was an appropriate combination of the symbols of colonial resistance. It was not, however, invented in America. Brunton had merely copied the English frontispiece, engraved by William Sharp (Baker 35).

Originally there had been ambitious plans for illustrating the English edition of the poem with an engraving after Benjamin West. A "fellow countryman" living in England wrote to Wharton in 1778 about plans for publishing the poem, adding that he had finally gotten a print of Washington from Paris, "a tolerably good likeness; but as it is a front face, and only of bust size, I got W— [Benjamin West] to promise to make a full length drawing, in order to get a print engraved;

but the artists in that way [engravers] ask such a confounded deal of money, that I doubt if my finances will allow me to get it struck off." In another letter, dated April 14, 1779, the correspondent wrote that if the poem were published with a biographical sketch,

> and a proper dedication to some distinguished personage, (suppose the Duchess of Devonshire, for she particularly distinguishes him as a toast at her table,) it may sell for half a crown or two shillings. Mr. West has formerly seen General Washington, and I think, with my recollection of him and description of his face a drawing may be made tolerably like him, so that a small full length may be got for the frontispiece of a quarto edition. I have spoken to West about it, but he cannot think of any thing else but two pictures he is finishing for the exhibition, which opens the 24th instant. (Doane, pp. xxii–xxiv.)

The print from Paris was probably a Washington portrait attributed to Jean-Victor Dupin and issued by the French publishers Esnauts and Rapilly (see Fig. 7). The cannon, cannonballs, banners, branches, and liberty cap in the French print are all repeated in Sharp's engraving. The motto above the portrait also had precedents. It first appeared on an official American flag raised on the ship *Alfred* in 1775. The flag was featured in the fictitious mezzotint of Esek Hopkins, published in London in 1775, as well as on the portrait of Hopkins published by Esnauts and Rapilly in Paris.

The likeness of Washington in Sharp's print strongly resembles the portrait painted by John Trumbull in 1780. The inscription on Sharp's engraving indicates that it was published on February 20, 1780, some months before Trumbull had even arrived in London. However, the details of the face and uniform, and the arm crossed over the chest, are so reminiscent of the Trumbull painting that it seems the inscription date must be wrong. Since Valentine Green's mezzotint engraving after the Trumbull portrait was published in January 1781 (Hart 84), Sharp could have copied an early proof of it for his illustration and the book could have been published at the end of 1780. The Sharp print inspired a number of European copies, as well as Brunton's version in America.

Hart 93 // Stauffer 282 // Bates, pp. 12, 42–43, 46 // Warren, p. 84 // Baker, *Washingtoniana*, pp. 1–2 // *DAB*—Wharton // Doane, pp. xxii–xxiv // Weitenkampf, pp. 54–55.

His Ex.cy George Washington Esq.

Captain General of all the American Forces

14.

John Norman (c. 1748–1817)

Engraving, 1781

15.2 × 9.2 cm

His Excy. George Washington Esqr. | Captain General of all the American Forces | J Norman Sc

❧ *An Impartial History of the War in America,* Volume 1 (Boston: Coverly and Hodge, 1781). Evans 17241; National Portrait Gallery (frontispiece only).

The three-volume history of the Revolutionary War published in Boston from 1781 to 1784, was, according to one bibliographer, "a polyglot affair at best, drawn from three sources." The first three chapters of the work were based on a 1779 Dublin history of the war. The rest came primarily from James Murray's *Impartial History of the Present War in America* (Newcastle-upon-Tyne, 1778–1780 or London: Baldwin . . . , 1778–1780), which in turn borrowed heavily from articles in the *Annual Register* (Libby, p. 425).

The illustrations for the Boston edition, engraved by John Norman, had an equally complex evolution and received their own share of criticism. One correspondent to a 1795 Philadelphia newspaper remarked:

> The expense of copper plates . . . might be spared, unless they could be executed in a different stile from those in the history of the American War, printed at Boston in 1781 and 82. There gen Knox and Sam Adams, are represented more frightful than Lord Blackney on a London ale house sign, and gen Greene the exact resemblance of Jonathan wild in the frontispiece of a two penny history. Surely such extraordinary figures are not intended to give the rising generation an improved taste in the arts of designing and sculpture. (*Freeman's Journal,* January 16, 1795; Andrews, p. 27.)

Norman's five full-length portraits of generals were copied from engravings in a 1780 London edition of the *Impartial History* published by Faulder. The title page of that edition advertised "beautiful Copper Plates, representing real and animated Likenesses of those celebrated Generals." Animated they may have been to some eyes, but likenesses they certainly were not. They in turn were based partially on a series of fictitious mezzotint portraits of the officers published in London from 1775 to 1778. Basically the first images available of the Revolutionary War generals, these mezzotints were widely copied throughout Europe in separate prints and in book illustration.

It was a reasonable assumption, therefore, that Norman's engravings were as fictional as his English models. In fact, however, he quite consciously changed the faces for a number of his portraits, in some cases copying from known paintings or prints. The figure of Washington, like its English prototype, leans on a cannon and holds a baton in his outstretched right hand. The military camp in the background, with tents, cannon, and soldiers, is also copied from the English engraving. The head, however, while not like any known Washington portrait, is entirely different from the fictional image. If Norman was attempting to make his portrait look more like Washington, he failed; though judging from his other portraits, a likeness was probably his intention.

Hart 761 // Stauffer 2355 // Baker 419 // Weitenkampf, pp. 59–60 // Andrews, pp. 24–27 // Libby, pp. 419–425.

15.

John Norman (c. 1748–1817), after Benjamin Blyth and Charles Willson Peale

Etching and engraving, 1782

29.2 × 23.5 cm

B. Blyth del. | J. Norman Sculp. | His Excellcy. George Washington, Esqr. | General and Commander in Chief of the Allied Armies, | Supporting the Independence of America. | Taken from an Original Picture in possession of His Excy Govr. Hancock | Published by John Coles, Boston, March. 26th. 1782. On pedestal: *Temperance, | Prudence, | Fortitude, | Justice.*

Print Collection, New York Public Library

John Norman moved from Philadelphia to Boston around 1780 to continue his career as a publisher and an engraver of maps, portraits, architectural plates, bills of lading, and, as he once commented, "many other Things too tedious to mention in an Advertisement" (Stauffer 1:191). Norman had already had occasion to engrave some of the early printed portraits of Washington, including an illustration for a primer of 1779, the ornamental heading of a broadside almanac for 1780, and a 1781 Washington plate for the Boston edition of *The Impartial History* [4, 5, 14]. In 1782, however, he published a pair of separate portrait engravings of the General and his wife for fram-

ing rather than for illustration. According to the inscription, the Washington print was after a portrait by the Salem pastel artist Benjamin Blyth, which in turn was "Taken from an Original Picture in the Possession of his Excy Govr. Hancock." The original source that Blyth copied was the painting by Charles Willson Peale made for John Hancock in 1776, an image that seems to have been the basic inspiration for a number of Norman's heads of Washington. This likeness is enclosed in an oval medallion frame set on a pedestal labeled "Temperance, Prudence, Fortitude, Justice" and surrounded by some of the same military ornaments employed in his portrait of Washington on the *Philadelphia Almanack for 1780* [5].

In May 1783 a group of Philadelphia booksellers issued a joint advertisement in the *Pennsylvania Gazette* announcing "New American Publications" for sale as well as "Beautiful Engravings of that most illustrious General and Patriot, his Excellency George Washington, Esq; Commander-in-Chief, of the Armies of the United States of America, and his Lady" (Prime 1:16). Although the advertisement could refer to Joseph Hiller's mezzotint portraits [2], particularly since the companion piece by Norman is entitled "Mrs." rather than "Lady" Washington, the date of the advertisement and Norman's previous close associations with the Philadelphia booksellers (Weiss, pp. 3–10) suggest that his prints, rather than Hiller's, may have been the pair offered for sale.

Hart 43 // Baker 26 and pp. 17–18 // Stauffer 2351 // Bowditch, p. 192 // Watkins, p. 132 // Sellers, *Portraits*, p. 242 // Andrews, pp. 21–22 // Hart, "Norman," pp. 395–396 // Weitenkampf, p. 60.

His Excellᵗ GEORGE WASHINGTON, Esqʳ
COMMANDER in Chief, of the Armies, of the UNITED STATES, of
America.

16.

John Norman (c. 1748–1817), after Benjamin Blyth and
Charles Willson Peale

Etching and engraving, c. 1782

29.1 × 23.1 cm

*J. Norman Sc. | His Excellcy. George Washington, Esqr. |
Commander in Chief, of the Armies, of the United States,
of | America.* On pedestal: *Temperance, | Prudence, |
Fortitude, | Justice.*

Print Collection, New York Public Library

This print is a copy, in reverse, of Norman's 1782
engraving of Washington [15]. Like its predeces-
sor, it was probably issued with a companion
piece of Martha Washington (Fielding 1140).

Hart 44 // Stauffer 2352.

17.

Attributed to John Norman (c. 1748–1817), after Charles
Willson Peale

Etching, c. 1783

23.7 × 18.6 cm

*The true Portraiture of his Excellency | George Washington
Esqr | in the Roman Dress, as Ordered by Congress for the
Monument to be erected | in Philadelphia, to perpetuate
to Posterity the Man who commanded the | American
forces through the late glorious Revolution.*

Mabel Brady Garvan Collection, Yale University Art
Gallery

George Washington in a full suit of sixteenth-
century field armor seems to be one of the more
preposterous and imaginative images of the hero
of the Revolutionary War. In fact, the head in
this print is based on a portrait by Charles Willson Peale, and the general idea was more appropriate than it first seems. The inscription on the
print refers to a monument ordered by Congress.
According to its *Journal,* on August 7, 1783, the
Continental Congress voted unanimously: "That
an equestrian statue of General Washington, be
erected at the place where the residence of Congress shall be established." On the advice of a
committee consisting of Arthur Lee, Oliver Ellsworth, and Thomas Mifflin, the Congress further
resolved:

> That the statue be of bronze: The General to be
> represented in a Roman dress, holding a truncheon
> in his right hand, and his head encircled with a laurel
> wreath. The statue to be supported by a marble
> pedestal, on which are to be represented, in basso
> relievo, the following principal events of the war, in
> which General Washington commanded in person,
> viz. The evacuation of Boston—the capture of the
> Hessians at Trenton—the battle of Princeton—the
> action of Monmouth, and the surrender of York. On
> the upper part of the front of the pedestal, to be
> engraved as follows: The United States in Congress
> assembled ordered this statue to be erected in the
> year of our Lord 1783, in honor of George Wash-
> ington, the illustrious Commander in Chief of the
> Armies of the United States of America, during the
> war which vindicated and secured their Liberty,
> Sovereignty and Independence. (*Journals of the
> Continental Congress 1774–1789,* pp. 494–495.)

The statue was to be executed by "the best artist
in Europe."

Charles Henry Hart attributed the engraving
on the basis of style to John Norman (Hart 45),
who was, by this time, familiar with the oval-
shaped Peale face of Washington. Norman's solution for approximating ancient dress was to copy
a plate from John Guillim's *Display of Heraldry.*
This volume was first published in 1611; and an
expanded edition, issued in 1724, was owned by
Norman's sometime partner John Coles, Sr., who

The true PORTRAITURE of his Excellency *George Washington Esqr*

In the Roman Dress, as Ordered by Congress, for the Monument to be erected in Philadelphia, to perpetuate to Posterity the Man who commanded the American Forces through the late glorious Revolution.

later specialized in heraldry painting (Bowditch, p. 174). Norman borrowed the figure, pose, and background battle from the engraving of Sir William de la More, changing only the head. Norman's crudely executed portraits often seemed to be caricatures when they were not, and the suggestion has been made that this portrait was published with satiric intent (Baker 426). However, a suit of armor could also be used symbolically as an indication of military strength. Paul Revere's 1774 portrait of John Hancock in the *Royal American Magazine* is flanked by Liberty on one side and a fully armored figure on the other, a design he had borrowed from an English engraving (Brigham, pp. 82–84). John James Barralet, in the 1790s, repeatedly used the device of a helmet and baton in his images of Washington [see entry 64, 65, 101]. Norman's engraving, while not similar to the described statue, may not have seemed ridiculous or satiric to his audience, but in fact appeared as an appropriate if somewhat unusual military image.

Hart 45 // Baker 426 // Andrews, pp. 8–9 // Weitenkampf, p. 67 // Thorpe, p. 30.

Wa'hington---Victory doth thy Trumpets found,
Who are with .Laurals cover'd round!

hero to mourn, the ingenious Norman created a
memorial to the British colonies in America: with
Washington featured on the obelisk, Britannia in
effect was mourning a native son whose loss to her
was as significant as the death of the Duke. Un-
necessary elements of the English print were
eliminated: the grieving "paupers," for instance,
who had been "cheared and employ'd" by the
Duke, had no place in an American engraving.
The allegorical figures, however—Minerva as Wisdom, Hercules with his club as Valour, an unidentified male, perhaps Mercury, and a dramatic,
foreshortened Fame with arms, legs, and trumpets
waving in the air—were all faithfully if crudely
copied. Even the small helmet above the oval
portrait, an appropriate symbol of military
strength, was not forgotten. Poorly cut, in fact
barely legible, the illustration was nonetheless a
sort of lifetime memorial that reflected Washington's legendary status among his countrymen by
the time the Revolution was over.

The American Antiquarian Society has attributed the authorship of these almanacs to Daniel
George.

Hamilton 100.

18.

Unidentified artist

Relief cut, 1783

13.7 × 8.6 cm

*Washington—Victory doth thy Trumpets sound, / Who are
with Laurals cover'd round!*

❧ Daniel George, *Weatherwise's Town and Country
Almanack for . . . 1784* (Boston: Norman and White,
[1783]). Evans 18164; Library of Congress.
Daniel George, *Weatherwise's Town and Country Almanack
for . . . 1784* (Boston: Coverly, [1783]). Evans 18163.

According to their title pages, these almanacs
were "Embellished with a plate, representing the
Victorious General Washington, survey'd in pleasing attitudes, by Wisdom and Valour, while
Britannia deplores her loss of America." John
Norman, one of the publishers, with his interest
in Washington and in allegory, no doubt planned
the illustration. Like other American engravers
Norman habitually copied plates from the English
magazines, adapting them to his own purposes.
In this instance he used an engraving designed as
a memorial to William Duke of Cumberland from
the *London Magazine* of 1765. Without a dead

19.

John Norman (c. 1748–1817), after Charles Willson Peale

Engraving and etching, 1784

14.3 × 8.8 cm

J Norman Sc

❧ *The Boston Magazine*, April 1784 (Boston: Norman,
White, and Freeman). Evans 18378; Library of Congress.

According to their proposal for the *Boston Magazine,* the publishers, John Norman and Joseph
White, were considering "how many sparkling
geniuses lay dormant for want of a proper vehicle
to discover themselves to the public." Along with
the usual literary miscellany they promised "two
copper-plate prints, and a song set to music," and
hoped the magazine would meet with "the appro-
bation of the learned, judicious, unprejudiced
reader, and do honour, and be a Benefit, to the
Publishers" (*Weatherwise's Town and Country
Almanack for . . . 1784*, Boston: Norman and
White, [1783]). It turned out to be neither an
honor nor a benefit to one of the publishers, Norman, who was also the engraver of the plates.
Norman and White had sold their interest in the
magazine in July 1784 (L. N. Richardson, p. 214).
The new publishers discontinued the engravings
at the end of the year, announcing in the press:

> Many of the Customers having found great fault with
> the Cuts, as being badly executed, has induced the
> Publishers to omit them, untill an Engraver can be

procured to do them in an elegant manner. In the mean time, to do justice to the Subscribers, the price will be reduced to Twelve Shillings per annum. (*Boston Gazette,* February 7, 1785; *Boston Magazine,* February 1785.)

John Norman had his own side of the story which he publicized in response:

The engraver for the late Boston Magazine, in vindication of his character from the ill-natured suggestions made by the Printers of a sunken performance bearing the same name, is obliged to observe, . . . that the Printers were always ready to accept of his services gratis, but when after repeated refusals to pay his account, he was obliged to seek redress thro' the law, they then found it an oeconomical measure to omit the plates. Whether the difficulty of finding an accurate engraver to work without pay, is, or is not the true reason of the present nakedness of this work he leaves the world to judge. (*The Gentleman and Lady's Town and Country Magazine,* December 1784; *Boston Gazette,* February 7, 1785.)

Norman's allegorical frontispiece, crude as it is, in fact is a rather sophisticated offering. While it can hardly be considered a great likeness, it is without question the oval-shaped Peale face of

Washington that was recognized by many. The rest of the print was modeled on a frontispiece portrait of Montesquieu, engraved by Noël Le Mire for *Le Temple de Gnide* of 1772 (a correlation discovered by Beverly Orlove, Doctoral Fellow at the National Museum of American Art). Changing a putto in the lower left to the figure of Fame, and removing Montesquieu's titles from the books in the corner, Norman followed the allegorical conception fairly closely. On the inside of the cover of the magazine he published an explanation of the plate: "Nature stands ready to strike the Lyre, while the Genius of Liberty presents a medal of the illustrious man who hath defended her standard in this new World.—Fame blows her trumpet, and Astrea finds a part of the earth where she may fix her residence" (*Boston Magazine,* April 1784). While Fame, Liberty in various forms, and Justice (Astrea) were familiar symbols in association with Washington, the multi-breasted figure of Nature was somewhat unusual. The fecundity of Nature was, by extension, a reference to the prosperity of the new nation which Washington's victory had made possible.

Hart 57 // Stauffer 2353 // L. N. Richardson, pp. 212–216.

20.
James Trenchard (1747–?)
Etching and engraving, 1787
15.6 × 9.4 cm

Columb. Mag. | General Washington. | Exitus Acta Probat | J. Trenchard Scpt.

The Columbian Magazine, January 1787 (Philadelphia: Spotswood for Proprietors). Evans 20280; National Portrait Gallery (frontispiece only).

James Trenchard's engraving accompanies a series of George Washington's letters assembled by his former aide David Humphreys in an attempt to defend Washington's position in the unfortunate Asgill incident of 1782, which had raised an international storm of protest and criticism. The case had occurred when a British captain executed an American prisoner in retaliation for the death of a Tory captive. Washington considered this reprisal a "most wanton, unprecedented, and inhuman murder" and decided that an enemy prisoner in American hands should be executed unless the British captain responsible was given proper punishment (Flexner, pp. 479–482). Unfortunately, the English prisoner, chosen by lot, turned out to be a popular young officer named Charles Asgill. When the British captain was acquitted, Washington turned the case of Asgill's execution over to Congress. While Congress stalled, sympathy for the young man and criticism

GENERAL WASHINGTON.

J. Trenchard sculp.

of Washington's actions were growing; and the prisoner's mother, Lady Asgill, wrote a tearful letter to the French minister, Comte de Vergennes. Eventually, when the King and Queen of France interceded on Asgill's behalf, Congress decided to release the prisoner.

No doubt sensing that Washington's personal feelings about the case were never publicly understood, Humphreys solicited the correspondence relating to the incident. In sending the letters Washington responded that he "judged it better that the whole tenor of the Correspondence should appear, that no part might seem to be hidden." But he admitted, "In what manner it would be best to bring this matter before the Publick eye I am at a loss, and leave it to you to determine . . ." (Fitzpatrick 29: 2–3). Stung by the criticism from abroad, Washington was grateful for Humphreys' effort in his defense. He considered the publication "the best that cou'd be devised; whilst the matter will prove the illiberality, as well as the fallacy of the reports which have circulated on that occasion" (Fitzpatrick 29:125).

James Trenchard's engraving accompanying the letters presents an appropriately serious image of the General that seems to confirm Washington's firm stance and personal sympathy for the prisoner. The integration into the title of Washington's coat of arms and motto, "Exitus Acta Probat" (the end proves the deed), is a straightforward but effective ornamentation. The likeness of Washington, however, was awkward, and its source is difficult to determine. While the uniform is similar to Charles Willson Peale's early painting of Washington, the shape of the face is noticeably different, as is the hair. William S. Baker suggested that Trenchard combined a Peale image with one by Robert Edge Pine, whose 1785 portrait of Washington was in Philadelphia at that time (Baker 37; see also Stewart, pp. 92–96). Another possible source, judging by the square-shaped jaw and the sculptural highlights on the face, was a bust of Washington by Jean Antoine Houdon. Trenchard was a good engraver and seemed to be struggling hard for a likeness. The awkwardness of his portrait may be another indication that he was attempting to translate from a three-dimensional image. When Trenchard engraved a copy of Peale's mezzotint likeness of Washington that was published several months later, the results were much more successful [see entry 22].

Trenchard was one of the publishers of the *Columbian Magazine,* which, according to its initial proposal, promised that each issue would be "elegantly printed" and "adorned with two engravings on copper-plate, executed by an American artist" (*Pennsylvania Gazette,* August 9, 1786; L. N. Richardson, pp. 276–277). Trenchard himself was usually the American artist. Unfortuately, this portrait of Washington was far from being his best plate; it has been criticized, with some justification, as a "harsh, none-too-flattering portrait" (Crompton, p. 384). Generally his engravings—particularly those after drawings by Peale—were the main reason the periodical has been called "the handsomest magazine of its century" (Mott 1:99; E. P. Richardson, pp. 175–181).

Hart 839 // Baker 37 // Stauffer 3277 // Fitzpatrick 29:2–4, 125 // Crompton, p. 384 // L. N. Richardson, p. 249n // Mott 1:94.

21.

Charles Willson Peale (1741–1827)

Mezzotint, 1787

18.9 × 14.6

His Excel: G: Washington Esq: L.L.D. Late Commander in Chief of the Armies of the U. S. of America & President of the Convention of 1787 / Painted & Engrav'd by C. W. Peale. 1787.

Metropolitan Museum of Art (third state)

As early as 1779, Charles Willson Peale was making plans to execute a series of portrait prints of Revolutionary War figures. On October 15 he wrote to his friend and patron Edmund Jenings that he had "requested Mr. Carmichael to send [from Spain] . . . paper and Copper Plates for me to etch a Set of Heads of the Principal Characters who have distinguished themselves during this contest" (Sellers, *Peale*, p. 183). The materials apparently never arrived, but in 1787 Peale returned to his scheme, which he described in a letter of February 2:

But of Late I have begun one other great work, the making of Mezzotinto prints from my collection of portraits of Illustrious Personages. This undertaking will cost me much labour as I am obliged to take the plates from the rough and doing the whole business myself, even the impressing. I have just finished one of Doctr Franklin which I am giving out as a specimen of the size & manner I intend this series of Prints. By the next packet I will be able to send you some, and will esteem it a favor if you will take the trouble to have them sold for me. My first intention was to have taken subscriptions for a Doz prints which I had selected out of the whole Collection of Heads, but on second thought I have judged it best to propose only one at a time which I expect I shall be able to deliver in 6 weeks after I begin the work. The price of each print will be 3 dollars in a double oval Frame, the inner part of the framed border under the Glass to be gilt—to each print without fraiming one Dollar. . . . By this business of Prints I hope I shall get something in return for my great Expense of time and labour in making my Collection of Portraits. (E. P. Richardson, p. 169.)

Peale sent a copy of his first mezzotint, the portrait of Benjamin Franklin, to George Washington on February 27, 1787, remarking, "yet I do myself injustice as this Print is much coarser than others will be" (Sellers, *Portraits*, p. 237). Washington encouraged him: "I wish you great success in the Mezzotinto Prints which you have undertaken, and have no doubt but your abilities in Works of Genius will ensure it" (Fitzpatrick 29:178). By April, Peale had finished an engraving of Lafayette, which was followed in May by one of a local clergyman, the Reverend Joseph Pilmore. On May 29 he wrote again to Washington, who had just been elected president of the constitutional convention, that he was the obvious subject of the next portrait of the series:

With the utmost reluctance I undertake to ask you to take the trouble of sitting for another portrait. It gives me pain to make the request, but the great desire I have to make a good mezzotinto print that your numerous friends may be gratified with a faithful likeness (several of whom I find is not satisfied with any of the portraits they have seen). My particular interest alone in this business would not have induced me to be thus troublesome, but if you can indulge me so far I will do everything in my power to make it convenient & easy to you. (Sellers, *Portraits*, p. 237.)

As usual, Washington cooperated, as his July 3, 1787, diary entry records: "Sat before the meeting of the Convention for Mr. Peale, who wanted my picture to make a print of Metzotinto by" (Sellers, *Portraits*, p. 238). He sat again for the painting on July 6 and 9. Peale was very pleased: "On the success of this undertaking depends much of my happiness," he wrote Washington. "If I am so fortunate as to make a good and faithful portrait, shall be enabled to gratify many of your warm friends by executing a good print, and the practice I lately had in this line is only bringing in my hand to execute something I hope more excellent" (Sellers, *Portraits*, p. 238).

On August 20, 1787, Peale advertised in the *Pennsylvania Packet* for subscribers for his new mezzotint, promising it would be "ready for delivery in two weeks." It was finished at least by September 26, when it was advertised in the *Pennsylvania Gazette* as "now compleated." "The likeness is esteemed the best that has been executed in a print," read the notice (Prime 2:20–21). Two days later the *Pennsylvania Packet* informed the public that the price of Peale's prints had been reduced from their cost, in frames, of two dollars a piece:

Mr. Peale has by his practice overcome difficulties in the execution of Mezzotinto Prints, which he had

to contend with; he therefore proposes to sell the prints, which are to compose his Collection of Portraits of illustrious Personages distinguished in the late Revolution, at two thirds of a dollar each, which is at or below the London prices; and the subscribers to this work who have been supplied with the first prints, shall be allowed the difference of price which they have paid above the present proposal, in deduction from the price of the succeeding prints. The double oval frame between print and glass being gilt, cannot be afforded by the artist for less than one dollar. (Shadwell, "Peale," p. 140.)

On September 27, 1787, Peale wrote Washington: "By this post I take the liberty of sending a few Prints for your acceptance. I have not been able to execute a greater number of plates as yet, but am preparing some others which I hope will be published some time in the ensuing fall and winter" (Sellers, *Portraits*, p. 238). Despite his enthusiasm and the lower prices, sales did not live up to Peale's expectations, and the Washington plate was his last mezzotint. On November 17 he sent some of the portraits to Benjamin West with the comment: "I have begun a work from my collection of portraits of which I send you by Mr. Clarkson some proof prints.—This is a work which I mean to pursue when I have no other business to do, for the sale is not such as to induce me to pursue it otherwise" (E. P. Richardson, p. 181). In 1789 he printed an impression of the Washington portrait "on white satin to ornament a muff" for Mrs. Christopher Hughes while she was sitting for her portrait. The last recorded sale of the engraving was May 29, 1790 (Sellers, *Portraits*, p. 239).

Peale gave up his plans to make more mezzotint portraits, but not before one final accomplishment in his limited but extraordinary career as a printmaker. He had printed the first lettered state of the Washington plate in brown as well as in black ink; the second was printed in black, in red, and in colors. His diary records that on July 30, 1788, he "Ground some colors and printed some plates of Genl. Washington" (Sellers, *Portraits*, p. 238; Shadwell, "Peale," p. 140). One of the earliest experiments with copperplate color printing in America, an impression of Peale's Washington in colors exists in the New York Public Library, a testament to the artist's extraordinary combination of technical inventiveness and aesthetic sensitivity.

During Washington's lifetime this portrait along with Peale's mezzotints of Franklin and Lafayette was hung in the music room at Mount Vernon (E. P. Richardson, p. 171).

Hart 3 // Baker 1 // Stauffer 2429 // Sellers, *Portraits*, pp. 237–239 // Sellers, *Peale*, p. 219 // Shadwell, "Peale," pp. 138–141 // E. P. Richardson, pp. 169–175 // Thorpe, p. 27 // Weitenkampf, p. 109.

His Excel: G: Washington Esq.

22.

Attributed to James Trenchard (1747–?), after Charles
  Willson Peale

Engraving, 1787

16.2 × 10 cm

His Excel: G: Washington Esq.

❧ Museum of Fine Arts, Boston
  Noah Webster, *An American Selection of Lessons in Reading
    and Speaking* (3rd ed., Philadelphia: Young and M'Cul-
    loch, 1787). Evans 20862.
  Noah Webster, *The American Spelling-Book* (7th ed.,
    Philadelphia: Young and M'Culloch, 1787). Evans 20864.

The frontispiece that once adorned Noah Webster's reading and spelling books, perhaps the most
beautiful of all the book illustrations of Washington, has been attributed to the engraver James
Trenchard by William S. Baker (Baker 38). As a
lifelong friend of Charles Willson Peale, Trenchard would have been aware of the mezzotint Peale
published in September 1787 [21], which was undoubtedly the source for this engraving. Furthermore, Trenchard's portrait is similar in style to
the signed engraving of Nathanael Greene that he

made for the *Columbian Magazine* in September
1786.

Judging from newspaper advertisements, the
Washington engraving was used by publisher William Young to illustrate several Philadelphia editions of Webster's books. Unfortunately, none of
the existing editions contains the print. In 1787
Young issued a seventh edition of the *American
Spelling-Book* (*Pennsylvania Gazette*, August 24,
1787), assumedly with this engraving as frontispiece. Webster had originally considered the use
of Washington's image disrespectful (Skeel, p. 11),
but this engraving seems to have changed his
mind. "I have procured a copy of Mr. Young's last
edition of the Spelling Book," he wrote to another
publisher. And, planning to use the engraving for
other editions, he continued, "I have sent to
Philadelphia to know on what terms I can procure
a Plate of Genl Washington's Portrait, which Mr
Young has prefixed to the works & which is pretty
well executed. I intend that all future impressions
shall be alike; & if I lower copy right, I shall
expect that you get a plate, for it will certainly
assist the sale" (*American Historical Record*, 1872,
1:374).

Contemporary advertisements indicate that
there was a Washington portrait in the eighth
edition of the spelling book published by Young
in 1788 (now unlocated; Skeel, p. 12); and there is
also evidence that the plate appeared in a 1789
twelfth edition of the speller (now unlocated;
Baker 38) and in a 1787 third edition of the
reader, *An American Selection of Lessons* (Littlefield, p. 156). Despite Webster's plan, the engraving seems to have appeared only in William
Young's editions. Several years later another
Washington portrait, cut by Alexander Anderson,
was substituted in a New York edition, but when
the copyright was secured by the publishers
Thomas and Andrews, the ubiquitous image of
Noah Webster became the standard frontispiece.

Hart 4 // Baker 38 // Stauffer 3276 // Skeel, pp. 10–12, 16,
  163–165 // Littlefield, pp. 154–156 // *American Historical
  Record*, 1872, 1:374.

97

Columb. Mag.

23.
Unidentified artist
Etching and engraving, 1788
15.6 × 9.8 cm
Columb. Mag.

❧ *The Columbian Magazine,* March 1788 (Philadelphia: Spotswood for Proprietors). Evans 21007; National Portrait Gallery (illustration only).

The publication of Johann Kaspar Lavater's book on physiognomy in the 1770s created a great interest during the last quarter of the century in the analysis of facial characteristics as an indication of personality traits and moral character. Before the Swiss author's four-volume work was even translated into English, a contributor to the *Columbian Magazine* chose from the French edition these two profiles, which he presented as "two of the most distinguished citizens of America," George Washington and Benjamin Franklin. Lavater "treats his subject as a science," wrote the contributor, adding that while the remarks seemed fanciful, they would have at least "the merit of novelty." He then quotes Lavater's analysis of the silhouetted profile which resembled the head of Washington:

> The first of these profiles, says Lavater, indicates a sound judgment; freedom from prejudice, and a

heart that opens itself to truth, which it imbibes and cherishes. It designates, likewise, taste, or if you please, a sense of beauty. The original must be distinguished by an indefatigable activity—a man who acts with prudence, and always with dignity. (*Columbian Magazine,* March 1788.)

While most of the plates in the *Columbian Magazine* are engraved by James Trenchard, two of his pupils, James Thackara and John Vallance, did some of the illustrations in the 1788 volume, and one or the other may have been responsible for this rather awkwardly executed engraving. At the Library Company of Philadelphia there is a copy of the magazine that belonged to the lawyer John Beale Bordley and is annotated in his hand. Bordley noted in the margin that the portrait on the right was "Doctor Franklin; no doubt; & the Profile very like him." He thought less of the likeness of Washington, writing "Genl. W. is meant, altho' the Profile is little like Him."

The magazine's subscribers were probably introduced to Lavater's "science" for the first time through this issue. Considering the quality of this illustration, however, they may well have agreed that his analysis seemed "fanciful."

Hart 810.

24.

Unidentified artist

Relief cut, 1789

10.1 × 7.3 cm

❧ *Bickerstaff's Boston Almanack, or, Federal Calendar, for 1790* ([Boston:] Russell, [1789]). Evans 22268; American Antiquarian Society.
Bickerstaff's Boston Almanack, or Federal Calendar for 1790 (3rd ed., [Boston:] Russell, [1789]). Evans 22270.

While these medallion portraits are not identified, their placement in a triumphal arch with thirteen stars and a federal eagle and shield suggests that they were intended to be George Washington and John Adams, just elected President and Vice-President. The almanac contains a "sketch of the life and character of our American Fabius," as well as a poem to Washington comparing him to ancient heroes.

Charles Evans commented that the "blurred portraits had formerly done duty as Washington and Gates" (Evans 22270), but this earlier appearance of the cut has not been located.

Hamilton 1357.

25.

Amos Doolittle (1754–1832), after James Trenchard (first state) and Joseph Wright (other states)

Etching and engraving, c. 1788–1789

51.8 × 42.3 cm

Display of the United States of America | To the Patrons of Arts and Sciences, in all parts of the World, this Plate | is Most respectfully Dedicated, by their most obedient humble Servants | Amos Doolittle & Ebnr. Po[rter.] | Printed & Sold by A. Doolittle New Haven where Engraving & Roling Press Printing is performed. In ink: *1790*.

❧ Independence National Historical Park Collection (second state)

Amos Doolittle's engraving *Display of the United States of America* was a celebration of the Constitution and the new federal government. In his ingenious design, the portrait of Washington is enclosed in a ring of fourteen interlocking circles containing the seals of the United States and the original thirteen colonies. In the upper left corner are the words "The United States were first declard Free and Independent July 4th 1776," and in the upper right corner is the inscription "The Present Constitution was formd by the Grand Convention held at Philadelphia Sept 17th 1787." Within the circular border of the state seals are the population statistics and the numbers of senators and representatives designated for each state. These figures are explained in the lower corners of the print. On the left is inscribed "The number of Inhabitants in the several States is according as they were reckoned in the Grand Convention held at Philadelphia in 1787," and on the right, "The number of Senators and Representatives is what the Constitution alloweth each State at Congress."

With this emphasis on the Constitution, Doolittle may have originally planned for his print to feature the portrait of Washington in civilian dress as president of the Convention. Charles Henry Hart assumed that the first state dated from 1788 before Rhode Island and North Carolina had ratified the Constitution, since their representation in Congress is left blank (Hart 840). However, it must not have been issued until 1789, after Washington's election, because the circular border around the portrait is inscribed "President of the United States of America. The Protector of his Country, and the Supporter of the rights of Mankind." With this inscription, along with the title, Doolittle's engraving becomes an image of Washington elevated from his relatively minor role as president of the constitutional convention

to his major role as the central figure of a newly strengthened federal government. The change from a loosely connected federation of states, split by factional differences, to a nation of states under a strong central government is dramatically presented by the visually indissoluble unity of interlocking circles. This heraldic ring of seals also gives particular prominence to the portrait. As a visual "display" of the importance of Washington's leadership and the strength of the government, Doolittle's impressively large engraving must have had considerable impact.

Since the print was dedicated to the "Patrons of Arts and Sciences in all parts of the World," Doolittle clearly had ambitious hopes for its sale and distribution. With the changing statistics of population, however, and the growing number of states and territories, the information in the *Display* was quickly outdated; and the plate had to be continually revised. During Washington's presidency it was issued in no less than six different states. (This second state, dated 1790 in ink on the copy in the Independence National Historical Park Collection, is not listed under Hart 840.)

For the central portrait in the first state (Fig. 21), Doolittle had made the unfortunate choice of copying James Trenchard's 1787 engraving of Washington from the *Columbian Magazine* [20]. This magazine illustration was an awkward composite image, and Doolittle's copy of it was the major weakness of his design. Apparently Doolittle realized its deficiencies, for by 1790 he had modified the plate to make the portrait resemble Joseph Wright's profile etching ([26]; Shadwell, *American Printmaking*, p. 44). In the succeeding states—the third and fourth were published in 1791, the fifth in 1794, and the sixth in 1796—the population numbers were changed and various insertions were made for "Main," Kentucky, Vermont, and the Northwest and Southwest territories (see Hart 840 a–d). Doolittle was never quite satisfied with the profile protrait—it is modified in every version. In the fifth state it is almost entirely reengraved, and in the sixth he changed the shape of the head so it only barely resembles the Wright etching.

The rarity of all the states of the *Display* suggests that it did not have as wide a distribution as Doolittle had no doubt anticipated. Nevertheless, he did not want to abandon his idea. In 1799 he engraved and published "A New Display of the United States" featuring the portrait of John Adams [reproduced in *Antiques* 101 (February 1922):266], and he apparently also issued a smaller version in 1803 with the portrait of Jefferson (Beardsley, p. 144). The concept of a circular chain of states had a life of its own: in 1776 it appeared on a half-dollar bill printed in Philadelphia (Leopold-Sharp, p. 51); it was featured on the inaugural buttons made in 1789 (MacNeil, pp. 14, 16); and later it was seen in various designs for ceramics (Ormsbee, pp. 5 ff.).

Hart 840 // Stauffer 521 // Shadwell, *American Printmaking*, 79 // Ormsbee, pp. 5 ff. // Leopold-Sharp, p. 51.

26.
Joseph Wright (1756–1793)
Etching with drypoint, c. 1790
6.5 × 4.8 cm
G. Washington. | J. Wright Pinxt. & Ft.
Print Collection, New York Public Library

Joseph Wright's exquisite print of George Washington had an important impact on the visual concept of the new President. The often-repeated and probably apocryphal story that Wright surreptitiously sketched Washington as he sat in a pew in St. Paul's Chapel, New York, was first recorded in 1857 by Gulian C. Verplanck, who added: "I do not know whether he painted any large portrait in oil or in crayon from the small likeness thus obtained, but he etched it himself, and published it here printed on a card" [*The Crayon* (August 1857):246–247]. Verplanck's story was correct at least in the fact that all known copies of the etching are printed on card stock. Although the story of the sketch cannot be documented, Wright had had a sitting with Washington in 1783 at which time he made a life mask and painted an oil portrait. The etching may thus derive its authenticity from Wright's original experience of modeling and painting Washington's face from life. The only other reference to a sketch is from William Dunlap, who in commenting on Wright's painting of Washington also noted: "He afterwards drew a profile of Washington and etched it, and it is very like" (Dunlap, *History*, 1:313).

The so-called Goodhue profile drawing in lead or crayon (Eisen, *Portraits*, pp. 444–445) was actually an impression of the Wright etching. It was sent by Benjamin Goodhue as a gift to William Bentley, who noted it in his diary on December 15, 1790 (Bentley 1:219). Goodhue had inscribed on the back of the etching: "This was done in New York, 1790, and is acknowledged by all to be a very strong likeness" (Hart, "Notice," p. 161).

Thomas Jefferson was one purchaser of Wright's print, paying eight shillings on June 10, 1790 (Jefferson Account Book for 1790). On June 27 he wrote Martha Jefferson Randolph, "I now inclose you an engraving of the President done by Wright who drew the picture of him which I have at Paris" (Boyd 16:577–578).

Wright's profile head was widely copied in prints, medallions, relief cuts, and medals both here and abroad (see Kimball, "Wright, Sculpture"). Closely related to his etching is Wright's painting of Washington now at the Cleveland Museum, with the head in profile but the body turned three quarters to the right. This image spawned its own progeny of prints, particularly in England.

In the opinion of Fiske Kimball, Wright's profile portraits of Washington, "with their wide currency in engravings, must be accounted among the most influential of his portraits, sharing with Stuart's three-quarter views and Houdon's bust the creation of the President's likeness as it exists in the mind of the public" (Kimball, "Wright, Paintings and Engravings," p. 382).

Hart 138 // Baker 74 // Stauffer 3418 // Hart, "Notice," pp. 161–165 // Kimball, "Wright, Paintings and Engravings," p. 382 // Kimball, Wright, Sculpture," pp. 38–39 // *The Crayon* (August 1857): 246–247 // Bentley 1:219 // Weitenkampf, p. 1.

27.
James Manly (active 1789–1793), after Joseph Wright

Etching and engraving, c. 1790

8.9 cm (diameter)

G Washington | Born Virginia Febry. 11th. 1732. | General of the American Armies 1775. | Resign'd 1783. | President of the United States 1789.

Historical Society of Pennsylvania (second state)

The engraving by James Manly (occasionally cited as John or Jacques) was based on the first portrait medal of George Washington to be produced in this country. On March 3, 1790, Manly advertised in the *Pennsylvania Packet* a medal of the newly elected President available in white metal, silver, and gold. Included in the notice was an endorsement dated February 22 and signed by Thomas Mifflin, Richard Peters, Christian Febiger, and Francis Johnston, who acknowledged that the medal was "a strong and expressive likeness and worthy the attention of the citizens of the United States of America." On March 20, "James Manly, Die Sinker" announced in the *Federal Gazette* that the medal, "a fine profile of the venerated President of these states has lately been executed."

Describing himself as an Irish artist who had lived in London, he informed his patrons that he had had "uncommon difficulties to contend with in executing so capital a branch of the fine arts in a country where the auxiliary arts have not yet arrived at perfection" (Prime 2:70–71).

Manly modeled his likeness, rather inexpertly, on Joseph Wright's profile etching [26]. The die for the medal was cut and signed by Samuel Brooks, a Philadelphia goldsmith and seal-cutter (Baker, *Medallic Portraits*, pp. 39–40, 43). The reverse of the medal featured the words "General of the American Armies, . . . 1775 . . . ," which were also in the inscription on the print.

Judging from a broadside with the heading "Medals, Miniature and Profile Painting and Shades," both Manly and Brooks may have been in Boston by September 23, 1790 (Storer, pp. 6–7). The broadside announced the one-month stay of "the Artists, who took the most correct likeness of the President of the United States, and executed a Medal of him." Along with their various talents, they advertised for sale "that most approved Historical Medal of the President."

An earlier state of the engraving was inscribed "J Manly," indicating that Manly had made the engraving as well as designing the medal. There are also restrikes of the print from a plate that was extensively reworked with the title removed from a ribbon on the arm and placed above the image (Hart 155b).

Hart 155 // Baker 97 // Stauffer 2171 // Stauffer 1:172 // Storer, pp. 6–7 // Baker, *Medallic Portraits*, pp. 39–40, 43 // Kimball, "Wright, Sculpture," p. 38.

THE PRESIDENT OF THE UNITED STATES.

28.

Unidentified artist, after Joseph Wright

Etching and engraving, 1791

6 × 4.8 cm

Massa. Mag. | The President of the United States.

❧ *The Massachusetts Magazine,* March 1791 (Boston: Thomas and Andrews). Evans 23558; Rare Books Division, New York Public Library.

Illustrating a biographical sketch of Washington by John Bell, the profile portrait in Isaiah Thomas' *Massachusetts Magazine* was an early copy after Joseph Wright's etching [26]. The distinctive figure-eight design of the epaulet in this image was imitated by other printmakers (Kimball, "Wright, Paintings and Engravings," p. 382).

The controversy over the engraved plates in this magazine, many of which were made by Samuel Hill, reveals the contemporary interest in illustration despite the lack of skill and originality. From its first issue, in January 1789, each number of the magazine was illustrated with an engraving. The publishers attempted to cut down on expenses by omitting the frontispiece. In the general preface to the 1791 volume they suggested that "eight pages extra, would at times be more gratifying, than the . . . trivial decoration of a plate, which only amuses the eye, without informing the mind, or meliorating the heart." However, they noted that "should any lovers of this really fine art, present us with original views, either of animate or inanimate nature, as yet unnoticed by the human pencil, they will be received with thankfulness, and faithfully deposited in the fronts of future Numbers." The suggestion was decidedly rejected;

the readers demanded engravings, original or not. As the publishers explained in the preface to the next year's volume: "Three month's experience was decisive: The admirers of this polite art earnestly called for their resumption: They were instantly gratified." This was followed by another plea for "any foreign or domestick designs, in which brilliancy of invention, or accuracy of delineation, are conspicuous."

Hart 143 // Baker 77 // Baker, *Washingtoniana,* p. 4 // Mott 1:108–111 // Kimball, "Wright, Paintings and Engravings," p. 382 // L. N. Richardson, pp. 354–361.

29.

William Rollinson (1762–1842), after Joseph Wright

Etching and engraving, c. 1791

7.2 × 5.2 cm

W Rollinson Sculpt. | N. York. NA. | Washing[ton]

❧ Print Collection, New York Public Library

William Rollinson's "first attempt at copperplate engraving," according to William Dunlap, was "a small profile portrait of General Washington done in the stippling manner" in 1791 (Dunlap, *History,* 1:188). Although other writers have confused Rollinson's first effort with his engraving of Washington after Edward Savage (Reid and Rollinson, p. 16), this badly trimmed image was identified by Charles Henry Hart as the profile Dunlap described (Hart 144). The engraving was probably copied directly, although not very carefully, from Joseph Wright's etching of Washington [26].

Hart 144 // Dunlap, *History,* 1:188 // Reid and Rollinson, p. 16 // *DAB*—Rollinson.

Georg Waschington,
Präsident der Vereinigten Staaten.
D [1792.]   Ler

30.

Unidentified artist, after Charles Willson Peale

Relief cut, 1791

9.2 × 7.3 cm

Georg Waschington, | Praesident der Bereinigten Staaten.

❧ *Der hoch-deutsche americanische Calender, auf das Jahr 1792* (Germantown: Billmeyer, [1791]). Evans 23444; Rare Books Division, New York Public Library.

The small cut of Washington used in this almanac was probably copied from Charles Willson Peale's 1787 mezzotint or James Trenchard's engraving after it [21, 22].

31.

Edward Savage (1761–1817)

Stipple, 1792

13.7 × 11.1 cm

Painted & Engraved by E. Savage | George Washington, Esqr. | President of the United States of America. | From the Original Picture Painted in 1790 for the | Philosophical Chamber, at the University of Cambridge, | In Massachusetts. | Publishd Feby. 7, 1792 by E. Savage, No. 29 Charles Street, Middx. Hospital.

❧ National Portrait Gallery
Washington's Monuments of Patriotism (Philadelphia: Baileys for Ormrod, 1800). Evans 39021.

In 1789 Edward Savage called on George Washington with a letter from Joseph Willard, president of Harvard: "Mr. Savage, the bearer of this . . . , [has] politely and generously offered to take your portrait for the university, if you will be so kind as to sit" (Sparks 10:64; Hart, "Savage," p. 4). Washington's diary records three sittings to Savage for the original painting, which was finished in January of 1790 (Hart, "Savage," p. 5). A

replica of the Harvard portrait, made for John Adams, required another sitting on April 6, 1790. There was probably another replica which Savage took to London to use as the basis of this stipple engraving, published there on February 7, 1792 (Morgan and Fielding, pp. 180–181).

Print historian Frank Weitenkampf has commented that this engraving, which was printed in brown and in colors as well as in black, "shows remarkably minute stippling in the face. It is almost entirely dotted, with a modicum of line work on coat and wig; an honest, careful job" (Weitenkampf, p. 70). Savage's instant mastery of various print techniques in London coupled with his later dependence on apprentices has caused speculation that his authorship was not so honest and that he signed his name to prints done by others (Dunlap, *History*, 1:321; Baker, *American Engravers*, p. 155; Hart, "Savage," pp. 1–19; Dickson, "Savage," pp. 6 ff.; Dickson, *Jarvis*, pp. 35–57). Dunlap's *History* quotes David Edwin as saying "Savage, a portrait painter, was the only publisher of prints at that time. He published prints from

Painted & Engraved by E. Savage

GEORGE WASHINGTON, ESQ.ᴿ

President of the United States of America.

From the Original Picture Painted in 1790 for the
Philosophical Chamber, at the University of Cambridge,

IN MASSACHUSETTS.

Publishd Feb.ʸ 7, 1792 by E. Savage, N.ᵒ 29 Charles Street, Mid.ˣ Hospital.

pictures of his own painting, being sometimes painter, engraver, and printer" (Dunlap, *History*, 2:68). However, Dunlap also quotes Savage's apprentice John Wesley Jarvis saying that Savage "painted what he called fancy pieces and historical subjects, and they were published as being designed and engraved by him, though his painting was execrable, and he knew nothing of engraving" (Dunlap, *History*, 2:75). Jarvis, who thought that Savage was "the most ignorant beast that ever imposed upon the public," undoubtedly exaggerated. Nevertheless, it is clear that many of the Savage plates were a group effort (see entry [55]).

In this 1792 print he was probably assisted by the English artist who taught him how to engrave, since, as Dickson points out, these prints are hardly the work of an amateur (Dickson, "Savage," p. 7). Joint effort or not, it was a fine production and had a wide circulation in America, being copied for a number of book frontispieces in the 1790s. A second state, with the title and imprint erased and "General George Washington" substituted, can be found as a frontispiece to *Washington's Monuments of Patriotism* (1800), although some copies of this volume have an English plate engraved by James Fittler.

Hart 214 // Baker 116, 117 // Stauffer 2753 // Hart, "Savage," pp. 4–7, 15 // Dickson, "Savage," p. 7 // Dickson, *Jarvis*, p. 36 // Weitenkampf, p. 70 // Andrews, p. 49 // Morgan and Fielding, pp. 180–181 // Dunlap, *History*, 1:321, 2:68, 75–76.

32.
Alexander Anderson (1775–1870), after Charles Willson Peale

Relief cut, 1792

14.3 × 8.3 cm

General Washington.

☙ Noah Webster, *The American Spelling Book* (14th ed., New York: Campbell, 1792). Evans 25000; Connecticut State Library.

In 1783, Noah Webster published the first part of *A Grammatical Institute of the English Language*, better known by its later title, *The American Spelling Book*. It was the first spelling book by an American author, and its success was immediate and long lasting. The influence of Webster's speller was credited for that "remarkable uniformity of pronunciation in our country which is so often spoken of with surprise by English travelers" (Littlefield, p. 132). It was still considered a popular book a century later, and its sales were recorded as having reached eighty million by 1880 (*American Historical Record*, 1872, 1:152–153; Littlefield, p. 132).

In 1787 some of William Young's Philadelphia

editions of Webster's work were illustrated with a portrait of George Washington (see entry [22]). For this "fourteenth edition," New York bookseller Samuel Campbell got Alexander Anderson to supply a Washington portrait. Anderson's frontispiece, a rather crude copy of a Charles Willson Peale image, was engraved on type metal in a style resembling the white-line engraving in which he eventually specialized. Anderson had started printmaking at the age of twelve by scratching a head of "Paul Jones" on copper with the back spring of his pen knife. He recalled later that "an obliging blacksmith afterwards made some tools for me and I began to work in type metal" (Burr, p. 84). Already familiar with working in relief, the so-called father of American wood engraving simply switched from type metal to boxwood cut on the end grain, and, inspired by the work of Thomas Bewick, perfected the art. William J. Linton in his *History of Wood-Engraving in America* states that "his type-metal work . . . was only wood-engraving on metal" (Linton, p. 5). This portrait of George Washington was part of that naive tradition of white-line relief work in eighteenth-century American book illustration that was a precedent to the wood engraving of the nineteenth century.

Baker 2 // Skeel, p. 19 // *American Historical Record*, 1872, 1:152–153.

George Washington Esq.r
PRESIDENT of the UNITED STATES of AMERICA.

33.

Edward Savage (1761–1817)

Mezzotint, 1793

45.6 × 35.2 cm

E. Savage pinx. et sculp. / George Washington Esqr. / President of the United States of America. / From the Original Portrait Painted at the request of the Corporation of the University of Cambridge in Massachusetts / Published June 25, 1793, by E. Savage, No. 54, Newman Street

✣ National Portrait Gallery

When the young artist John Wesley Jarvis saw in Philadelphia "the prints displayed at the shop windows," he recognized "something much more perfect and more to my taste" than painting and decided to become an engraver (Dunlap, *History*, 2:75). Since Savage's name was on several of the prints he admired, Jarvis went to him as an apprentice. This large Washington mezzotint published in London on June 15, 1793, was undoubtedly one of the pieces (along with Savage's print of

Benjamin Franklin published in London the same year), that had so impressed Jarvis. The Washington print, in particular, had all the refinement of technique—softness of texture, subtlety of shading, and richness of effect—that had made English mezzotint engraving so popular for over a century. Although Jarvis' admiration for Savage did not last long, it is no wonder that he was impressed by the quality of these prints.

Savage's own participation in the production of his prints became a controversial question after Jarvis' disparaging remarks to William Dunlap (Dunlap, *History*, 1:321, 2:75–76; see entry [31]). The portrait of Washington may indeed look like an English mezzotint partly because Savage was materially assisted by an English engraver, and partly because in London a technician was generally available to prepare the plate and a skilled printer to print it.

The inscription on the Washington print indicates that it was copied from the painting Savage made for Harvard (Fig. 26), although this must have referred only to the face. Savage probably took a replica of the Harvard painting with him to London where he painted a three-quarter-length portrait on a wooden panel that was the more immediate source for the mezzotint (Fig. 28). The panel painting, now at the Chicago Art Institute and very similar to the mezzotint in size and in details of composition, is signed and dated 1793.

Savage sent impressions of his two London mezzotints to George Washington on October 6, 1793, with an accompanying letter.

> I have taken the liberty to send two prints. The one done from the portrait I first sketched in black velvet, labours under some disadvantages as the Likeness never was quite finished. I hope it will meet with the approbation of yourself and Mrs. Washington as it is the first I ever published in that method of Engraving. The portrait of Doctor Franklin which is published as the companion, is done from a picture in the possession of Mr. West. (Hart, "Savage," p. 7.)

A dignified presidential-looking image of Washington in his second term in office, the engraving depicted him seated at a table, his hand resting on a plan for the new federal city lettered with the words "Eastern Branch." Judging from the number of copies still in existence, the Savage print was quite popular in America. It was copied once, supposedly by Savage (see [34]; Baker 119), and again, in several versions, by William Hamlin of Rhode Island [76, 77, 78].

Hart 228 // Baker 118 // Stauffer 2752 // Shadwell, *American Printmaking*, 82 // Hart, "Savage," pp. 6–8 // Dickson, "Savage," p. 7 // Dickson, *Jarvis*, pp. 36–37, 41 // Eisen, *Portraits*, 2:451–452, 458–461 // Morgan and Fielding, pp. 79, 181 // Weitenkampf, p. 110 // Andrews, p. 48.

George Washington
PRESIDENT of the UNITED STATES of AMERICA

34.
Attributed to Edward Savage (1761–1817)

Mezzotint, c. 1793

46 × 35.5 cm

George Washington / President of the United States of America, / From the Original Portrait Painted at the request of the Corporation of the University of Cambridge in Massachusetts

Historical Society of Pennsylvania

Copied from the preceding print [33] and probably also by Edward Savage (Baker 119), this mezzotint of Washington has a slightly coarser grain and is not as smoothly executed. Nevertheless, the draftsmanship is still quite good.

Hart 229 // Baker 119.

The figure of America wears Minerva's plumed helmet, carries a liberty pole and cap, and has a cornucopia resting at her feet. She tramples on a wolflike creature representing "Oppression" and points upward with her right hand as a gesture of immortality in reference to the two heroes, Benjamin Franklin and George Washington. Franklin's portrait is surrounded by books, a lyre, and a bolt of lightning. Washington's image, which is no attempt at a likeness, is ornamented with military banners and a liberty cap.

The authorship of the book, which was advertised in the *Vermont Gazette* on May 2, 1794, has been questioned. It has also been attributed to Richard Johnson (McCorison, p. 60).

Hart 821, 822 // McCorison, p. 60.

35.
Unidentified artist
Etching and engraving, 1793
11.1 × 6.3 cm

Frontispiece | America trampling on Oppression
  In medallions: *Docr Benn Franklin | Gen. Geo. Washington*

W. D. Cooper, *The History of North America* (Bennington: Haswell for Spencer, 1793). Evans 25347.

ꙮ W. D. Cooper, *The History of North America* (Lansingburgh, N.Y.: Tiffany for Spencer, 1795). Evans 28480; Metropolitan Museum of Art.

The 1789 edition of W. D. Cooper's *History of North America,* published in London, had as a frontispiece an allegorical engraving entitled "America trampling on Oppression" (Fleming, "1783–1815," p. 48). The print was copied for the 1793 Vermont edition of the book and then re-engraved and reissued as the frontispiece for a 1795 Lansingburgh, New York, edition.

36.
Joseph Hiller, Jr. (1777–1795), after Joseph Wright
Etching, 1793
5.3 × 3.2 cm

G: Washington | Jos. Hiller Junr Sculp. 1793

ꙮ Print Collection, New York Public Library

While undoubtedly based on Joseph Wright's etched profile, the first portrait of Washington by the sixteen-year-old Joseph Hiller, Jr., is somewhat awkward in technique and inaccurate in the squarish shape of the head. It may have been an experimental piece, for a much closer copy of the Wright etching was signed by Hiller in 1794 [37].

Fielding 700.

108

37.

Joseph Hiller, Jr. (1777–1795), after Joseph Wright

Etching with drypoint, 1794

6.6 × 4.9 cm

G. Washington. | J. Hiller. Jur. Sculp 1794.

❧ Print Collection, New York Public Library

In 1794, at age seventeen, Joseph Hiller, Jr., made his second, and much more successful, attempt to copy Joseph Wright's etched profile of Washington [26]. Except for the unworked background, it was a close rendition of Wright's portrait; Hiller even used a similar heavy card stock. In fact, most of the impressions are actually printed on the backs of playing cards. Charles Henry Hart located four original Hiller etchings in 1907, as well as the copperplate, which he used to publish a restrike as frontispiece to his monograph (Hart, "Hiller," passim). The Essex Institute in Salem owns a seal with a very similar image of Washington; and Hart records the suggestion that the etching was made to send to London as a model for the seal-cutter. This impression is a variant state of the print not listed in Hart (see Hart 140), with more periods in the inscription and without a *t* in the word *Sculp.*

Hart 140 // Fielding 699 // Hart, "Hiller," pp. 1–6 // Eisen, *Portraits,* 2:540–541.

38.

Unidentified artist, after John Trumbull

Relief cut, 1794

7.5 × 5.8 cm

Genl. Washington.

❧ [Jedidiah Morse], *The Life of General Washington, Commander in Chief . . . and Present President* (Philadelphia: Jones, Hoff and Derrick, 1794). Evans 27221; Library Company of Philadelphia.

John Trumbull's images of Washington were rarely copied in American prints. This simple relief cut, however, with the sharply arched eyebrow, the folded-back flap of the coat, and the pose and shape of the head, is distinctly reminiscent of various Trumbull paintings of the General, particularly *Washington at Trenton.* This cut illustrated a Washington biography which was reprinted, along with one of Richard Montgomery, from sketches in Jedidiah Morse's *American Geography* of 1789 (Baker, *Washingtoniana,* p. 5). The biography was a modest publication, yet its illustration of Washington implies that a valiant effort was made to copy Trumbull's heroic image.

Rosenbach 177 // Baker, *Washingtoniana,* p. 5.

LIBERTAS

E PLURIBUS UNUM

Printed by R.Roberton.

Engraved by R.Field.

GEORGE WASHINGTON,

PRESIDENT of the UNITED STATES.

Published by Walter Roberson, Philadelphia & New York 1st August 1795.

39.

Robert Field (c. 1769–1819), after Walter Robertson and John James Barralet

Stipple, 1795

27.9 × 22.9 cm

Jon. Jas. Barralet | Invenit 1795. | Painted by W. Robertson. | Engrav'd by R. Field. | George Washington, | President of the United States. | Published by Walter Robertson, Philadelphia & New York 1st. August 1795.

Historical Society of Pennsylvania

At about the time this print was published, in August 1795, the three artists involved—Walter Robertson, John James Barralet, and Robert Field—were boarding together at the house of Mrs. Janet Clarke in Philadelphia (Piers, p. 12). In an unusual combination of talents, Field engraved the stipple plate after a miniature painted by Robertson (Fig. 37) adding to the portrait a symbolic border designed by Barralet. Field had written to Robert Gilmore in January 1795 describing his plan for the engraving: "Mr. Robinson's [sic] miniature of the President is as good a likeness and as fine a piece of painting as I ever saw. I have engaged to engrave it the same size with some ornaments to surround & make it more interesting" (Piers, p. 10).

On April 23, 1795, a New York newspaper printed the proposal to publish companion prints of Washington and Alexander Hamilton "Engraved by Robert Field, late of London, from the original painting by Walter Robertson. The size, including an emblematical border to be 11 × 15 inches; the price to subscribers to be five dollars each print." Subscriptions were to be taken in Philadelphia by Barralet and Field as well as in New York (*American Minerva*, April 23, 1795; quoted in Kelby, p. 38). At the same time the artists advertised in the *Maryland Journal* (April 20, 1795; Piers, p. 13; Prime 2:68). Apparently the trio had ambitious plans for other publications. Both advertisements included mention of an equestrian engraving of Washington attended by Hamilton, and the Baltimore newspaper mentioned "Four Plates in Commemoration of the Western Expedition" after drawings by Barralet (Prime 2:68). However, the Hamilton portrait after Robertson was later engraved by George Graham (Stauffer 1163), while the equestrian engraving of Washington and the plates from the Western expedition were probably never published.

An early state of the Field engraving had a radiating sun above the oval and the hilt of a sword appearing to the right of the eagle's head

(*Anderson Gallery Auction Catalogue*, No. 335, November 16, 1904). In its final state, however, the sword—topped with a liberty cap—and the word "Libertas" enclosed in a laurel wreath were added above the oval as a crowning motif, both visually and symbolically. Flanked by palm branches and military banners and supported by a realistic eagle holding an "E Pluribus Unum" ribbon in his beak and the scales of justice on his back, the Washington portrait is suspended in a heavenly atmosphere of clouds and radiating light. It was apotheosis imagery that skillfully presented two accomplishments of Washington's leadership: liberty through military strength, and justice and unity through wise governance. In the middle of a stress-ridden and controversial second term in office, Washington was presented in this print as nearly godlike.

The print was published by the painter, Walter Robertson, in both Philadelphia and New York. The Robertson likeness from this print, with its characteristic black stock (William Dunlap was critical of this feature of the portrait; see Dunlap, *History*, 1:430), was copied by William Rollinson for a book illustration [44], by an engraver named Walker in London, and by unknown engravers in both Dublin and Belfast (Hart 250, 252, 253).

Hart 249 // Baker 169 // Stauffer 1004 // Taylor, pp. 29–30 // Kelby, p. 38 // Dunlap, *History*, 1:430 // Piers, pp. 10–14, 193.

40.

John Scoles (active 1793–1844), after Edward Savage

Engraving, 1795

12.8 × 10.1 cm

I Scoles. del et sculp. | George Washington, | President of the United States of America. | Publish'd by Smith, Reed, and Wayland.

William Winterbotham, *A Geographical, Commercial, and Philosophical View of the Present Situation of the United States of America*, Volume 1 (New York: Tiebout and O'Brien for Reid, . . . , 1795). Evans 29912; National Portrait Gallery (illustration only).

William Winterbotham, *An Historical, Geographical, Commercial and Philosophical View of the United States*, Volume 3 (New York: Tiebout and O'Brien for Reid, 1796). Evans 31647.

William Winterbotham, who had never been to America, wrote his four-volume commentary on the United States while he was a prisoner at Newgate in 1795. It was, as one author has stated, "an impudent compilation of extracts, made without any judgment, from various authors" (Bartlett, p. 385). Nevertheless, the first two volumes were republished in New York that same year, and the third and fourth, along with a second issue of the first two, came out the following year with a

GEORGE WASHINGTON,

PRESIDENT of the UNITED STATES of AMERICA.

Publish'd by Smith, Reed, and Wayland.

J.Scoles, del.t sculp.

slightly different title. The plates in the second issue were rearranged.

John Scoles copied his portrait of Washington from Edward Savage's mezzotint [33], eliminating the background curtain and lettering the plan on the table "City of Washington" (this may indicate another state, since Stauffer documents this lettering as "Eastern Branch"). Except for a second engraving of Washington by Rollinson (see entry [44]), all the other portraits in the work were copied from the 1795 London edition.

Hart 233 // Baker 134 // Stauffer 2809 // Bartlett, p. 385.

41.

Unidentified artist

Relief cut, 1795

6.4 × 4.9 cm

History of America. | His Excellency Gen. Washington, | President of the United States. | "Great without pomp, without ambition brave, | "Proud not to conquer fellow-men, but save.

  ❀ *The History of America Abridged for the Use of Children* (Philadelphia: Wrigley and Berriman for Curtis, 1795). Evans 28831; Historical Society of Pennsylvania.

This one-volume history was, according to its title page, "abridged for the use of children of all denominations" and "adorned with cuts." It was probably the earliest American history to be edited specifically for young people (Rosenbach, p. 81), which apparently provided an excuse for extremely crude illustration. The cuts were at least profuse. They included two scenes—Columbus' first interview with the natives of America, and Israel Putnam captured by the Indians—and twenty small profile portraits. The profiles seem

History of America. 47

His Excellency GEN. WASHINGTON, President of the United States.

" Great without pomp, without ambition brave, " Proud not to conquer fellow-men, but save.

to have been inspired initially by the portraits in John Andrews' *History of the War,* published in London in 1785 (see portrait of Clinton in Cresswell, p. 12). However, the artist quickly abandoned the attempt to provide likenesses. Thus all the portraits are quite similar, varying mainly by the addition of a tricornered hat with or without a rosette. In fact, several of the blocks sufficed for more than one hero. The Samuel Adams cut reappeared as General Bradley and as Henry Lee, the Richard Montgomery profile became Richard Howell, and the Benjamin Franklin was also Thomas S. Lee and Isaac Shelby. Eleven blocks were used to portray twenty different men.

Beneath the portrait of Washington was the verse: "Great without pomp, without ambition brave, Proud not to conquer fellowmen, but save." The talent of the poet was well matched to that of the artist. The publisher clearly had the common attitude that quantity rather than quality was of primary importance for the illustration of children's books.

Rosenbach 192 // Hamilton, p. 39.

42.

John Scoles (active 1793–1844), after Joseph Wright

Engraving, 1795

7.5 × 5.9 cm

Scoles sc. | General Washington. | [Publish'd by Smith, New York.]

❦ Charles Smith, *The Gentleman's Political Pocket-Almanac for . . . 1796* (New York: Wayland & Davis for Smith, [1795]). Evans 29520; American Antiquarian Society.

Charles Smith's almanac was advertised on January 15, 1796: "This day is published (Price 4s) And to be had of C. Smith . . . and of all the principal Booksellers in New York, & throughout the United states, Smith's Political Almanack, for the Year 1796. It is ornamented with a well-engraved likeness of Gen. Washington . . ." (*The Argus or Greenleaf's New Daily Advertiser,* January 15, 1796). John Scoles' image of Washington, used as the frontispiece, was related to the etching by Joseph Wright [26], except that the body was turned to a three-quarter pose rather than a profile. In this respect it resembles the painting of Washington by Joseph Wright now at the Cleveland Museum of Art (Kimball, "Wright, Paintings and Engravings," p. 382).

After publishing this portrait, the author apparently sold the plate. In a letter dated January 5, 1796, the Baltimore bookseller George Keatinge wrote to the publisher Mathew Carey asking help in procuring plates for the magazine that he planned to publish. "The first No. will be published on the 1st of Feby," he wrote, "with an

GENERAL WASHINGTON.

engraved Likeness of the President the plate I purchased from Mr. Smith of New York & it is the one he has in the political magazine" (Weems 1:5). Keatinge was referring either to this almanac or to Smith's magazine, *The Monthly Military Repository,* which also had a portrait of Washington [43].

Hart 163 // Baker 95 // Stauffer 2808 // Weems 1:5 // Kimball, "Wright, Paintings and Engravings," p. 382.

GEN.ᴸ WASHINGTON.

Engrav'd for C. Smith N-YORK.

43.

Elkanah Tisdale (1771–?)

Etching and engraving, 1796

16.7 × 10 cm

Genl. Washington Takes Command of the | American Army at Cambridge July 3d 1775. | Tisdale Sc. | Genl. Washington. | Engrav'd for C. Smith N–York.

☙ Charles Smith, *The Monthy Military Repository*, 1796 (New York: Davis for Author). Evans 30807; Rare Books Division, New York Public Library.

Charles Smith, *The American War, from 1775 to 1783* (New York: Smith, 1797). Evans 32842.

New York bookseller Charles Smith edited a series of articles about the Revolution, based supposedly on descriptions by the generals Baron von Steuben and Horatio Gates (*Appletons' Cyclopedia—Smith*). Illustrated with portraits and plans, the articles were originally published in Smith's periodical the *Monthly Military Repository* and then collected into a single volume, *The American War*. The illustrations apparently differ in various reported copies of the latter work.

The exact source of Elkanah Tisdale's frontispiece engraving of Washington remains elusive. Both Walter Robertson (Baker 173) and Archibald Robertson (Hart 248) have been suggested as the original portraitist, but no exact prototype has yet been identified. It is possible that Tisdale combined several images. He probably did design the small vignette of Washington taking command at Cambridge. Hart documented a "modern copy" of this plate which is inscribed across the top "Engraved for C. Smith N. York."

Hart 248 // Baker 173.

44.

William Rollinson (1762–1842), after Walter Robertson

Engraving, 1796

10.2 × 7.9 cm

Rollinson Sculpt. | G. Washington | President of the United States | Publish'd by I. Reid New York 1796.

☙ William Winterbotham, *An Historical, Geographical, Commercial and Philosophical View . . . of the United States of America*, Volume 3, Part 3 (New York: Tiebout and O'Brien for Reid, . . . , 1796). Evans 29912; National Portrait Gallery (illustration only).

William Winterbotham, *An Historical, Geographical, Commercial, and Philosophical View of the United States of America*, Volume 1 (New York: Tiebout and O'Brien for Reid, 1796). Evans 31647.

Rollinson's engraving and one of Washington by John Scoles were the only two plates in Winterbotham's work that were not copied from the English edition. Rollinson based his image on the 1795 engraving by Robert Field [39] after a miniature by Walter Robertson. (For discussion of Winterbotham's work, see entry [40].)

Hart 251 // Baker 172 // Stauffer 2719.

G. WASHINGTON

President of the United States

Publish'd by I. Reid New York 1796.

GEORGE WASHINGTON
President of the United States

45.

William Rollinson (1762–1842), after Edward Savage

Aquatint and stipple, 1796

12.8 × 11.8 cm

Savage Pinxt. / Rollinson sct. / George Washington / President of the United States.

☙ *Epistles Domestic, Confidential, and Official, from General Washington* (New York: Robinson and Bull for Rivington, 1796). Evans 30392; American Antiquarian Society.
Roswell Shirtliff [Shurtleff], *An Oration on the Illustrious George Washington* (Walpole, N.H.: Carlisle for Thomas and Thomas, 1800). Evans 38504.

In 1796 a young Episcopal clergyman forged a series of letters which he published as George Washington's, apparently "in order to make his fortune in England, in the character of a loyalist" (Bartlett 2:400). Washington wrote to Secretary of State Timothy Pickering on March 3, 1797, claiming "that the letters herein described are a base forgery, and that I never saw or heard of them until they appeared in print" (Fitzpatrick 35:415). Illustrating both the *Epistles* and a eulogy published in New Hampshire four years later—*An Oration on the Illustrious George Washington*—is the first state of William Rollinson's engraving, executed mainly in aquatint. This plate after Savage has been confused with the profile portrait of George Washington that was Rollinson's first attempt at printmaking (Reid and Rollinson, p. 16). Rollinson's engraving was later reengraved in stipple (Hart 217).

Hart 217 // Baker 132 // Stauffer 2718 // Bartlett 2:400 // Reid and Rollinson, p. 16.

46.

Samuel Hill (active 1789–1803), after Edward Savage

Etching and engraving, 1796

10.3 × 7.8 cm

Engraved by S. Hill / George Washington, / President of the United States of / America.

☙ George Washington, *Official Letters to the Honorable American Congress*, Volume 1 (2nd Boston ed., Boston: Manning and Loring for S. Hall, . . . , 1796). Evans 31422; Library of Congress.

Another version of Edward Savage's 1792 engraving [31], Samuel Hill's portrait was the frontispiece to an authorized edition of official letters. According to Charles Evans the book was issued both with and without a portrait, with an extra charge for its inclusion. Both Evans (29737) and Joseph Sabin (101726) list the same portrait in the first edition, but no copy can be located with the print. The second edition was advertised as being "ornamented with a striking Likeness" (*Massachusetts Mercury*, January 17, 1800).

Hart 216 // Baker 129 // Stauffer 1382.

GEORGE WASHINGTON,
president of the UNITED STATES of AMERICA.

G. WASHINGTON.

Love righteoufnefs, ye that be judges of the earth : think of the Lord with a good heart, and in fimplicity of heart feek him.

47.
Unidentified artist, after Pierre Eugène Du Simitière

Relief cut, 1796

5.9 × 6 cm

G. Washington. | Love righteousness, ye that be judges of | the earth: think of the Lord with a good | heart, and in simplicity of heart seek him.

🪶 *The New-England Primer: Much Improved* (Germantown, 1796). Evans 30847; Rare Book Department, Free Library of Philadelphia.

Pierre Eugène Du Simitière's 1779 drawings of Washington and other American statesmen were engraved in Paris by Bénoit Louis Prévost in 1781 and in London in 1783 in two separate versions (Donnell, pp. 17–21). The English sets inspired numerous copies on textiles and creamware. Despite its popularity in Europe, the Du Simitière profile of Washington was rarely copied in America. This relief cut in a Germantown *Primer,* however, appears to be based on Du Simitière. The medallion portrait is surrounded by fifteen stars and symbols from the arms of Pennsylvania: a plow, a ship, and sheaves of wheat. With the placement of a biblical quotation beneath the portrait—"Love righteousness, ye that be judges of the earth: think of the Lord with a good heart, and in simplicity of heart seek him"—Washington was presented to the youthful readers of the *Primer* as a symbol of exemplary behavior.

Rosenbach 214.

48.
H. Houston (active 1796–1798), after John James Barralet

Stipple, c. 1796–1798

25.6 × 20.8 cm

J. J. Barralet del. | H. Houston sculpt. | General Washington, | President of the United States of | America.

🪶 Print Collection, New York Public Library

John James Barralet and H. Houston were both immigrant artists from Dublin working in Philadelphia when they collaborated on this dignified portrait engraving of George Washington. In 1795 Barralet had designed another Washington print, engraved by Robert Field, after a miniature by Walter Robertson [39]. Robertson's miniature no doubt influenced Barralet's likeness in this engraving as well; the black stock in both prints is a particularly distinctive feature. However, the slightly broader and more idealized face with upward-glancing eyes suggests that Barralet might also have been influenced by a Houdon bust.

The allegorical embellishment in the center of the title was typical of Barralet. Constrained by the size of the margin, he designed a somewhat awkward but nevertheless appropriate grouping of a helmeted Minerva-America with a cornucopia on one side and on the other an eagle bearing a shield with Washington's arms. The female figure holds an olive branch in one hand and in the other the same sword topped with a liberty cap that Barralet had added to the Field engraving of 1795. In this very small vignette he was able to suggest all the principal themes that were readily associated with Washington's image, including peace, prosperity, federal union, and military strength.

Although the engraving cannot be dated exactly, Houston was working in Philadelphia from about 1796 to 1798 (Stauffer 1:133), and this print fits logically within that period.

Hart 212 // Baker 171 // Stauffer 1464 // Jacobs, p. 118.

J.J. Barralet del.   H. Houston sculp.t

GENERAL   WASHINGTON,

President OF THE   United Stataes OF

AME   RICA.

For the American Universal Magazine.

GENERAL WASHINGTON.

49.

Attributed to H. Houston (active 1796–1798), after Joseph
  Wright

Stipple, 1797

9.7 × 7.8 cm

*For the American Universal Magazine. | General Wash-
ington.*

❧ *The American Universal Magazine,* February 6, 1797
  (Philadelphia: Budd and Bartram for Lee). Evans 31728;
  National Portrait Gallery (illustration only).

Although this engraving was not signed, the
wrapper cover of the *American Universal Magazine* for January 23, 1797, advertised that the next
number would contain "a truly elegant Portrait
of the President by Houston." The original source
for the engraving was the profile etching by
Joseph Wright. An earlier engraved copy of the
Wright etching was published in 1791 in the *Massachusetts Magazine* with a distinctive figure-eight
design in the epaulet [28]. This engraving in turn
was modified by Thomas Holloway in England for
the *Literary Magazine* (August 1792) with changes
in the uniform. The Houston engraving was based
on the Holloway print (Kimball, "Wright, Paintings and Engravings," p. 382), completing a trans-

atlantic circle of borrowed visual imagery that
was characteristic of the period.

The Houston engraving apparently was designed to be the monthly ornament to the magazine rather than an illustration to a particular
essay. The publishers, like many of their com-
petitors, spent considerable effort and expense
procuring engravings. In the "Conditions" for the
magazine, printed on the wrapper cover of the
January 2, 1797, issue, the publishers found it
necessary to apologize "for delaying the publication of our first number—the unexpected severity
of the weather prevented the finishing of the paper
in time, and likewise arrested the progress of the
engraver." Their problems made them cautious
about promising engravings for future numbers:

> Portraits are preparing for this work in the same
> elegant stile as our first:—but we do not thereby
> pledge ourselves, that every future engraving shall
> be equal to these; the length of time required would
> render it impossible; nor could the very great
> expense be supported by so cheap a work.—We are
> however determined that no possible exertion shall
> be wanting to render the work satisfactory.

Hart 171 // Baker 89 // Stauffer 1467 // Kimball, "Wright,
Paintings and Engravings," p. 382.

50.

Unidentified artist, after Charles Willson Peale

Relief cut, 1797

4.9 × 4.3 cm

Geo. Washington Esq.

❧ *The South-Carolina Weekly Museum,* Volume 1, 1797–
  1798 (Charleston: Harrison and Co.). Evans 32860; William L. Clements Library, University of Michigan.

The *South-Carolina Weekly Museum* was the only
magazine published south of Baltimore in the
eighteenth century (Mott 1:32). Printed on the
paper wrapper of each number as well as on the
title page of this semi-annual volume was a relief
cut of Washington. The egg-shaped face in an
oval frame ornamented with banners is reminiscent of the Charles Willson Peale image.

SOUTH-CAROLINA
WEEKLY MUSEUM,

AND

COMPLETE MAGAZINE

OF

Entertainment and Intelligence.

CONTAINING,

A great variety of Original and Selected Essays, on different subjects,	Poetry, Foreign and Domestic Intelligence, &c. &c.

VOLUME I.

EYE NATURE'S WALKS, SHOOT FOLLY AS IT FLIES,
AND CATCH THE MANNERS LIVING AS THEY RISE.—*POPE.*

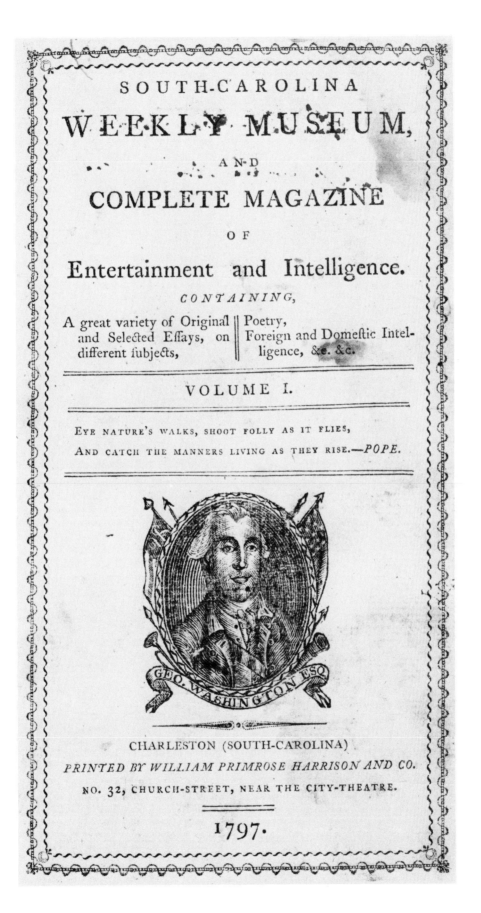

GEO. WASHINGTON ESQ

CHARLESTON (SOUTH-CAROLINA)

PRINTED BY *WILLIAM PRIMROSE HARRISON AND CO.*

NO. 32, CHURCH-STREET, NEAR THE CITY-THEATRE.

1797.

51.
Unidentified artist, after Charles Willson Peale
Relief cut, 1797
7 × 5.7 cm
Washington.

⚘ *The New-England Primer* (New York: Harrisson, 1797).
Evans 32528; Library of Congress.

Like most frontispiece portraits from the *New-England Primer*, this grim-faced warrior was probably derived from a Charles Willson Peale image. However, it is too poorly drawn to suggest much of a resemblance to Washington.

52.
Unidentified artist
Etching, 1797
12.7 × 7.8 cm
Frontispiece.

⚘ *The Nightingale of Liberty* (New York: Harrisson, 1797).
Evans 32584; Library of Congress.

The subtitle of *The Nightingale of Liberty* explains the contents of the book: *Delights of Harmony: a Choice Collection of Patriotic, Masonic, & Entertaining Songs. To which are added Toasts and Sentiments, Moral, Humorous, and Republican.* The frontispiece engraving is loosely based on an illustration in the *Sentimental and Masonic Magazine* published in Dublin in 1795 (see Fig. 25). The American artist combined three figures from the Irish print into one. Justice, Freedom, and a winged cupid with a liberty cap and pole are synthesized into a single personification of America, wearing a Masonic apron and leaning casually against a medallion portrait of Washington. A helmeted Minerva, copied from the Irish print, peers at the portrait from the other side.

The scrawny bird at the top is invoked on the title page: "Thou sweetest songster of the feather'd tribe, Carol, with notes harmonious, songs to Liberty." Several of the songs in the collection are in praise of Washington.

53.
Unidentified artist, after Joseph Wright
Engraving, 1797
29.3 × 20.7 cm

G. Washington | The Battle of Trenton | A Sonata | For the | Piano-Forte | Dedicated | To | General | Washington | New York Printed & sold by James Hewitt at his Musical Repository No. 131 William Street | B Carr Philadelphia [& J Carr] Baltimore—Price [10s]

⚘ *The Battle of Trenton, A Sonata for the Piano-Forte* (New York: Hewitt; Philadelphia: B. Carr; Baltimore: J. Carr, [1797]). Evans 33381; Library of Congress.
New Yankee Doodle Sung with Great Applause at the Theatre (New York: Hewitt; Philadelphia: B. Carr; Baltimore: J. Carr, [1797–1798]). Evans 48535.
Joseph Hopkinson, *The Favorite New Federal Song Adapted to the President's March* [Philadelphia: Carr, 1798]. Evans 33896.

A goddess of Liberty wearing Minerva's helmet is the principal figure of this print, which was designed as a cover for "The Battle of Trenton," a song composed and published by James Hewitt. Although the song was "dedicated to General Washington," the small portrait of him after Joseph Wright seems almost an afterthought, stuck in between two spears above the large oval space reserved for the title. An even smaller figure of Victory points toward heaven while crowning Washington with a laurel wreath. Hewitt's song was advertised in the New York *Minerva* on August 23, 1797.

Incorporated into Hewitt's song was the familiar tune of "Yankee Doodle," well known to American audiences since before the Revolution. Shortly after "The Battle of Trenton" was issued, Hewitt published the "New Yankee Doodle" ornamented with the same image of Washington. In-stead of using the full cover, however, the profile bust of Washington and the ribbon beneath it were trimmed to a small oval and mounted onto the music in the center of the title. Parts of a spear on the right and a banner on the left are still visible from the larger image.

Having sold the "New Yankee Doodle" at his shop in Philadelphia, Benjamin Carr repeated the idea of mounting a portrait onto the music sheet in his 1798 publication of "The Favorite New Federal Song." Better known as "Hail Columbia," this patriotic song was ornamented by several different portraits (see entry [57]), one of which was the trimmed profile from "The Battle of Trenton."

Hart 157 // Sonneck and Upton, pp. 39, 173, 479–480 // Hart, "Hail Columbia," opposite p. 162 // Howard, pp. 88–89, 113–121.

54.

David Edwin (1776–1841), after Gilbert Stuart

Stipple, 1798

14.6 × 11.6 cm

Inscription from Fielding 425: [*T. B. Freeman Excudit—D. Edwin Sculpt | George Washington Esquire | Philadelphia Published by T. B. Freeman Febry | 12th 1798*]

❧ Historical Society of Pennsylvania

When the English engraver David Edwin arrived in Philadelphia in December 1797, he considered the conditions for engraving very poor. In a letter to William Dunlap, he recalled that "copperplates were finished rough from the hammer; no tools to be purchased, he (the engraver) had to depend upon his own ingenuity to fabricate them for himself, or in directing others qualified for the work; but worse than all was the slovenly style in which printing was executed" (Dunlap, *History*, 2:68).

Edwin's first job was working for the print publisher T. B. Freeman. By February 12, 1798, Edwin had engraved a stipple print of Washington after Gilbert Stuart's "Vaughan" likeness. Although this impression, printed in black ink on satin, has no inscription, the original lettering was recorded by Mantle Fielding from the actual copperplate (Fielding 425, p. 15). Freeman announced the publication of the Washington print along with one of John Adams in the *Federal Gazette* on February 8, 1798:

Striking Likenesses of John Adams and George Washington, Esquires. On Monday the 12th inst. will be ready for delivery, the above Portraits, engraved by two eminent English artists from pictures painted from the life; to be had elegantly framed in best burnish gold frames, with enamel glasses, &c. at six dollars a pair; Printed in colours on white Sattin, at Eight Dollars. Those desirous of securing early impressions are requested to apply to the publisher and subscriber, at his store, No. 40 south Water street. . . . (Prime 2:80.)

As Fielding pointed out, Edwin's print of Washington was badly drawn (Fielding, p. 15). Freeman published Edwin's second, more successful, Washington portrait [56] just a few months later, on May 1, 1798.

Hart 273 // Baker 391 // Fielding 425, p. 15.

55.

Edward Savage (1761–1817) and David Edwin (1776–1841), after Edward Savage

Stipple, c. 1790–1798

46.8 × 62.3 cm

Painted and Engrav'd by E: Savage. | The Washington Family. | La Famille de Washington. | George Washington his Lady, and her two Grandchildren by the name of Custis. | George Washington, Son Epouse, et Ses deux petits Enfants du Nom de Custis. | Philadelphia. Publish'd March 10th. 1798. by E: Savage & Robt. Wilkinson No. 58 Cornhill London.

❧ National Portrait Gallery

Edward Savage's *Washington Family* print depicted the President surrounded by his wife, her grandchildren, Eleanor Custis and George Washington Parke Custis, and the servant Billy Lee. Few American prints of this period were as financially successful as this engraving seems to have been. Although Savage started the copperplate around 1790, shortly after he painted the portraits of George and Martha Washington and her grandchildren, the published print was a collaborative effort not issued until March 1798. Some of the history and success of the engraving was related in Savage's letter to George Washington on June 3, 1798:

Agreeable to Col. Biddle's order I delivered four of the best impressions of your Family Print. They are choose out of the first that was printed. Perhaps you may think that they are two [*sic*] dark, but they will change lighter after hanging two or three months. The frames are good sound work. I have varnished all the gilded parts which will stand the weather and bare washing with a wet cloth without injury. The likenesses of the young people are not much like what they are at present. The Copper-plate was begun and half finished from the likenesses which I painted in New York in the year 1789. I could not make the alterations in the copper to make it like

The WASHINGTON FAMILY.   La FAMILLE de WASHINGTON.

George Washington his Lady and her two Grandchildren by the name of Custis   George Washington Son Épouse et Ses deux petits Enfants du Nom de Custis

Philadelphia, Published March 10th 1798 by E. Savage & Ro.t Wilkinson N.o 58 Cornhill London

the painting which I finished in Philadelphia in the year 1796. The portraits of yourself and Mrs. Washington are generally thought to be likenesses. As soon as I got one of the prints ready to be seen I advertised in two of the papers that a subscription would be open for about twenty days. Within that time there was 331 subscribers to the print and about 100 had subscribed previously, all of them the most respectable people in the city. In consequence of its success and being generally approved of I have continued the Subscription. There is every probability at present of its producing me at least $10,000 in one twelve month. As soon as I have one printed in colours I shall take the liberty to send it to Mrs Washington for her acceptance. I think she will like it better than a plain print. Mrs Savage joins me in respectful compliments to Mrs Washington. (Hart, "Savage," pp. 9–10.)

Savage abandoned his work on the copperplate when he went to London in 1791. It was not published until he had returned to America, settled in Philadelphia, and hired David Edwin, a skilled

English stipple engraver. The authorship of Savage's prints in general, and this one in particular, has occasioned a lively controversy ever since the publication in 1834 of William Dunlap's *History of . . . the Arts of Design* (see also [31, 33]). Dunlap reported that *The Washington Family* was "engraved by Edwin, who made it tolerable," and that Savage habitually "published prints from his own wretched pictures, mended and engraved by Edwin, but inscribed with Savage's name as engraver." This information came from John Wesley Jarvis, Savage's apprentice, who apparently was also involved in the production of the print. "I assisted in engraving it," Jarvis told Dunlap, "I printed it, and carried it about for sale" (Dunlap, *History*, 1:321). Another Philadelphia printmaker, Alexander Lawson, informed Dunlap that before either Edwin or Jarvis arrived, Savage had brought back from London a "dull engraver" who "after engraving Savages Washington family, took legal advice on his thraldom & was set free" (Dunlap,

Diary, 3:706). The case has since been argued both for and against Savage as a printmaker (for example, Baker, pp. 74–75; Hart, "Savage," pp. 9–11; Dickson, *Jarvis,* pp. 35–57), yet there is no reason to doubt that Dunlap's story, although mostly based on the memory of a disgruntled apprentice, was largely factual. Savage must have known how to engrave but no doubt drew upon the greater skills of assistants, particularly David Edwin, for some of his prints. *The Washington Family* was probably engraved primarily by Edwin, although Savage started it, an unnamed temporary employee dabbled with it, and Jarvis printed and peddled it.

On March 3, 1798, Savage announced in the *Philadelphia Gazette* that *The Washington Family* would be ready by March 15, and subscribers were promised the best prints at a reduced price of one and a half guineas. An "unfinished impression" was on display at Mr. McElwee's Looking Glass store. As reported by the *Pennsylvania Gazette* (March 21, 1798), the print was ready by March 19:

> An elegant Engraving, 20 by 26 inches, executed by Savage from an original picture, painted by himself, is just published. The Print represents General Washington and his Lady (two capital likenesses), sitting at a table on which lies a plan of the Federal City. A perspective view of the river Potomac and of Mount Vernon, forms an agreeable and appropriate embellishment in the picture. The whole is executed in a style evincive of the rapid progress of an elegant art, which has hitherto been in a very crude state in this country. (Stauffer 1:311–312.)

Savage also had subscribers in New York City, where he advertised the print on May 2, 1798, in the *New York Daily Advertiser* (Gottesman 2:18). He may have been considering international distribution as well, since the title in the inscription is in both English and French.

As he had indicated in his letter, the outdated images of the children could not be changed, but in 1795 Savage did get new sittings from George and Martha Washington. He finished *The Washington Family* canvas, now in the National Gallery of Art, in 1796.

The engraving seems to have been brought to Washington's attention by Clement Biddle, not Savage himself. "In consequence of the opinion given by you of Mr. Savages Print (presuming it is his you allude to)," Washington wrote Biddle on March 19, 1798, "I pray you to request him to chuse four for me; and have them put into handsome, but not costly, gilt frames, with glasses (supposing them to be of a size to admit glasses) and send three of them to me; the other, Mrs. Washington (I believe) is under promise of presenting to Mrs. Green (now Mrs. Miller)" (Fitzpatrick 36:188–189). On June 17, 1798, Washing-

ton wrote to Savage that the four prints had been received and thanked him for taking the trouble. Whereas Savage intended to present Martha Washington with the impression printed in colors, the other four engravings were paid for as a regular order (Fitzpatrick 36:294, 295).

Savage's plans to do the color printing were delayed by the yellow fever epidemic in Philadelphia in 1798; the print he had promised, therefore, was not ready until March 1799. Savage wrote Washington on June 17, 1799, that he had finally arranged a shipment for it and was enclosing as well his two aquatints of the *Chase* and the *Constellation* (Hart, "Savage," pp. 10–11). Washington responded on June 30: "Your letter of the 17th instant and the Print (which is exceedingly handsome, and well set) have come safe; and receives, as it highly deserves the thanks of Mrs. Washington; to whom you have had the kindness, and politeness to present it" (Fitzpatrick 37:255). In her will Mrs. Washington made a special bequest to Eleanor Parke Lewis of "a print of the Washington Family in a box in the garret" (Hart, "Savage," p. 11).

Hart 235 // Baker 120 // Stauffer 2754 // Hart, "Savage," pp. 9–11, 17 // Dickson, "Savage," pp. 6 ff. // Dickson, *Jarvis,* pp. 36, 38, 45–47, 50–51, 56 // Stauffer 1:311–312 // Fitzpatrick 36:188–189, 293–295, 373; 37:255 // Eisen, *Portraits,* 2:462–465 // Morgan and Fielding, pp. 183–186 // Dunlap, *History,* 1:321 // Dunlap, *Diary,* 3:706.

56.
David Edwin (1776–1841), after Gilbert Stuart

Stipple, 1798

15 × 12.1 cm

Engraved from an Original Picture by D. Edwin. T. B. Freeman Excudit / George Washington Esqr. / Philadelphia Published by. T. B. Freeman May 1st. 1798.

Collection of Stanley D. Scott

The Philadelphia printseller T. B. Freeman imported and sold European engravings, but by 1796 he was beginning to contemplate the publishing of American prints, "bringing forward works of Artists in this country, that will convince the rest of mankind that America is their equal in elegance and taste" (*Federal Gazette,* March 11, 1796; quoted in Prime 2:77). When Freeman advertised a print of Anthony Wayne on June 7, 1796, he described the publication as "the commencement of a series of interesting American Characters" (*Aurora;* quoted in Prime 2:79). Edwin's nicely executed engraving of George Washington was also a part of Freeman's scheme for publishing portraits. Soon after his arrival in Philadelphia in December 1797, Edwin was set to work, and on February 12, 1798, Freeman published Edwin's

first engraving of Washington [54]. Apparently it was not satisfactory, and Edwin engraved this second version, after Stuart's "Athenaeum" likeness. It was published by Freeman, along with Edwin's portraits of the actors John Harwood and John Bernard (Dunlap, *History*, 1918 ed., 1:381n) on May 1, 1798.

Edwin's plate was entirely reengraved and published by John Scoles in New York. Hart lists several states of this reworked image with changes in inscription (Hart 359).

Hart 359 // Baker 208 // Stauffer 892.

57.
Attributed to David Edwin (1776–1841), after Gilbert Stuart

Stipple, 1798

3.6 cm (diameter)

  Joseph Hopkinson, *The Favorite New Federal Song Adapted to the President's March* [Philadelphia: Carr, 1798]. Evans 33896; Library of Congress.
Francis Hopkinson, *Brother Soldiers All Hail* (Philadelphia: B. Carr; Baltimore: J. Carr; New York: J. Hewitt, [1799]). Evans 35637.
Benjamin Carr, *Dead March and Monody* (Baltimore: Carr [1799]). Evans 37105.

"Hail Columbia," first published as "The Favorite New Federal Song Adapted to the President's March," was written by Joseph Hopkinson in April 1798 at the request of his friend Gilbert Fox. In an 1840 letter to Rufus Griswold, Hopkinson recalled that the song was written at a time "when war with France was thought to be inevitable." Internal tension between Federalists and anti-Federalists was mounting daily. Hopkinson intended the words to arouse "an American spirit which should be independent of, and above the interests, passion, and policy of both belligerents" (Elson, pp. 160–161). The singer and actor Gilbert Fox, worried about filling the theater for his benefit performance, had asked Hopkinson to write a "patriotic song adapted to 'The Presidents March.'" The song and the play were advertised in *Porcupine's Gazette* on April 24, 1798, the day before the performance. Abigail Adams, curious to hear the words to the song, attended the performance incognito and reported to her sister the next day that her head still ached from the thunderous applause that greeted each chorus as the audience demanded repeated encores (S. Mitchell, pp. 342–343).

To Hopkinson's surprise, "Hail Columbia," written to an already familiar and popular tune composed by Philip Phile, soon became a favorite national song, played at all musical performances, and if not scheduled, demanded by the audience. Hopkinson sent a copy of it to George Washington on May 9, 1798, with the remark, "As to the song it was a hasty composition, and can pretend to very little extrinsic merit—yet I believe its public reception has at least equalled any thing of the kind. The theatres here [Philadelphia] and at New York have resounded with it night after night; and men and boys in the streets sing it as they go" (Sonneck, *Report*, p. 46). Washington thanked him for the "Pamphlet and Song," and his "favourable sentiments," observing that "to expect that all men should think alike upon political, . . . or other subjects, would be to look for a change in the order of nature; but at so dangerous a crisis as the present, when everything dear to Independence is at stake, the well disposed part of them might, one would think, act more alike" (Fitzpatrick 36: 274–275).

On April 27, 1798, two days after the performance, *Porcupine's Gazette* had announced the publication, at Carr's Musical Repository, of "the very favourite New Federal Song; written to the tune of the 'President's march' by J. Hopkinson, Esq. and sung by Mr. Fox, at the New Theatre with great applause, ornamented with a very elegant portrait of the President." The first issue of the song bore the image of President John Adams (see

The favorite new Federal Song

Adapted to the Presidents March

Sung by Mr. FOX

Written by J. HOPKINSON Esqr.

[1798?]

For the Voice, Piano Forte, Guittar and Clarinett.

Hail! Columbia happy land haill ye Heroes heavn born band Who fought and bled in

freedoms cause who fought & bled in freedoms cause and when the storm of war was gone en_

_joy'd the peace your valor won let Inde pen_dence be our boast ever mindful

what it cost ever grateful for the prize let its Altar reach the Skies

2d time Chorus

Firm uni __ ted let us be rallying round our Li_ber _ty as a band of

Library of Congress copy). The small circular portrait was a separate engraving, neatly trimmed and pasted on the music sheet in the center of the title above the words "Behold the Chief who now commands!"

On July 3, 1798, George Washington was appointed Commander in Chief of the American forces in anticipation of war with France. This event apparently prompted Benjamin Carr, the publisher, to substitute a portrait of Washington for that of John Adams (Sonneck, "Hail Columbia," pp. 180–189). Since all the portraits were mounted onto the music sheets, different engravings of Washington are found on various copies of the song. Charles Henry Hart mentioned having seen four separate types (Hart, pp. xii–xiii), some of which, he suggested, were mounted at a later date. At least three Washington prints on the song appear to be contemporary 1798 issues by Benjamin Carr in Philadelphia (see entry [53, 58]).

This miniature Washington clearly was engraved by the same hand that did the John Adams, and the most likely artist for the work is David Edwin. When Edwin first arrived in Philadelphia, T. B. Freeman introduced him to Benjamin Carr, who asked him to engrave a title page for a book of Scottish airs (Dunlap, *History*, 2:67). Not only was he already associated with Carr, but the miniature engravings closely resemble Edwin's style, and the Washington image (probably issued in July) is very similar to the print he had just finished for Freeman a couple of months before [56]. Having discovered this formula for ornamenting an engraved music sheet, Benjamin Carr used the same miniature engraving for the patriotic song "Brother Soldiers All Hail," and again for his own composition "Dead March and Monody," which was performed for George Washington's funeral in Philadelphia on December 26, 1799, and published, with an "elegant likeness of the late General," on December 31 (*Philadelphia Gazette*, December 30, 1800).

The question of the first issue of the song caused much speculation before the discovery of the Adams music sheet. The controversy is summarized by Sonneck and Upton (pp. 171–174), who include a bibliography. Confusing the discussion further was the appearance on some music sheets, with and without the mounted portraits of Washington, of an eagle and sunburst engraved onto the original music plate in the center of the title.

Hart, pp. xii–xiii // Sonneck and Upton, pp. 50, 100–101, 171–174 // Sonneck, *Report*, pp. 43–72 // Sonneck, "Hail Columbia," pp. 180–189 // Elson, pp. 155–165.

58.
Unidentified artist, after Gilbert Stuart

Engraving, c. 1798

4 × 3.3 cm

❧ Joseph Hopkinson, *The Favorite New Federal Song Adapted to the Presidents March* [Philadelphia: Carr, 1798]. Library of Congress.

This is one of the several portraits of Washington that were mounted onto the song sheet in the middle of the title. It was copied from the miniature engraving attributed to David Edwin. Printed beneath the mounted portrait on this issue of the song are the words: "Behold the Chief who now commands." (For further discussion see entry [57].)

59.

Attributed to David Edwin (1776–1841), after Gilbert Stuart

Stipple, c. 1798

3.5 cm (diameter)

Genl. Washington.

⚓ Print Collection, New York Public Library

Reversed but very similar in style to the miniature image mounted on music sheets published by Benjamin Carr [57], this tiny stipple portrait can also be attributed to David Edwin. No music sheets have yet been located which bear this engraving, and the inscription beneath the print has been trimmed.

60.

Unidentified artist, after Gilbert Stuart

Engraving, c. 1798

5.9 × 4.8 cm

The Ladies | Patriotic Song | Sung by Mrs. Hodgkinson. | With Universal Applause | At the Columbia | Gardens

⚓ *The Ladies Patriotic Song* (New York: Gilfert, [1798]). American Antiquarian Society.

According to the inscription, "The Ladies Patriotic Song" was sung in New York by the actress Frances Brett Hodgkinson, on July 4, 1798. The portrait of George Washington, engraved on the plate in the center of the title (as opposed to being mounted onto the music sheet, as in Benjamin Carr's publications), has a curious resemblance to white-line wood engraving. This distinctive style reappears in the portrait of John Adams on Gilfert's publication of *Adams and Liberty* (Sonneck and Upton, p. 4).

Sonneck and Upton, p. 222.

61.

David Edwin (1776–1841), after F. Bartoli and John James Barralet

Engraving, c. 1798

28.7 × 22.6 cm

F. Bartoli Pinxt. | D. Edwin Sc. | His Excellency George | Washington Lieut. Genl. | of the | Armies | of the United | States of America. | Respectfully Dedicated to the | Lovers of their Country | and Firm Supporters | of its Constitution. | Published by D. Kennedy, 228 Market St. Philada.

⚓ Mabel Brady Garvan Collection, Yale University Art Gallery

Washington's reappointment as Commander in Chief no doubt inspired David Edwin's impressive military portrait. Although the inscription reads "F. Bartoli Pinxt.," this artist has not been identified nor is any such painting known to exist. While Bartoli may have designed the pose and the setting, the head of Washington was based on Gilbert Stuart's "Athenaeum" likeness with which David Edwin was already familiar [56, 57, 59].

After the General's death, John James Barralet was responsible for the metamorphosis of the print into a memorial image. Erasing the title and the federal eagle vignette, he added a ruled border surrounding the entire image, with a tablet inscribed "Washington, Sacred to Memory" above the portrait and two mourning figures flanked by military armaments below. The framing device had the effect of uniting the tablet and vignette with the portrait and giving the whole image an appropriate formality. "Revised by I. J. Barralet" was added at the bottom.

Hart 788 // Baker 216 // Stauffer 905 // Grote, p. 132.

F. Bartoli Pinx.   D. Edwin Sc.

His Excellency GEORGE   WASHINGTON Lieu.t Gen.l
                of the   Armies
        of the United   States of America.
Respectfully Dedicated to the   Lovers of their Country
    and firm Supporters   of its Constitution.
            Published by P.Kennedy, 228 Market St Philad.a

129

This Plate is with our RESPECT Inscribed to the CONGRESS of the United States BY

62.

Cornelius Tiebout (c. 1773–1832), after Charles Buxton and Gilbert Stuart

Engraving and etching, 1798

61.6 × 55.2 cm

Geo. Wa--ington | Sacred to Patriotism. | Designed & Drawn by Charles Buxton M.D. | C. Tiebout sc. | This Plate, is with due Respect Inscribed to the Congress of the United States. By | Chas. Smith | New York. Published by C. Smith, 1798.

Print Collection, New York Public Library

Charles Buxton, a New York physician and designer of this large and symbolically complex engraving, wrote to George Washington on April 27, 1799, enclosing "two Proof prints" and an introductory letter from their mutual friend Dr. John Bard. The publication of the drawing "was not originally intended," Buxton explained,

> but the flattering encomiums of a Bookseller, after repeated application, obtained the temporary use of the Drawing for that purpose, & by whom I was presented with a small number of the first Impressions; Your acceptance of those forwarded will prove an ample gratification To, Sir, One who feels all the gratitude which ought to warm the heart of every American, & ardently inspire him with the most lively wishes for the continuation of your life & happiness. (Charles Buxton to Washington, April 27, 1799, Washington Papers, Library of Congress, Washington, D.C.)

Buxton informed Washington that Bard had recently died and enclosed the doctor's letter of introduction written "about twelve months past." In the letter Bard mentioned that Buxton had

> employed himself during a Season of Bodily indisposition to design and finish an emblematical picture with a view to perpetuate the idea of the American revolution, of which those persons among us of Judgment and taste in these things speak very well. Doctor Buxton is desirous of presenting you with a copy of this Picture as a proper acknowledgment of the event. (John Bard to Washington [April 1798], Washington Papers, Library of Congress, Washington, D.C.)

The engraver of the print was Cornelius Tiebout. The bookseller was, according to the inscription on the print, Charles Smith, who had published the engraving in 1798 with a dedication to the United States Congress. Smith may indeed have had some "judgment and taste in these things," since he had previously published a series of articles on the Revolution (see entry [43]).

Washington responded to Buxton on May 30, 1799, that the "last Post" had brought him the "two proof Prints elegantly executed (one of Satten) engraved from your emblematic Picture, designed to perpetuate the idea of the American Revolution." In acknowledging the gift he added, "Was not the late President of the United States a conspicuous character in the Piece I might say more than would now become me of the fruitfulness of the Design" (Fitzpatrick 37:217). The presentation copy referred to, printed on satin, was exhibited at the Grolier Club of New York in 1900 with a note that it had formerly belonged to General Robert E. Lee, who inherited it from the Washington family (Grolier Club, *Centenary Exhibit*, p. 32). It has recently returned to the collection at Mount Vernon.

Buxton's elaborate design is an amalgam of patriotic symbols referring to Washington's military achievements and his role in forging the new nation. The figure (with an "Athenaeum" head) stands on a pedestal ensconced in a niche and flanked by two obelisks labeled "Liberty" and "Independence." An eagle at the top of the arch holds a ribbon from which hang tablets representing the first sixteen states. The large urn in front of the figure obviously cannot be a mourning image and is probably the Masonic pot of incense, an emblem of a pure heart. Some of the other imagery, particularly the columns, arch, and patterned floor, also seem to have Masonic allusions. The key to the whole design, however, lies in the background view of Bowling Green, New York, which depicts an empty pedestal where a statue of George III formerly stood. Statements that the figure of Washington in the print was modeled on a wooden statue that was erected at Bowling Green have been proven false (Stokes 5:1999). But in Buxton's design he stands on his pedestal as a symbolic replacement for the King. The background scene alludes to the evacuation of the British from New York on November 25, 1783 (Stokes 1:413); a similar view of Bowling Green had appeared in the background of John Trumbull's portrait of Washington painted for New York City Hall.

Although impressions of the original engraving are quite scarce, the image was known in the nineteenth century from a printed cotton textile made in Glasgow in 1819 (Hart 676).

Hart 676 // Baker 407 // Stauffer 3196 // Bailey, pp. 137–138 // Stokes 1:413, 5:1999 // Stokes and Haskell, p. 60 // Marks, pp. 73–74 // Fitzpatrick 37:217 // Grolier Club, *Centenary Exhibit*, p. 32 // Anderson 33 // Weitenkampf, p. 69.

GEORGE WASHINGTON ESQᴿ.

Philadᵃ. Published for Thoˢ. Condie Bookseller.

63.

H. Houston (active 1796–1798), after Edward Savage

Stipple, 1798

12.5 × 10.6 cm

*Houston Sc | George Washington Esqr. | Philada. Published
for Thos. Condie Bookseller.*

❧ *The Philadelphia Monthly Magazine, or, Universal
Repository,* January 1798 (Philadelphia: Condie). Evans
34365; Rare Books Division, New York Public Library.
Philadelphisches Magazin oder unterhalter Gesellschafter,
May 1798 (Philadelphia: H. and J. R. Kammerer, Jr.).
Evans 34369.
John Searson, *Mount Vernon, A Poem* (Philadelphia: Fol-
well for Author, [1800]). Evans 38479.

The publisher of the *Philadelphia Monthly Magazine* wrote at the beginning of the first (and only)
volume that he had determined "at the commencement of the work . . . that the copperplates
should be finished in a stile calculated to please
even connoisseurs; those already published are
equal, if not superior, to the engravings that generally accompany Magazines, whether foreign or
domestick, nor is their number disproportionate."
The frontispiece for January 1798 was a portrait
of Washington, which showed H. Houston's mastery of the stipple technique. As William S. Baker
noted, Houston's portrait of Washington was cop-

ied from Edward Savage's 1792 stipple print
(Baker 130). Charles Henry Hart suggested that it
was based on a miniature by John Ramage, but
judging from the treatment of the buttons, the
collar, and the upward glance of the eyes, it appears that Baker was correct. When Houston's
print was reused for the German-language magazine, it was entirely reengraved, the publisher's
line was erased, and all the subtlety was lost. In
the John Searson poem *Mount Vernon,* the stipple
border around the portrait also disappeared.

Searson may have had greater ambitions for the
frontispiece of his poem. On the title page is the
statement: "This rural, romantic and descriptive
poem of the seat of so great a character, it is hoped
may please, with a copper-plate likeness of the
General. It was taken from an actual view on the
spot by the author, 15th May, 1799." If Searson
himself did make a drawing of Washington at
Mount Vernon, it was probably never engraved.
Hart noted that a few copies of the poem do have
a frontispiece of Washington seated in front of his
mansion (Hart 787). The print he referred to,
however, was clearly engraved much later, probably for *Aesop Junior in America* (1834) and therefore could not have been an original frontispiece
for the 1800 edition of the Searson poem. Most
copies of *Mount Vernon* have the Houston portrait.

Hart 210 // Baker 130 // Stauffer 1466 // Baker, *Washingtoniana,* pp. 6–7.

64.

Alexander Lawson (1773–1846), after Gilbert Stuart and
John James Barralet

Engraving and etching, 1798

16.2 × 10.2 cm

*G. Washington | Barralet Direxit | Lawson sc. | Publish'd
by R. Campbell and Co | From a Copy Painted by J. Paul.*

[Tobias George Smollett], *The History of the British
Empire,* Volume 2 (Philadelphia: Bioren for Campbell,
1798). Evans 33879.
❧ [Tobias George Smollett], *The History of England,*
Volume 6 (Philadelphia: Bioren for Campbell, 1798).
Evans 34565; Rare Books Division, New York Public
Library.

William Dunlap in 1834 wrote that the engraver
Alexander Lawson first worked for John James
Barralet, then formed "a kind of co-partnership
with him," and eventually quarreled with the
"eccentric Irishman" (Dunlap, *History,* 1:434).
Lawson's engraving of Washington for the *History
of the British Empire,* written by a "Society of
Gentlemen" as a continuation of the work of
Tobias Smollett, bears beneath the portrait an
unmistakable Barralet device, the helmet, sword,
and baton of a knight. Barralet used this symbol
of Washington's (and the new nation's) military

Barralet Direxit Published by R.CAMPBELL and C° Lawson Sc
From a Copy Painted by J.Paul.

G.WASHINGTON

65.

Alexander Lawson (1773–1846), after John James Barralet

Engraving and etching, 1799

12.6 × 9.8 cm

Barrelet Invt & Direxit | Lawson sculp | General Washington's | Resignation. | Published by B. Davies Philada 1st Feby 1799.

The Philadelphia Magazine and Review, January 1799 (Philadelphia: Davies). Evans 36114; Library of Congress.

Deciding the proper way to accept George Washington's resignation as Commander in Chief in 1783 threw Congress, in James Thomas Flexner's words, into "an agony of dignity" (Flexner, p. 526). Sixteen years after the event his action was memorialized in a very dignified fashion in an allegorical frontispiece designed by John James Barralet. It was published in 1799 in the first number of the *Philadelphia Magazine and Review* (dated January 1799 but actually published on February 9 according to *Porcupine's Gazette* of that date; quoted in Deutsch and Ring, p. 405). In the "Explanation of the Frontispiece," included in the magazine, the print is called an "emblem of the American Cincinnatus retiring from public office" and clearly relates the event to Washington's 1797 retirement to Mount Vernon after his second term in office. In fact, the allegory is based on an entertainment held at the time of his retirement, as described in the "Explanation":

> At the end of his second Presidentship, in March, 1797, General Washington retired from the illustrious office of the first Magistrate of the United States. . . . At this interesting period, the merchants of Philadelphia gave a splendid public dinner, in honor of the Statesman and the Hero. . . .
>
> The company, in which were all the Foreign Ministers, many of the Members of both Houses of Congress, the Governor of the State and all the principal Merchants of the city, met at Oeller's hotel, and from thence marched in procession to the place of entertainment. On their entering the Circus, Washington's march resounded through the place when a curtain was drawn up, and there was presented to view a transparent full length female figure, as large as life, representing America, seated on an elevation, composed of sixteen marble steps; on her right side stood the Federal shield and eagle, and at her feet lay the Cornucopia; in her right hand she held the Indian calumet of peace, and in her left a scroll, inscribed, "Valedictory:"—in the perspective appeared the Temple of Fame; on her left hand stood an altar, dedicated to public gratitude, on which incense was burning; and at the foot of the altar lay a plumed helmet and sword, from which a figure of George Washington, as large as life, appeared retiring down the steps, pointing with his right hand to the emblems of power, which he had resigned, and with his left, to a beautiful land-

strength in his allegorical design of the resignation, also engraved by Lawson, as well as in his apotheosis print [65, 101]. The helmet is placed against a background of oak and olive branches on a base lettered "G. Washington." Barralet included his name in the inscription with the word "Direxit" (= directed), implying that he organized the picture although he did not paint the portrait or engrave the plate.

The actual image of Washington was "From a Copy Painted by J. Paul" after Gilbert Stuart's "Athenaeum" likeness. According to Dunlap, "when Stuart painted Washington for [William] Bingham, [Jeremiah] Paul thought it no disgrace to letter the 'books'" (Dunlap, *History,* 1:417). Having thus worked for Stuart, Paul would have had an opportunity to copy the "Athenaeum" painting.

Lawson's portrait was also used in the sixth volume of the longer edition of the Smollett work, entitled *The History of England.* Some copies of this edition have a later state of the print with Barralet's and Lawson's names removed.

Hart 409 // Baker 273 // Stauffer 1688.

Barrelet Invt & Direxit   Lawson sculp

GENERAL WASHINGTON'S

RESIGNATION.

Published by B. Davies Philadª 1ˢᵗ Febʸ 1799.

scape, representing Mount Vernon, in front of which were seen oxen harnessed to the plough.

The entertainment display (probably a transparency) was still at Ricket's Circus on February 14, 1799, when it was described in *Claypoole's American Daily Advertiser* as "a view of Mount Vernon, and George Washington's retirement" (Deutsch and Ring, p. 405). It was created by John James Barralet, the designer of this print, not by Charles Willson Peale, as suggested by Hart (776). The words "Invt" (for *invenit*) and "Direxit" on the print imply it was Barralet's own invention, and the allegory is similar to other prints he engraved or designed. Charles Willson Peale had constructed a triumphal arch in 1783 entitled "George Washington's Resignation." One scene depicted on the structure was "Washington, in the character of Cincinnatus, returning, laurel-crowned, to his plow," and a "gigantic figure of Peace" was also featured at the event (Sellers, *Artist,* p. 226; Jacobs, pp. 120–121). However, the entire structure had burst into flames from a rocket fired at the beginning of the ceremony. While Barralet may have heard of Peale's idea, the Cincinnatus and peace themes were obvious ones, and Barralet's treatment of them was quite different.

Prominently placed in the front of the print was the federal eagle with his shield, olive branch, and "E Pluribus Unum" ribbon. The other elements are derived from the standard allegorical vocabulary of European art published in emblem books such as Cesare Ripa's *Iconologia.* The concept of Peace, for instance (according to George Richardson's 1779 English edition, *Iconology*) was "allegorically expressed by the figure of a woman, holding a cornucopia full of fruit and flowers, with an olive branch in one hand, and with the other setting fire to trophies of armour" (G. Richardson 2:31; see also Jacobs, pp. 120–121). Although most of the allegorical components of Peace were included, Barralet did not copy directly from *Iconology.* He gave the olive branch and the cornucopia to the eagle, alluding to the abundant resources of America as well as to the prosperity that comes with peace. He added a specifically American symbol by giving Peace an Indian calumet to hold. The knight's helmet, sword, and baton—symbols of military strength—were included in other Barralet images (see entry [64, 101]).

Although Barralet's allegorical conceit was lucid and well designed both in terms of its composition and its implied meaning, the figure of Washington was probably pieced together from several sources. The face may have been inspired by a Houdon bust, which it resembles slightly; the

coat looks vaguely like a uniform with the epaulet removed. Barralet may have combined a number of images in order to create a younger, idealized Washington.

Hart 776 // Stauffer 1689 // Jacobs, pp. 119–121 // Deutsch and Ring, p. 405.

66.

John Roberts (1768–1803), after Gilbert Stuart

Mezzotint, 1799

7.9 × 6.5 cm

In ink: *Engraved by John Roberts a native / of Dumfries, an intimate friend of / Robert Burns / 1799.* In pencil: *John Roberts*

Historical Society of Pennsylvania

"The ingenuity of [John] Roberts in mechanics," wrote William Dunlap in 1834, "was as great as his taste for the fine arts. He made engraving tools, and even invented new to answer the exigencies of his work" (Dunlap, *History,* 1:428). A musician, mathematician, and artist, Roberts came to America from Scotland in 1793. The story of his engraving of Washington was also recorded by Dunlap:

His friend Trott had executed a beautiful miniature of Washington from Stuart's portrait of the hero, and Roberts engraved a plate from it, but after he had finished his work to the satisfaction of his friends, he was retouching it, when Trott came in, and some misunderstanding taking place between the engraver and the painter, Roberts deliberately took up a piece of pumice and applying it to the copper obliterated all trace of his work. . . A few impressions, taken as proofs, only exist. (Dunlap, *History*, 1:428.)

Roberts' technique resembled mezzotint, and he apparently invented new tools to roughen his plate. According to Dunlap:

> While he was engraving the Washington from Trott's miniature, he invented a new mode of stippling, produced by instruments devised and executed by himself, and which I have been assured, were "of such exquisite finish and workmanship, that a microscope was necessary to discover the teeth in some of the rollers." He made a printing-press for proving his work. (Dunlap, *History*, 1:428.)

In the annotated copy of his own *Engraved Portraits of Washington* (at the Historical Society of Pennsylvania) William Baker wrote that this impression, in his personal collection, was the only one he had seen as originally finished. It was "presented to Alexander Anderson," he noted, "by the engraver, and came to me from a Grandson. It was much valued by the Dr. who made a fine copy of it, on wood, and also used it as a model for other blocks. It was engraved by Roberts in 1799." The wood engraver, Alexander Anderson, was a pupil of Roberts for a short time and confirmed to Dunlap Roberts' reputation as a "universal genius" (Dunlap, *History*, 2:8).

Restrikes from the defaced plate were made in the mid-nineteenth century (Baker 314).

Hart 486 // Baker 314 // Stauffer 2701 // Dunlap, *History*, 1:428.

67.
Unidentified artist

Relief cut, 1799

7.1 × 6.2 cm

George Washington, Esq.

Nathaniel Low, *An Astronomical Diary, or an Almanack for . . . 1773* (Boston: Kneeland, 1773). Evans 12438.
The New-England Primer Improved (Hartford: Patten, 1777). Evans 15451.
❧ *The American Primer; or Young Child's Horn-Book* (Newfield, Conn.: Beach, 1799). Evans 48773; American Antiquarian Society.

By the late eighteenth century a portrait of George Washington was considered an ideal frontispiece for a child's primer. For Lazarus Beach's edition of the *American Primer* published in Newfield, Connecticut, in 1799, a cut of Washington was not readily available, so he used a twenty-six-year-old relief-block portrait of John Dryden. The portrait had been cut originally as the cover illustration for a 1773 Boston almanac by Nathaniel Low. It was copied from one of a number of English engravings after a painting of Dryden by Godfrey Kneller. Four years later the block had lost its

identity and made its way to Hartford, where it was used for a *New England Primer* as a portrait of Samuel Adams. In 1799 it was resurrected as "George Washington Esq." to inspire another generation of children.

Reilly 1560.

68.
Cornelius Tiebout (c. 1773–1832), after Gilbert Stuart

Stipple, 1800

23 × 17.9 cm

Painted by G. Stewart | Engraved by C. Tiebout | George Washington. | Published by C. Tiebout No. 28 Gold Street New York January 8th. 1800

❧ Museum of Fine Arts, Boston

On January 1, 1800, Cornelius Tiebout advertised his print of Washington in the New York *Commercial Advertiser*:

> George Washington.—To those who revere the memory of the Great and Good Washington. A Portrait as natural as life, from a painting of the masterly Stewart, is in hand, and will be ready for delivery on the 8th. inst—Price to subscribers, one dollar and fifty cents. Subscriptions received at this office, and by C. Tiebout, engraver and publisher, no. 28 Gold-street. (Gottesman 3:48.)

A few months later, on April 17, 1800, Tiebout advertised in the same newspaper a collection of his portraits, including one of Washington, which was probably this engraving (Gottesman 3:47).

Although it was not one of Tiebout's best engravings, it probably sold well in 1800, the year after Washington's death, and it served as a model for frontispieces in the many eulogies, collected writings, and biographies that appeared during that year.

Hart 454 // Baker 343 // Stauffer 3195.

136

Painted by G. Stewart   Engraved by C. Tiebout

GEORGE WASHINGTON.

Published by C. Tiebout, N.º 28 Gold Street New York January 8.th 1800

D. Edwin. Fecit

69.

David Edwin (1776–1841), after Gilbert Stuart

Stipple, 1800

13 × 11.3 cm

D. Edwin. Fecit

❦ George Washington, *George Washington to the People of the United States* (Philadelphia: Maxwell for Dickins and Maxwell, 1800). Evans 38990; American Antiquarian Society.

Washington's Farewell Address, given on September 17, 1796, was first widely circulated through the newspapers and was then frequently reprinted in bound volumes. This edition was issued shortly after Washington's death. It was advertised in the *Philadelphia Gazette* on January 1, 1800:

> In the Press, and in a few days will be published at Dickins's Bookstore, a superb edition of Washington's Address To the People of the United States, on retiring from Public Life . . . Ornamented with a capital Portrait by one of the first artists: Neither exertions nor expence have been spared to render this Publication worthy of patronage, and although all the materials and workmanship are entirely American, the paper printing and engraving, have been allowed, by good judges, to excel anything ever attempted in the U. States.

Copies of the book contain either this state of the Edwin engraving or impressions with the additional line of inscription: "Philadelphia Published Jany. 1st. 1800 by A: Dickins" (Hart 360).

A 1796 broadside edition of the Farewell Address, published by Charles and George Webster in Albany, was supposedly ornamented with a stipple portrait of Washington (Sabin 101549), but no copy can be located. Another edition, a miniature volume entitled *Columbia's Legacy* and published in Philadelphia in 1796 by Sweitzer and Ormrod, has a crude engraved portrait after Stuart in one copy only (at the Historical Society of Pennsylvania; see Paltsits, p. 320). That print, however, was probably made for a German-language volume on Washington which was published in Chambersburg, Pennsylvania, in 1816 (see Hart 430), and it may have been bound into *Columbia's Legacy* at that time.

The publisher and bookseller Asbury Dickins also advertised for sale, on January 11, 1800, "The Best Likeness of the Celebrated Washington which has ever been published . . . at the moderate price of one dollar" (*Philadelphia Gazette*). Although his claim seems exaggerated, he was apparently selling Edwin's small frontispiece engraving as a separate print. When the book was sold in Boston, extra copies of the engraving were sent along as well. In August and September 1800, James White advertised that he had "Just received from Philadelphia, and for sale . . . Washington's Address to the People of the United States, a superb edition, ornamented with a capital portrait, price 2 dollars. A few copies of the Portrait may be had separate, at one dollar each" (*Independent Chronicle,* August 25, 1800; *Massachusetts Mercury,* September 9, 1800).

Hart 360 // Baker 209 // Stauffer 893.

70.

James Akin (c. 1773–1846) and William Harrison, Jr. (active 1797–1819), after Joseph Wright (state 1), James Sharples (state 2), and unidentified artist (state 3)

Etching and engraving, 1800

29.4 × 18.7 cm

America lamenting her Loss at the Tomb of | General Washington | Intended as a tribute of respect paid to Departed Merit & Virtue, in | the remembrance of that illustrious Hero & most Amiable man who died Decr. 14. 1799. | Design'd Engraved & Published by Akin & Harrison Junr. Philada. Jany. 20th. 1800. Inscribed on tomb: *G. Washington. | Born 11th Feby. O.S. 1732. | Comr Contl. Army 1775 | Prest. Fed: Convention 1787. | Prest. United States 1789. | Declined Election 1796. | Comr. Fedl. Army 1798.*

❦ Historical Society of Pennsylvania (second state)

On January 20, 1800, less than seven weeks after George Washington's death, James Akin and William Harrison, Jr., published their memorial print. Taking advantage of the early publication date, and no doubt sensing the competition ahead as engravers hastened to produce portraits and

America lamenting her Loss at the Tomb of
GENERAL WASHINGTON
*Intended as a tribute of respect paid to departed Merit & Virtue, in
the remembrance of that illustrious Hero & most Amiable man who died Dec.14.1799*

Design'd Engraved & Published by Akin & Harrison Jun.r Phila.d June 20.th 1800

memorials for a grieving nation, they advertised heavily in the newspapers and issued a broadside carrying the same message (Deutsch, pp. 324–325). "Having taken considerable pains to engrave an Elegant Design in remembrance of the late illustrious General Washington," they informed their readers, they

> now offer it for public patronage. A good likeness is preserved in front of an obelisk elevated upon a tomb, at the base of which a female figure, mournfully habited, represents America, who leaning upon it is lamenting her loss. The American Eagle at her feet appears greatly agitated at the distressing scene. The print is 14 by 8½ inches, and is admirably calculated to ornament the parlour, or hang as a centre-piece, between any two other prints—it will also suit to enrich the labours of the needle upon white satin, and will be found an agreeable pastime for the Ladies. (*Philadelphia Gazette*, January 23, 25, 28, 30, February 4, 6, 8, 11, 1800; see also "Akin and Harrison, Junior" broadside at the Library Company of Philadelphia; Deutsch, pp. 324–325.)

In her research in contemporary newspapers, Davida Deutsch has discovered that many Washington memorial prints were based on decorations and stage sets designed for monodies and eulogies delivered after Washington's death. Akin and Harrison apparently were influenced by the monody presented by Thomas Wignell "with appropriate scenery and decorations, designed and executed by Mr. Milbourne, Mr. Holland and Mr. Barralet" (*Gazette of the United States*, December 21, 1799; quoted in Deutsch, p. 324). The staging was described as a

> Tomb in the centre of the Stage in the Grecian stile of Architecture, supported by Trusses. In the Centre of it was a Portrait of the General, incircled by a wreath of oaken leaves; under the Portrait a sword, shield and helmet and the colours of the United States. The top was in the form of a Pyramid, in the front of which appeared the American Eagle, weeping tears of Blood for the loss of her General and holding in her beak a scroll, on which was inscribed "A Nations Tears." (*True American*, December 24, 1799; quoted in Deutsch, p. 324.)

One of the "airs" that followed the monody that evening began with the words "Glory, bring thy finest wreath, Place it on thy Hero's urn" (*True American*, December 24, 1799). One theme of both the performance and the print was the grandeur of a hero's immortality emphasized by the pyramid, the urn, the crowning wreath, and the list of his accomplishments lettered on the tablet beneath the portrait. The next air on the program suggested the other aspect of the print: "Hold not back the sacred tear, Give to him the sigh sincere." Akin and Harrison reinforced this theme of mourning by including the grieving woman "representing America" (according to their adver-

tisement) and by their title "America lamenting her Loss at the Tomb of General Washington."

The Grecian mourning figure, dressed in white, was a popular neoclassical ornament in the last quarter of the eighteenth century, appearing on Wedgwood medallions, on architectural borders, on transfer printed pitchers, and other arts (see Schorsch, *Mourning Becomes America*; and Schorsch, "Mourning Art"). Angelica Kauffmann's painting *Fame Decorating the Tomb of Shakespeare*, copied as a print by Francesco Bartolozzi in 1782, was one influential example of this classically garbed mourning figure; illustrations from Goethe's story of Charlotte mourning Werther were another. James Akin, who advertised that he had "employed a considerable part of [his] life in acquiring a knowledge of the fine arts, from the most celebrated and esteemed masters in Europe," and who owned "pictures" by the English artist Thomas Stothard, had probably studied in England, where he would have become familiar with European mourning imagery (Quimby, pp. 60–61). The urn, the pyramid with a portrait, and the grieving female combined with the willow and pine trees make the Akin and Harrison engraving a prototype for the American mourning art that was to flourish in the decades after the death of Washington.

In the first state of this engraving, the portrait of Washington was modeled on the Joseph Wright profile. Although this image was widely known through numerous print copies, the engravers felt compelled to change the face of Washington not once but twice. In the second state it is altered to appear more like the profile by James Sharples than that by Wright (Hart 147a). In the third state (Deutsch, p. 324), possibly as an attempt to present a more classical image of the hero, the profile has been changed to resemble a sculpted bust.

Akin and Harrison were particularly conscious of the possible use of their print. By suggesting in their advertisement that it was "admirably calculated to ornament the parlour, or hang as a centre-piece, between any two other prints," they were implying that it had a significance beyond the average decorative picture and that it should have a special place of honor. They even promised that with some evidence of sufficient interest, they would print impressions in color. At the same time they anticipated the demand for such an image to use for needlework pictures and promised to print it on white satin for that purpose. "Those who wish to have any printed in colours, or upon sattin," they advised, "will please to leave word as above; because the expence attending such a mode would be too great without a sufficient list of names to encourage it" (*Philadelphia Gazette*, January 23, 1800). The second state of the print

140

did in fact inspire several needlework memorials (Deutsch and Ring, pp. 406–407), and it was also copied on an English transfer-printed jug (Schorsch, *Mourning Becomes America,* 31; Deutsch, p. 324).

Hart 147 // Baker 400 // Stauffer 22 // Anderson 9 // Deutsch, pp. 324–325 // Deutsch and Ring, pp. 406–407 // Quimby, p. 108.

71.

Unidentified artist, after engraving by Akin and Harrison

Relief cut, 1800

17.1 × 13.9 cm

Within ribbon: *Washington*

❧ *Der neue hoch deutsche americanische Calender, auf das Jahr Christi 1801* (Baltimore: Saur [1800]). Evans 38032; American Antiquarian Society.

The designer of this memorial in a German-language almanac produced a simplified relief-cut copy of James Akin and William Harrison's engraving *America Lamenting her Loss,* published early in 1800 [70]. Like the third state of the Akin and Harrison print (Deutsch, p. 324), the artist has used a sculpted bust image of Washington but has modified it from a profile to a three-quarter pose. For the single figure of America he substituted twin mourning females. The one on the right, holding a trumpet, is meant to be the ubiquitous figure of Fame, the most common alle-

gorical companion to the great hero. The one on the left holds the palm branch which had appeared crossed with a sword on the base of the pyramid in the Akin and Harrison print. The weeping eagle remains a dominant element.

72.

Unidentified artist, after Joseph Wright (state 1) and Gilbert Stuart (state 2)

Etching, 1800

26.7 × 24.4 cm

Lived respected and Fear'd—Died Lamented and rever'd / Columbia lamenting the loss of her Son / Who redeem'd her from Slav'ry & Liberty won / While Fame is directed by Justice to spread / The sad tidings afar that Washington's dead / Philadelphia published by Pember & Luzarder 1800. Inscribed on step beneath urn: *Born Feby 11th 1732 O.S. Died Decmr. 14th 1799*

❧ Museum of Fine Arts, Boston (second state)

The memorial print inscribed "Lived respected and Fear'd—Died Lamented and rever'd" required no mention of Washington's name. Everyone recognized both the Wright-type portrait in the first state and the Stuart image in the second, and everyone understood the sentiment. In contrast to the factual reporting of its companion piece, "G. Washington in his Last Illness" [73], this print published by Edward Pember and James Luzarder has all the allegorical components of a mourning picture. Even without the verse, viewers of the engraving would know that the figure on the left was "Columbia lamenting the loss of her Son" and the figure on the right was Justice directing Fame to spread the word of Washington's death. The enormous urn between the allegorical mourning figures leaves little room for the portrait of Washington that had to fit within the confines of an obelisk. The palm trees, somewhat unusual for American prints in this era, were found in earlier depictions of the exotic new continent.

Like Akin and Harrison's memorial [70], the portrait of Washington in the first state of the engraving resembled the Wright profile (Hart 644a) and later was changed. The image in the second state was based on a Gilbert Stuart portrait, possibly Cornelius Tiebout's engraving published in January of 1800 [68].

Because printed handkerchiefs based on this pair of prints were imported from Scotland and advertised in the newspaper by July 24, 1800 (*Mercantile Advertiser,* New York; quoted in Deutsch, p. 326), the engravings must have been published early in 1800. The advertisement describes the mourning picture as "representing the Genius of Liberty weeping over the urn of her Hero."

Although the technique is crude and the com-

Columbia lamenting the loss of her Son
Who redeemed her from Slavery & Liberty won

While Fame is directed by Justice to spread
The sad tidings afar that Washington's dead

Philadelphia Publish'd by Pember & Luzarder 1800

position awkward, the unknown engraver has combined some of the most common allegorical symbols and figures—Justice, Fame, the exaggerated urn, the obelisk, and the grieving Liberty-Columbia—into a memorial image that could be easily understood by the least sophisticated viewer.

Hart 644 // Baker 408 // Deutsch, p. 326 // Mount Vernon Ladies' Association, Report, 1940, pp. 25–28.

73.
Unidentified artist

Etching, 1800

25.1 × 24 cm

G. Washington in his last Illness attended by Docrs. Craik and Brown | Americans behold & shed a grateful Tear | For a man who has gained yor. freedom most dear | And now is departing unto the realms above | Where he may ever rest in lasting peace & love

Museum of Fine Arts, Boston

Shortly after Washington's death, on December 14, 1799, Tobias Lear's letter to John Adams describing the event was published in nearly every newspaper (Deutsch, p. 329). Washington's complaint was an "inflammatory sore throat," Lear reported, and he was attended by Drs. James Craik, Elisha Cullen Dick, and Gustavus Richard Brown. "His last scene corresponded with the whole tenor of his life; not a groan, nor a complaint escaped him in extreme distress. With perfect resignation, and in full possession of his

reason, he closed his well-spent life" (Adams 9:163–164). The hand-colored engraving of "G. Washington in his last Illness" probably was published shortly after his death. There was no attempt to capture likenesses, nor were there classical allusions or symbols to elevate the importance of the man or the moment. Although the scene was certainly fictional, it had the appearance of factual reporting. Only the two older doctors are depicted, but their names are properly recorded. Furthermore, details such as the bottles of medicine on the table, the miniature portrait hanging around Martha's neck, the taking of the pulse with the aid of a watch, all contribute to the authenticity of the image. In its stark and unadorned simplicity, and its depiction of all the important characters at this climactic moment of a man's life, it is truly a prototype for that favorite of lithographic images in the nineteenth century, the deathbed scene.

The companion piece to this print, engraved by the same artist, was a mourning print inscribed: "Philadelphia Published by Pember & Luzarder 1800" [72]. Shortly after their publication, the pair of prints must have been shipped off to Scotland, where the images were copied on printed handkerchiefs. By July 24, 1800, the New York *Mercantile Advertiser* could report: "In the stores of some of our dry-good merchants, we observe a neat tribute to the memory of the illustrious Washington.—It is a pocket handkerchief, lately imported from Glasgow . . . on which is wrought a scene representing the Death of the General. . . . To this print is a companion, representing the Genius of Liberty weeping over the urn of her Hero" (Deutsch, p. 326). One of these handkerchiefs is preserved in the collections of the New York Public Library. The deathbed scene, taken from the Pember and Luzarder print, is surrounded by quotations from Henry Lee's funeral oration, Lear's letter, and other sources (Deutsch, p. 329; Waddell, p. 201; Lefèvre, p. 17).

Deutsch, p. 329 // Waddell, p. 201 // Mount Vernon Ladies' Association, Report, 1940, pp. 25–28 // Jacobs, p. 117.

74.
Charles Balthazar Julien Févret de Saint-Mémin (1770–1852)

Engraving, 1800

1.6 × 1.2 cm

National Portrait Gallery

The two small engravings of George Washington by the French refugee artist Charles Balthazar Julien Févret de Saint-Mémin were made shortly after Washington's death to insert into mourning rings. Working in America from 1793 until his return to France in 1814, Saint-Mémin produced

G.WASHINGTON *in his last Illness   attended by Doc.rs Craik and Brown*

Americans behold & shed a grateful Tear   And now is departing unto the realms above
For a man who has gained yo.r freedom most dau.   Where he may ever rest in lasting peace & love

hundreds of profile portraits with the aid of the physiognotrace, a mechanical device invented in France by Gilles-Louis Chrétien in about 1786. He habitually reduced these life-size drawings to a copperplate by means of a pantograph and engraved a circular profile print about two inches in diameter. The Washington engravings, however, were made smaller to fit into mourning rings. They were based on Saint-Mémin's drawing of Washington (now lost), which is believed to have been the last portrait drawn from life (Morgan and Fielding, p. 416; Norfleet, p. 218). The original plate of this version of the engraving, depicting Washington in uniform, is now owned by the National Portrait Gallery. At some later date the engraver Charles P. Harrison added on the copperplate the inscription "Printed by C. P. Harrison."

Philadelphia and New York jewelers advertised the rings for sale in January and February 1800 (Deutsch, p. 331). Simon Chaudron, a jeweler and silversmith, placed his notice in the Philadelphia *Aurora* January 6 through February 4: "Mourning Rings with an elegant Portrait of the late Illustrious General Washington to be had at S. Chaudron's No. 12 South Street."

Along with the miniature profile in uniform, Saint-Mémin engraved another Washington likeness for mourning rings which was designed "à l'antique" as a sculpted bust with a laurel wreath [75]. One Philadelphia jeweler, John B. Du-Moutet, who mentioned a ring with a "false" likeness of Washington, may have been referring to the sculpted bust engraving which he felt was misleading compared with the "true" likeness in uniform. His advertisement in the *Aurora* for February 26, 1800, read:

Hairwork & Jewelry Manufactory No. 55, South-Second, corner of Chestnut Street John B. DuMoutet having discovered that there are a quantity of Rings

& with false likenesses of the late General Washington informs his customers and the Public, That he is the only person in Philadelphia that is in possession of the plate, with a true likeness of General Washington in uniform dress. As has been allowed by the best artists.

Some authors have assumed that these rings were connected to a bequest in Washington's will (Eisen, *Portraits*, 2:549):

To my Sisters in law Hannah Washington & Mildred Washington,—to my friends Eleanor Stuart, Hannah Washington of Fairfield, and Elizabeth Washington of Hayfield, I give, each, a mourning Ring of the value of one hundred dollars.—These bequests are not made for the intrinsic value of them, but as mementos of my esteem & regard. *(Last Will and Testament, pp. 17–18.)*

There is no proof, however, that the will referred to the Saint-Mémin rings. There is also no documentation to support Elizabeth Johnston's statement that only six copies of the print were made (Johnston, p. 135). Mourning rings with the engraving still survive at the Metropolitan Museum and at Yale University. Occasionally the engravings in the rings were colored by hand to resemble miniatures (Deutsch, p. 331).

Hart 709 // Baker 395 // Johnston, pp. 134–135 //Morgan and Fielding, pp. 415–417 // Eisen, *Portraits*, 2:494, 546, 549 // Morgan, p. 23 // Lincoln, p. 159 // Deutsch, p. 331 // Norfleet, pp. 218–219.

75.
Charles Balthazar Julien Févret de Saint-Mémin (1770–1852)
Engraving, 1800
1.6 × 1.2 cm
[St M]
 National Portrait Gallery

Like Saint-Mémin's miniature engraving of Washington in uniform [74], his laureated version was made for insertion in mourning rings. The actual

profiles in the two prints are identical, and both seem to be based on the drawing (now lost) Saint-Mémin supposedly did from life in 1798. However, this engraving has often been associated with Saint-Mémin's second drawing of Washington (Morgan and Fielding, pp. 416–417; for discussion of drawing, see *Philadelphia*, pp. 202–203), which is also a sculpted bust image crowned with a laurel wreath. Ellen Miles has determined, however, that the second drawing is closer to a wax medallion signed by Joseph Wright (Kimball, "Wright, Sculpture," p. 37) than it is to this engraving. (Dr. Miles is preparing a definitive catalogue for the National Portrait Gallery on the work of Saint-Mémin.)

Many authors have mentioned the bust or life mask of Washington by Jean Antoine Houdon as the source for this engraving. Even if the influence was not direct, Saint-Mémin would have been aware of the increased use of the sculpted bust profile which appeared on Wedgwood plaques, on the Duvivier medal in Paris, in miniatures, and in other depictions of Washington that Houdon's work inspired.

Hart 710 // Johnston, p. 165 // Morgan and Fielding, pp. 415–417 // Lincoln, p. 159 // Morgan, pp. 22–23 // Deutsch, p. 331.

Gen! George Washington.

Obt Deck! 14th 1799. Æ. 68

76.

William Hamlin (1772–1869), after Edward Savage

Mezzotint, c. 1800

18.1 × 14.2 cm

E. Savage pinxet / Wm Hamlin Sculp. Providence / Genl, George Washington. / Obt, Decbr, 14th, 1799, AE 68

Rhode Island Historical Society

The engraver William Hamlin, of Providence, Rhode Island, served his apprenticeship to a gold- and silversmith (Lane, p. 133). While he would have learned the rudiments of decorative engraving on metal during his training, his printmaking technique—described as a "somewhat weak mixture of mezzotint and stipple, frequently worked over with the roulette" (Stauffer 1:117)—seems to have been largely self-taught. Supposedly he also made his own engraving tools (Lane, p. 133). Hamlin apparently had seen Washington on the latter's visit to Providence (Stauffer 1:117), and impressed with his character, he made a series of engraved portraits of the first President. It was Edward Savage's 1793 print of Washington [33] which provided inspiration, and Hamlin made several copies of it in mezzotint (see also entry [77, 78]). This version, a straightforward copy without any memorial imagery, may have been the one advertised in the *Providence Journal* on March 12, 1800: "For Sale, By the subscriber, and at the different bookstores in this town, a handsome mezzotinto engraving of General George Washington; Pronounced by good judges to be an excellent likeness. William Hamlin. Those who apply soon, may have proof prints of the above."

The impression of this print at the Rhode Island Historical Society appears to be an unrecorded first state of a plate that was significantly reworked and frequently reprinted in the nineteenth century. A restrike at the New-York Historical Society that belonged to collector Thomas Addis Emmet has a notation in ink at the bottom: "a very scarce print as the plate was injured after two or three impressions." On the restrike (catalogued as Hart 231 and Baker 124), the title was changed from "Genl. George Washington" to "George Washington Esqr." and substantial changes were made to the image, particularly in the back of the chair and in the drapery. Stauffer and Lane confused the issue of Hamlin's Washington engravings by describing the figure in this print as "seated to right at table" (Stauffer 1239; Lane 18, 19). Stauffer also noted that the map on the table was inscribed "Eastern Branch," but no copy with this lettering has been found.

Hart 231 // Baker 124 // Stauffer 1239 // Lane 18, 19.

Genl George Washington.

77.

William Hamlin (1772–1869), after Edward Savage

Mezzotint, 1800

45 × 35.3 cm

E Savage Pinxt. | Wm Hamlin Sculpt. | Genl. George Wash-
ington. | Published July 1800. by Wm. Hamlin. Provi-
dence R.I.

Rhode Island Historical Society

William Hamlin made several different copies of
Edward Savage's mezzotint portrait of Washington
[33]. In this large version, Washington is depicted
in uniform rather than in the velvet coat of the
Savage print, and the portrait has been made into
a memorial image by the addition in the background of an urn on a pedestal. The urn is inscribed "G.W. Obt. Decbr. 14th 1799 AE 68." The
pedestal bears on one side the words "The Grateful Tribute of his Admiring Countrymen" and on
the adjacent side the verse "Death ere thou hast
slain another Wise and Great and Good as He,
Time shall throw his dart at thee." William S.
Baker recorded that only one hundred impressions
of this plate were taken for subscribers (Baker
123).

Washington is shown seated at a table, his arm
resting on the plan of the new federal city (lettered "Eastern Branch," as in the Savage print).
In changing his dress to a uniform, Hamlin may
have wanted to suggest Washington's military
achievements as well as his political career for the
memorial print.

Hart 230 // Baker 123 // Stauffer 1236 // Lane 13.

78.

William Hamlin (1772–1869), after Edward Savage

Mezzotint, c. 1800

18.5 × 14.2 cm

E. Savage pinxet. | Wm Hamlin. Sculp. Providence. | Genl,
George Washington. | Obt, Decbr, 14th, 1799, AE 68

Historical Society of Pennsylvania

This memorial print of Washington by William
Hamlin is reversed, reduced in size, and poorer in
execution than his otherwise similar engraving
[77]. In this version the urn, labeled "G.W.," is
topped with a figure of Fame, and the hilt of a
sword rests against the table. The orginal source
was Savage's 1793 mezzotint engraving [33].

Hart 232 // Baker 125 // Stauffer 1238 // Lane 17.

79.

William Woolley (active c. 1800)

Mezzotint, 1800

53 × 47 cm

Woolley | David Longworth Direxit. | Pinxit et Sculpsit. |
This Print, from the Original Picture in | the Possession

of Longworth and Wheeler | Is by them Dedicated, To
the Memory of | His Excellency Geo Washington Esqr. |
Published at the Shakespeare Gallery. No. 11 Park, N.
York.

Historical Society of Pennsylvania

William Woolley was an English engraver who appeared in New York in 1800 when this print was
published and rapidly disappeared again. Woolley's memorial to Washington was announced by
the publisher David Longworth in both the *New*
York Gazette and the *Commercial Advertiser*:

Because All revere Washington, D. Longworth has
employed an Artist of distinguished merit on a
Picture, the subject of which is The Memory of
Washington which he expects to exhibit for subscription in a short time—when the size of the Print
now copying from it, and the price of each, will be
known. The Likeness, he presumes, will Excell, and
the Other Emblems he flatters himself, will afford
peculiar satisfaction. (January 3, 1800. I am grateful
to Davida Deutsch for supplying me with all the
newspaper references in this entry.)

Since Woolley was only known to have made
three American plates (see also entry [80]), David
McNeely Stauffer assumed that Longworth
ordered the portrait and the engraved plate of
Washington from England and printed the plate
once it arrived in New York (Stauffer 1:296). However, Longworth's first advertisement was dated
January 3, less than three weeks after Washing-

This Print from the Original Picture in the Possession of Longworth and Wheeler Is by them DEDICATED to the MEMORY of His Excellency GEO. WASHINGTON Esq.r

ton's death. Since there was not enough time to send an order to London, much less to hear about the artist's plans for including "Other Emblems" in the picture, Woolley must have been residing in New York at the time. William Dunlap recalls an English painter named Woolley living in New York and Philadelphia around 1797 (Dunlap, *History*, 2:63). Although some of the paintings attributed to him, such as the portrait of Ashbel Green at Princeton University (Dunlap, *History*, 2: opposite p. 63), are actually by William Woollett, Dunlap's Woolley may have been the same artist who made the Washington painting and print.

By January 23, 1800, Longworth had put Woolley's painting on display to encourage subscribers for the engraving. The allegory of the memorial is explained in his notice in the *Commercial Advertiser*:

> To The Memory Of Washington An Original Painting, Is now exhibiting at no. 11 Park, . . . designd and executed by Woolly, Being A Portrait of Washington, Which is supported by three emblematic figures, On the left of the Picture is Liberty. On the right is Justice. And the centre represents Virtue holding over the Portrait her Crown, and pointing to Heaven as the reward of her Hero.
>
> In the foreground, on the left, is represented under the form of two beautiful female figures, Poetry and History, who, with dulcet verse and noble sentiment, applauds the merit of the great and good. In the right, America is personified in the figure of a female Aboriginal, whose grief evinces the deep regret impressed on the minds of all real Americans—Also that those unfortunate people have lost a Just Friend.
>
> The general gloom which pervades the whole surrounding group, proves the universal sensibility created by his death.

At the end of their advertisement, Longworth and Wheeler issued their proposal for publishing the engraving. The plate, which measured 24 by 19 inches, was to be ready in about six weeks. The mezzotints would cost four dollars to subscribers, and "not less than 5 dollars to non-subscribers." A month later, on February 4, 1800, the publishers advertised the print in the *Centinel of Freedom* in Newark, New Jersey, where Mr. Johnson Tuttle was taking subscriptions. The original was described as "an emblematical painting of General Washington . . . the likeness from the celebrated picture of Steward" (*sic*). Apparently the engraving of the plate took longer than the six weeks they had expected, but by May 23, 1800, Longworth and Wheeler could finally inform their public that the Washington print was completed (*Daily Advertiser*, New York).

Although the mournful face in the center of the engraving was a poor copy of the Stuart likeness, and the look-alike allegorical maidens were less

than inspiring, Woolley's prominently displayed portrait reinforced, soon after Washington's death, the apotheosis imagery that had already appeared in Washington prints [see 39]. The beam of light from above, the heavenly clouds, the medallion on a pedestal, and the allegorical figures of Liberty, Immortality, and grieving America all became common elements in the memorial images.

At some point in the nineteenth century the engraved plate was cut down and restrikes made of the central portrait with all of the allegorical scenery removed (Baker 354).

Hart 467 // Baker 354 // Anderson 34 // Taylor, p. 32 // Grote, p. 133.

George Washington Esqr.

80.
William Woolley (active c. 1800)

Mezzotint, 1800

29.5 × 25.1 cm

Woolley Pinxit | et Sculpsit. | George Washington Esqr. | [Publish'd at the Shakespeare Gallery. No. 11 Park, N York]

Metropolitan Museum of Art

At the time he made his allegorical memorial engraving of Washington [79], William Woolley also made an unembellished mezzotint portrait with a companion print of Martha Washington. The likeness, a somber version of the Stuart "Athenaeum" image, was the same as the one in the memorial. (For discussion of Woolley, see entry [79].)

Hart 466 // Baker 355 // Stauffer 1:296 // Grote, p. 132.

TRENTON
PRINCETOWN
MONMOUTH
YORKTOWN.

PATER
PATRIÆ.

Sacred to the Memory of the
truly Illustrious
GEORGE WASHINGTON, Renowned in
War, Great in the Senate, and
possessed of every Qualification
to render him worthy the Title of
a GREAT and GOOD MAN.

BORN Feb. 22. 1732. Ob. Dec. 14. 1799.

Painted by John Coles jur.   Engd by E.G.Gridley.

81.

Enoch G. Gridley (active 1800–1818), after John Coles, Jr., and Edward Savage

Etching and engraving, c. 1800

33.1 × 22.4 cm

Trenton | Princetown | Monmouth | Yorktown. | Pater | Patriae | Sacred to the Memory of the | truly Illustrious | George Washington, Renowned in | War, Great in the Senate, and | possessed by every Qualification | to render him worthy the Title of | a Great and Good Man. | Born Feb. 22. 1732. Ob. Dec. 14. 1799. | Painted by John Coles, jun. | Engd. by E. G. Gridley.

National Museum of American Art

The Sons of Columbia in Boston stated in a broadside entitled "Monumental Engraving" and dated March 13, 1801, that they felt it was their duty "to approve, and patronize the Engraving, agreeable to this Description, as the Design of a monument, sacred to the Memory of the late General George Washington; that posterity may see his Effigies, as well as hear the great and noble Deeds of the Father of His Country." (A copy of the broadside is at the Historical Society of Pennsylvania.) The ensuing description set forth in detail the allegorical implications of the memorial print designed by John Coles, Jr., and engraved by Enoch Gridley.

1st. An high finished white marble Monument, rising in a pyramidical form.

2d. On the left of the Piece, a war-worn Veteran, with his arms grounded, in awful surprise at the sight of his General's Funeral Pile; with his right hand he wipes the falling tear; and with his left he motions his distress of mind. In the Person of the war-worn Veteran, you behold a lively representation of the Grief of all the Army of America, for the loss of their beloved General and Commander in Chief.

3d. The Genius of Columbia, on the right reclining on her Spear erect in her right hand; and her left responsive to her deep distress. In the Genius of Columbia, you see a lively Emblem of the Grief of all America, for the loss of the Father of his Country.

4th. Minerva retires from her Shield, and seated near the Trophies of War, presents and supports the Likeness of the departed Hero. As Minerva is called the Goddess of Wisdom, in the heathen Mythology; and she supports his likeness, it shews in the Design, that he was always supported by Wisdom, in all his Measures and Transactions. In the Goddess Minerva, you see Wisdom grieving for the loss of one of the wisest Men of the Age.

5th. The Genius of Mars approaches with the Helmet of Defence; but finding the General is no more is stunned with surprize. In the Genius of Mars, you behold Valour and Courage grieving for the greatest Hero of the Age.

6th. The Genius of Minerva, attending with the Shield of the Gorgon head. As this is the Shield of Minerva, it supposes in the Design, that he was shielded by Wisdom in all his Difficulties and Dangers.

7th. Fame, with wings expanded, holding the Trump, on the Banner of which is inscribed the Names of those places where signal victories have been obtained; and in her left hand a Wreath, enclosing the Pater Patriae. You likewise see Fame, grieving for the most famous Man of the Age.

8 & 9. The Genii of Liberty and Truth, with their Emblems, both assisting to adorn his brow with Laurels; and on the top of the Pile, an Urn, blazing with the incense of Memory and Love, which will never be extinguished. And above, Liberty and Truth, grieving for the loss of the greatest Supporter they have had for several Ages past.

The source for this allegorical monument was discovered by Davida Deutsch to be the orator's platform for a eulogy given in Burlington, New Jersey, in March 1800. As described in a Trenton newspaper, "a beautiful emblematic obelisk, 15 feet high" was erected on stage, painted in imitation of marble, and ornamented with the figure of Fame holding a trumpet from which hung a scroll emblazoned with the names of Washington's battles at Trenton, Princeton, Monmouth, and Yorktown (*Federalist, or New-Jersey Gazette,* March 10, 1800; Deutsch, p. 325).

The young John Coles, Jr., just starting in his father's business of heraldry painting (Bowditch, p. 196), may have read the description of the New Jersey obelisk and reconstructed the design for a memorial engraving, interpolating freely and using putti for the "Genii" of most of his allegorical figures. Since "third edition" is printed on the March 1801 broadside, and a note is included that the piece already had nearly six hundred subscribers, it can be assumed that the print was made the previous year. In the Baker and Whelen catalogues the publication date is given as July 28, 1800 (Baker 403; Whelen, pp. 71–72). The engraving had been "patronized" by Governors Strong, Gilman, and Bowen, according to the broadside, and would continue to be published only by subscription. The image of Washington in the medallion was based on a Savage portrait, possibly his 1792 stipple engraving [31].

Hart 221 // Baker 403 // Stauffer 1184 // Anderson 22 // Shadwell, *American Printmaking,* 80 // Deutsch, p. 325 // Taylor, pp. 30–31 // Bowditch, p. 196 // Whelen, pp. 71–72 // Andrews, p. 23 // Schorsch, "Mourning Art," p. 14 // *Antiques* 69 (Feb. 1956): frontispiece.

One Dollar
No
1
WASHINGTON
The President Directors and Company of
Washington Bank in Westerly promise
to pay to or Bearer, on demand
ONE DOLLAR.
Westerly
Cash.r
Presid.t
ONE DOLLAR
One Dollar
No
1
WASHINGTON
The President Directors and Company of
Washington Bank in Westerly promise
to pay to or Bearer, on demand
ONE DOLLAR.
Westerly
Cash.r
Presid.t
ONE DOLLAR
One Dollar
No
1
WASHINGTON
The President Directors and Company of
Washington Bank in Westerly promise
to pay to or Bearer on demand
ONE DOLLAR.
Westerly
Cash.r
Presid.t
ONE DOLLAR
One Dollar
No
1
WASHINGTON
The President Directors and Company of
Washington Bank in Westerly promise
to pay to or Bearer, on demand.
ONE DOLLAR.
Westerly
Cash.r
Presid.t
ONE DOLLAR
PRINTED IN 1976

82.

Amos Doolittle (1754–1832), after Joseph Wright

Engraving, 1800

2.2 cm (diameter of profile in circle)

From strike from original copperplate: *Washington. / Engraved & Printed by Amos Doolittle New Haven 1800* (repeated on each banknote)

Washington Trust Company, Westerly, Rhode Island

Early in 1800 the citizens of Westerly, Rhode Island, a community with expanding agricultural, fishing, and shipbuilding activities, established the Washington Bank, to provide "those little assistances, from time to time, which banks only can give" (Cooney, p. 8). Receiving their charter from the state legislature in the spring, the new bank directors turned their attention to having banknotes engraved. While one of the directors rode off to Philadelphia in July 1800 to get the proper paper, the cashier headed for New Haven to engage Amos Doolittle to do the engraving (Cooney, p. 11). Three original copperplates, still owned by the Washington Trust Company in Westerly, document Doolittle's accomplishment. The first banknotes to bear the portrait of Washington, each of Doolittle's twelve notes (in five different denominations) is ornamented with a tiny profile in a circle. Two paper proofs of the Washington portrait [84, 85], this plate of four "one dollar" notes, and another plate of one "twenty-five dollar" and three "three dollar" notes (see entry [83]) were engraved in 1800. The third copperplate—with one "ten dollar" and three "five dollar" banknotes—is inscribed with the date 1803.

During the 1790s, on his print *Display of the United States* (see entry [25]), Doolittle had periodically revised the profile of Washington after Joseph Wright. While the banknote portraits are all from the same basic source and are all similar in design, each profile seems quite different. There is, however, no particular evolution of the image. Clearly the engraver's inability to make perfect copies explains the variety of profiles, some of which seem fairly close to the Joseph Wright etching and others hardly related at all. Retaining the uniform of the Wright portrait, Doolittle added a crown of laurel leaves, the symbol of victory that had been associated with Washington ever since the almanac cut of 1778 (see entry [3]).

Cooney, pp. 9–11, 16 // Newman, p. 351.

83.

Amos Doolittle (1754–1832), after Joseph Wright

Engraving, 1800

2.2 cm (diameter of profile in circle)

From strike from original copperplate: *Washington. / New Haven. Engraved & Printed by A. Doolittle / 1800* (repeated on each banknote)

Washington Trust Company, Westerly, Rhode Island

Amos Doolittle's plate of "three dollar" and "twenty-five dollar" banknotes was engraved in 1800 for the Washington Bank in Westerly, Rhode Island (for discussion, see entry [82]). An original three-dollar banknote from this plate is now at the Connecticut Historical Society (see Fig. 44).

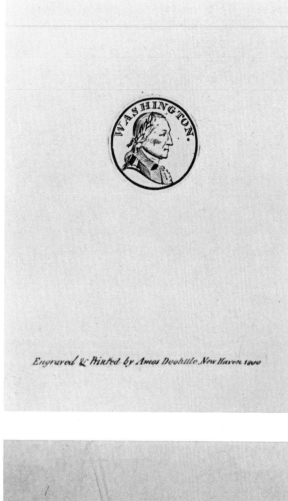

Engraved & Printed by Amos Doolittle New Haven 1800

84.

Amos Doolittle (1754–1832), after Joseph Wright

Engraving, 1800

2.2 cm (diameter)

Washington. | Engraved & Printed by Amos Doolittle. New Haven 1800

⚘ Connecticut Historical Society

Doolittle's tiny profile portrait is a proof for the banknote engravings he made for the Washington Bank in Westerly, Rhode Island (see entry [82]).

85.

Amos Doolittle (1754–1832), after Joseph Wright

Engraving, 1800

2.2 cm (diameter)

Washington. | Engraved & Printed by Amos Doolittle. New Haven 1800

⚘ Connecticut Historical Society

Varying only slightly from the preceding, this profile is another proof for Doolittle's banknotes for the Washington Bank in Westerly, Rhode Island (see entry [82]).

Engraved & Printed by Amos Doolittle New Haven 1800

86.

David Edwin (1776–1841), after Rembrandt Peale

Stipple, 1800

28.7 × 23 cm

R. Peale Pinx | D Edwin sc | General George Washington, | Born Feb. 22, 1732 in Westmoreland County Virginia, and Died Dec. 14, 1799 at Mount Vernon. | Published by J. Savage 1800.

⚘ National Portrait Gallery

Stipple engraver David Edwin had already published Washington portraits after Edward Savage and Gilbert Stuart when he issued this print after Rembrandt Peale the year after Washington's death. Edwin's engraving was large and imposing—a dignified image of the President which suggested, without benefit of military or allegorical symbols, the leadership and accomplishments of a deeply mourned national hero. Nevertheless, in prints the Rembrandt Peale image was not able to compete with the growing popularity of Gilbert Stuart's "Athenaeum" likeness, which as early as 1800 was frequently copied in separate prints and illustrations.

About a decade after its initial publication, the plate was reissued by Henry S. Tanner, and "Printed in Colours, by H. Charles" (Hart 701b).

Hart 701 // Baker 9 // Stauffer 903.

GENERAL GEORGE WASHINGTON.

Born Feb.22, 1732 in Westmoreland County Virginia, and Died Dec.14,1799 at Mount Vernon.

Published by J.Savage 1800.

Painted by R. Peal.   Published by A. Kennedy, No. 170, Chesnut Street, corner of 4th, Philadelphia.   Engraved by Edwin.

APOTHEOSIS OF WASHINGTON

156

87.

David Edwin (1776–1841), after Rembrandt Peale

Stipple, 1800

53.1 × 37.5 cm

Painted by R. Peale. | Published by S. Kennedy No. 129, Chestnut Street, corner of 4th. Philadelphia. | Engrav'd by Edwin. | Apotheosis of Washington.

National Portrait Gallery

On December 20, 1800, two New York newspapers, the *Mercantile Advertiser* and the *Temple of Reason,* carried a notice that Samuel Kennedy

is about publishing an elegant Engraving of the apotheosis of Washington, wherein there is at one view descried all that can be said of the Soldier, the Statesman, the Husband and the Friend. We hear the composition of the plate represents a whole length portrait of Washington, rising gently in a graceful attitude on light clouds, from Mount Vernon, which appears underneath: On one side are the portraits of Warren and Montgomery, among clouds, descending in an inviting attitude toward our principal Hero: on the other side, a figure of Cupid, suspended in the air, attentively admiring Washington, and holding a wreath of Immortality over his head. (Gottesman 3:51; Deutsch, p. 328.)

Charles Coleman Sellers had suggested that the two figures in the clouds were Martha Washington and John Parke Custis (Sellers, *Supplement,* p. 33). But although the faces do not look much like Richard Montgomery and Joseph Warren, the two slain generals seem more appropriate than Martha Washington, who was still alive, and her son.

As Sellers pointed out, the treatment of light in the print suggests that the original painting was a transparency (Sellers, *Supplement,* p. 33). During a celebration of the Louisiana Purchase on May 12, 1804, a transparency by Rembrandt Peale entitled *Apotheosis of General Washington* was set in a Philadelphia window, and the same image was exhibited again in 1808 for the Fourth of July. These references undoubtedly describe the lost original for the print. The engraving itself, if properly treated and colored on the back, could also have served as a transparency (Sellers, *Supplement,* p. 33).

Rembrandt Peale's design was inspired by Robert Strange's 1786 engraving of Benjamin West's *Apotheosis of Princes Octavius and Alfred* (Jacobs, p. 131). In the West composition the two boys meet on a cloud with Windsor Castle beneath them and welcoming cherubs above. Similarly, Mount Vernon appears in the lower corner of the Edwin print while a cherub hovers above Washington's cloudy perch with a laurel crown.

Hart 702 // Baker 402 // Stauffer 904 // Anderson 17 // *Classical Spirit* 15 // Jacobs, p. 131 // Deutsch, p. 328.

G. WASHINGTON.

88.

Benjamin Tanner (1775–1848), after Edward Savage

Stipple, 1800

12.9 × 10.2 cm

Savage pinx. | Tanner sc. | G. Washington.

National Portrait Gallery
The Washingtoniana (Baltimore: Sower, 1800). Evans 39018 and 39019.

Benjamin Tanner's copy of the Savage print of Washington seems to have been published first as a separate engraving. It was then bound into the *Washingtoniana,* a volume containing Washington's will and various "outlines of his character, from pens of different eminent writers both in Europe and America." Although the title of the print, which was too low on the sheet, was moved closer to the oval portrait, the engraving never quite fits into the bound volume. Nevertheless, the publisher added "Engraved for the Washingtoniana" across the top of the print and included on the title page the words "Embellished with a good Likeness."

Hart 218 // Baker 253 // Stauffer 3105 // Baker, *Washingtoniana,* pp. 11–12.

157

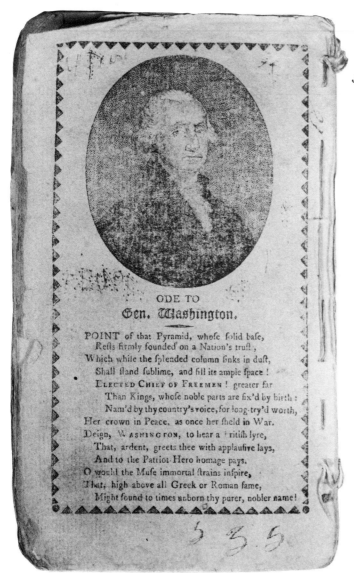

90.

Attributed to Samuel Hill (active 1789–1803)

Etching and engraving, c. 1800

12.2 × 8.7 cm

❧ Batty Langley, *The Builder's Jewel* (Charlestown, Mass.: Etheridge for Hill, [1800]). Evans 37778; Rare Books Division, New York Public Library.

The "First American Edition" of Batty Langley's architectural book was printed for the engraver Samuel Hill, who probably made the frontispiece, a grouping of Masonic symbols in a landscape. The three pillars—Masonic emblems of Wisdom, Strength, and Beauty—are adorned with stonemasons' instruments, which are commonly used symbols of Freemasonry. Placed on top of the pillars are the sun, the moon, and a bust which was identified by Mantle Fielding as an Houdon-type image of Washington (Fielding 666). Hill's design was copied from the frontispiece designed by Batty Langley in 1741, engraved by his brother Thomas, and published in a 1746 London edition (and perhaps other editions) of *The Builder's Jewel*. Clearly the original bust did not represent Washington, and it is doubtful that Hill's version was intended to portray him, particularly since the image appears bald and perhaps bearded. Masonic imagery of the federal period frequently incorporated the portrait of the Masons' most prominent member as well as other patriotic and national symbols (Franco, p. 31), but it seems an unlikely identification in this instance.

Fielding 666.

89.

Unidentified artist, after Gilbert Stuart

Relief cut, 1800

7.8 × 6.4 cm

❧ *Greenleaf's New-York, Connecticut, & New-Jersey Almanack, for . . . 1801* (Brooklyn: Kirk, [1800]). Evans 37543; Library Company of Philadelphia.

The back cover of Greenleaf's almanac features an ode to Washington illustrated by a portrait. The image is a standard one after Gilbert Stuart, but the technique is very unusual. It appears to be an imitation of stipple engraving done in relief.

91.

Unidentified artist, after Joseph Wright

Relief cut, 1800

6.3 × 5.4 cm

Immortal Washington

[Mason Locke Weems], *The Life and Memorable Actions of George Washington* ([Baltimore:] Keatinge, [1800]). Evans 39065; American Antiquarian Society.

This small and modest relief cut is the frontispiece to what bibliographers believe is the first edition of Mason Locke Weems' biography of George Washington. Extraordinarily popular both in its own day and in succeeding generations, the book was to appear in at least fifty-eight editions by 1850. Although many of Parson Weems' most famous anecdotes were not included until the revised and expanded 1806 version of the biography, the colorful style of his more modest early editions proved irresistible. On the market just months after Washington's death, Weems' work was printed in four editions in its first year. The inaccuracy as well as the popularity of Weems' account is summed up in one critic's assessment:

> Reckless in statement, indifferent to facts and research, his books are full of popular heroism, religion and morality. . . . Everything rages and storms, slashes and tears. . . . It is in vain that the historians, the exhaustive investigators, the learned and the accurate rail at or ignore him. He is inimitable. He will live forever. (Fisher, pp. 65–66.)

Weems was a traveling bookseller. He knew what people wanted to buy: "The Cowl knows best wt will suit in Virginia," he wrote, with reference to his ecclesiastical training (Weems 2:131). Significantly, from his first suggestion of a book on Washington, in a June 24, 1799, letter to publisher Mathew Carey, he contemplated a frontispiece portrait:

> I have very nearly ready for the press a piece . . . to be christen'd, "The Beauties of Washington." tis artfully drawn up, enlivin'd with anecdotes, and in my humble opinion, marvellously fitted "ad captandum gustum populi Americani!!!" What say you to printing it for me and ordering a copper plate Frontispiece of that Hero, something in this way. [sketch of head with inscription:] George Washington Esqr. The Guardian Angel of his Country. "Go thy way old George. Die when thou wilt we shall never look upon thy like again." (Weems 1: between pp. 2 and 3.)

By January 1800 Carey had still not responded to Weems, despite the fact that Washington's death the previous December made a biography all the more salable. "Millions are gaping to read something about him," Weems reminded Carey,

> I am very nearly primd & cockd for 'em. 6 months ago I set myself to collect anecdotes of him . . . My plan! I give his history, sufficiently minute—I accompany him from his start, thro the French & Indian & British or Revolutionary wars, to the Presidents chair to the throne in the hearts of 5,000000 of People. . . . All this I have lind and enlivend with Anecdotes apropos interesting and entertaining. (Weems 2:126.)

Frustrated with Carey's slowness in publishing his book, Weems admitted that he had "resolvd to strike off a few on my own acct" (Weems 2:127). The Keatinge edition was probably the result of his effort to get the work in print as quickly as possible. Although there was not time to get an engraved illustration, the book was published with a frontispiece. Simple and rather crudely cut, the relief cut was nevertheless a pleasing design of an eagle holding a medallion image of Washington. The portrait was based, no doubt, on one of the many copies after Joseph Wright's profile etching. (For other editions of Weems' biography, see entry [92, 93].)

Weems 1:2–6.

Engraved for the Rev.ᵈ M.L. Weems.

thing save plain fold & stitch" (Weems 2:129), but he originally had intended to illustrate the work with an engraved frontispiece portrait. "There is a beautiful likeness of Washington in one of the Ladies Magazines," he wrote Carey; "he was young, beautiful and interesting when that was taken. If you have to have that engravd on Copper as a Frontispiece to our little book it might have a happy effect" (Weems 2:127).

In May 1800 Weems sent Carey half of the manuscript with instructions to "put it to press instantly." He asked for an edition of 5,000, confident that he could "sell 10,000 Copies in Virginia alone!" (Weems 2:130). This "second edition improved" was printed by John Bioren, and Weems was not entirely pleased with the result. He referred to the printer as "Bioren, alias Black-Beard" on one occasion, and wrote to Carey in July 1800, "I beg you to keep in mind that the sooner you can dispose of the present (the 2d) edition of Washington's life the better. Hang me, if I am not dog-sick, on looking at it. And nothing but necessity cou'd make me lug it out even on Journeymen, Hatters & Blacksmiths" (Weems 2:131–132). Nevertheless, the edition seemed to sell. "You may thank Washington & the Bachelor [*The Bachelor's Almanac*] for most of the remittances made you," he told the publisher (Weems 2:136).

The frontispiece of this edition, a small engraving by Benjamin Tanner after the Stuart "Athenaeum" likeness, was an improvement over the relief cut in the Baltimore edition, but it may still have been a disappointment to Weems. Another engraving by Tanner was substituted for the "third" Bioren edition [93] published a few months later. (For further discussion of Weems, see entry [91, 93].)

Hart 524 // Baker 338 // Stauffer 3103 // Baker, *Washingtoniana*, pp. 13–14 // Weems 1:11–13.

92.

Benjamin Tanner (1775–1848), after Gilbert Stuart

Stipple, 1800

8.1 × 6 cm

G. Washington. | Tanner. sc. | Engraved for the Revd. M. L. Weems.

❦ Mason Locke Weems, *A History, of the Life . . . of . . . Washington* (2nd ed., Philadelphia: Bioren, [1800]). Evans 39062; American Antiquarian Society.

"Washington, you know is gone!" Mason Locke Weems wrote to publisher Mathew Carey in January 1800; "Millions are gaping to read something about him." Parson Weems had ready for the press an anecdotal biography of the President that he was certain would make his—and Carey's—fortune. When the Philadelphia publisher did not respond, Weems issued one edition in Baltimore (see entry [91]) and an unillustrated version in Georgetown (Weems 1:2–10). He continued, however, to negotiate with Carey for a Philadelphia edition. He asked for the cost of an inexpensive volume, "No Engravings—No Binding—no any-

93.

Benjamin Tanner (1775–1848), after Gilbert Stuart

Stipple, 1800

12.2 × 10.3 cm

B. Tanner, Sc. | G. Washington.

❦ Mason Locke Weems, *A History, of the Life . . . of . . . Washington* (3rd ed., Philadelphia: Bioren, [1800]). Evans 39063; Library of Congress.

"I must have a capital edition this Fall," wrote Mason Locke Weems in July 1800 to the publisher Mathew Carey (Weems 2:132). He was referring to his popular biography of George Washington and complaining about the "second edition improved," printed by John Bioren, which he urged Carey to dispose of as quickly as possible. By August he was planning a "third" edition (prob-

G. WASHINGTON.

might as soon borrow a ton of brimstone from the Devil as get my Washingtons . . . & other books . . . from you" (Weems 2:152).

The 1800 editions of Weems' biography had a greater impact than their modest frontispiece portraits would suggest. By March 1801 Weems wrote Carey frantically:

Washington is gone—the people are tearing me to pieces. Pleasants has sold all—he begs I wd get out another edition—& promises it will outsell any book in America. Can you print me speedily a Neat edition of 1600, on Octavo size, with my large plate of Washington . . . I'll wholesale like fury, and send you the money . . . very soon. (Weems 2:178.)

Already Parson Weems' little book was launched on its spectacular career. (For further discussion on Weems, see entry [91, 92].)

Hart 523 // Baker 340 // Stauffer 3106 // Baker, *Washingtoniana*, pp. 14–15 // Weems 1:13–15.

Gen. GEORGE WASHINGTON,
Commander in chief of the Armies of the United States.
Born Feb: 11th 1732, O.S.
Died December 14th 1799

94.

Amos Doolittle (1754–1832), after Joseph Wright

Engraving and etching, 1800

8.3 × 4.1 cm

A. Doolittle Sculp | Gen. George Washington, | Commander in chief of the | Armies of the United States. | Born Feb: 11th: 1732 O.S. | Died December 14th: 1799

❧ Benjamin Trumbull, *The Majesty and Morality of Created Gods* (New Haven: Read and Morse, 1800). Evans 38679; American Antiquarian Society.

Benjamin Trumbull's funeral elegy on the death of Washington was sold both with and without the frontispiece (Hough, pp. 269–270). The engraving,

ably actually the fourth), which he proposed to sell as a school book. He wrote to Carey, "If you have not already done it, 'twere well to put to press an edition of the Life of Washington in Duodo. The Likeness, in small, first done by Tiebout will be excellent" (Weems 2:141, 140). Weems may have been suggesting the engraving after Stuart that Cornelius Tiebout published on January 1, 1800 (see entry [68]). Shortly afterwards he sent Carey an engraving. "May it not do well to get this engravd for edition of Washington, alter'd for [from?] the Gallant Mercer [?]" (Weems 2:142). This ambiguous statement suggests that Weems had sent a portrait of General Hugh Mercer which he thought could be reengraved to represent Washington. Seemingly unconcerned about the accuracy of the image, Weems cared only that the book was illustrated. The suggestion that the "third" Bioren edition was issued both with and without Benjamin Tanner's engraved frontispiece is borne out by Weems' comment: "I left 80 or 90 Washington's Life with Mrs. Smith, without the cuts" (Weems 1:14, 2:169).

By September Carey was paying John Bioren for the cost of printing the edition. By November Weems wrote from Annapolis, "I brought with me the last of the 3d edition of Washington. I sold them all in 20 minutes, very sorry am I that we have not a 4th edition" (Weems 2:150). He referred, probably, to the last of his shipment rather than the last of the edition, and he complained that Carey was too slow in sending him more: "I

by Amos Doolittle, was a simple but effective image of Washington in uniform with an eagle hovering overhead with a laurel wreath. Doolittle had already copied this Joseph Wright profile in his engraving *Display of the United States* (see entry [25]). The eagle and laurel wreath motif is repeated in the facing title-page vignette, which featured a large urn marked "G. W." flanked by two classically garbed females.

Hart 145 // Baker 81 // Stauffer 519 // Hough, pp. 269–270.

Genl. Geo. Washington

95.

William Harrison, Jr. (active 1797–1819), after Edward Savage

Stipple, 1800

11 × 8.1 cm

W. Harrison Junr. sculpt.— | Genl. Geoe. Washington

❧ [George Washington], *Legacies of Washington* (Trenton: Sherman, Mershon and Thomas, 1800). Evans 38995; National Portrait Gallery (frontispiece only).

Appended to this collection of Washington's writings are eulogies by Henry Lee, Thomas Paine, and "a member of the Senate of the United States." The "biographical outline" was written by J. M. Williams (Baker, *Washingtoniana*, p. 16).

Hart 222 // Baker 128 // Stauffer 1290 // Baker, *Washingtoniana*, p. 16.

Farnsworth's Edition.

GEN. GEORGE WASHINGTON.

96.

William Hamlin (1772–1869), after Edward Savage

Etching and engraving, 1800

10.3 × 8.3 cm

Farnsworth's Edition. | E. Savage. Pinxt. | Wm. Hamlin, Sct. Provid. | Genl. George Washington.

❧ *Memory of Washington* (Newport: Farnsworth, 1800). Evans 37951; American Antiquarian Society.

The biographical sketch of George Washington in this volume was written by Jedidiah Morse. The frontispiece was engraved by the Providence engraver William Hamlin, who had published memorial images of Washington in 1800 [76, 77, 78].

Hart 223 // Baker 126 // Stauffer 1240 // Lane 20 // Baker, *Washingtoniana*, p. 12.

OBIIT, NUNQUAM REVERSURUS, ET DOLEO.

HE HAS GONE, NEVER TO COME BACK, TO MY GREAT
SORROW.

Introduction to the Funeral Oration.

IT may not be improper, dear fellow-citizens, before I begin this difcourfe, to remind you of a paffage in fcripture that correfponds well with the melancholy Oration which I am now to deliver. St. Paul, in one of his epiftles to the Hebrews, the 9th chapter, 27th verfe, fays—*And as it is appointed unto men once to die*—our late and great hero, WASHINGTON, could not of courfe be exempted from the facred, fure and irrevocable decree of God.

97.

Unidentified artist, after Joseph Wright

Relief cut, c. 1800

7.8 × 9.1 cm

Obiit, Nunquam Reversurus, et Doleo | He Has Gone, Never to Come Back, to My Great Sorrow.

❧ Michael Gabriel Houdin, *Et Sicut illud Statutum est Hominibus . . . A Funeral Oration on . . . Washington* (Albany: Barber and Southwick, [1800]). Evans 37653; American Antiquarian Society.

The author's own engraved portrait is the frontispiece to this eulogy, while the relief cut of Washington is printed on the introductory page. The embellishments to the Joseph Wright type of profile include the usual cannon, bayonets, and furled banner, but their unfortunate placement makes them all look upside down. Also unusual is the obvious funereal symbol of the coffin among the standard military ordnance.

GEORGE WASHINGTON

98.

Cornelius Tiebout (c. 1773–1832), after Gilbert Stuart

Stipple, 1800

8.7 × 6.8 cm

G. Stewart Del. / C. Tiebout Sculp. / George Washington.

☙ Uzal Ogden, *Two Discourses, Occasioned by the Death of . . . Washington* (Newark: Day, 1800). Evans 38154; National Portrait Gallery (frontispiece only).

According to the title page, the Reverend Uzal Ogden had on two occasions—December 29, 1799, and January 5, 1800—delivered eulogies on the death of Washington. They were printed together and published in Newark, New Jersey. For the engraved frontispiece Cornelius Tiebout no doubt copied the engraving after Stuart which he had published on January 1, 1800 (see entry [68]).

Hart 455 // Baker 344 // Stauffer 3194.

99.

Unidentified artist

Etching, c. 1785–1800

30.1 cm (diameter)

His Excellency George Washington Esqr. Commander in chief of the American Armies.—The Protector of his Country. The Supporter of Liberty. And the Benefactor of Mankind. May his name never be forgotten

☙ New Haven Colony Historical Society

Very little is known about this equestrian engraving of George Washington, of which there seem to be at least two versions as well as a nineteenth-century imitation. This version, which was

eventually reengraved entirely and exists in a number of different states, is distinguished by dark tents in the background with white interiors. The other version [100] and the imitation have white tents with dark interiors.

This equestrian image has been associated with the fictitious "Alexander Campbell" mezzotint of Washington (Fig. 6) published in London in 1775 (see Carson 118 and Mitchell Catalogue 99). However, its more immediate source was an English printed handkerchief (Fig. 10). The artist of the textile may have been inspired by one of two medals, designed in Paris and struck in the late 1780s, commemorating Generals Daniel Morgan and William Augustine Washington (see Loubat, Plts. 8, 9). Both medals have equestrian images with their arms outstretched.

This print could have been made any time after the late 1780s and may even have been produced as a memorial image in 1800. There is also a possibility that the plate was engraved in Europe and imported, with reengraved states printed in America.

The plate went through a number of different states. The frontispiece for Carl Drepperd's *Early American Prints* reproduces the same engraving with such changes as cross-hatching added to the rear leg of the horse. The print once owned by the Old Print Shop is probably another state, in which the face of Washington and much of the shading on the horse have been reengraved (*Old Print Shop Portfolio*, Vol. 14, No. 3 and Vol. 36, No. 2).

Drepperd, frontispiece // *Old Print Shop Portfolio*, Vol. 14, No. 3 and Vol. 36, No. 2 // Mount Vernon Ladies' Association, Report, 1940, p. 44.

100.

Unidentified artist

Etching, c. 1785–1800

29 × 28.8 cm

*His Excellency George Washington Esqr. Commander in
chief of the American Armies.—The Protector of his
Country. The Supporter of Liberty. And the Benefactor
of Mankind. May his name never be forgotten*

❧ Print Collection, New York Public Library

This crude engraving was probably copied from
the previous image [99] and is distinguished from
it by white tents in the background with dark interiors. The New York Public Library also owns
an imitation of this second equestrian print. It
was made in the nineteenth century and lacks
punctuation in the inscription (Hart 725). Stan
Henkels described an imitation as "one of those
which have emanated from the Miller Mill, whose
copper was not large enough, and about ¼ inch
of leaf border is missing at the top" (Mitchell
Catalogue 99). It is not known whether this is the
same imitation that Hart described.

Hart 725 // Carson 118 // Mitchell Catalogue 99.

101.

John James Barralet (c. 1747–1815)

Engraving and etching, 1800–1802

61 × 47 cm

Philadelphia Published by Simon Chaudron / and John J. Barralet, Jany. 1802. On tomb and lid of tomb: *Sacred / to the Memory of / Washington. / OB 14 Dec AD 1799. / AEt 68. / I. J. Barralet Fecit.*

Metropolitan Museum of Art

Although John James Barralet's *Apotheosis of Washington* was not actually published until 1802 (*Aurora*, February 3, 1802; quoted in Jacobs, pp. 133–134), proof prints were on view for potential subscribers by December 19, 1800 (*Aurora;* quoted in Prime 2:80–81). Since a partially engraved plate probably would not have lured subscribers, we can consider the print on exhibition and nearly finished in 1800. As Patricia Anderson has pointed out, the imagery of the engraving was connected to a Masonic funeral elegy presented in January of that year. Simon Chaudron, French emigré silversmith and copublisher of the print, gave a funeral oration which employed the apotheosis theme, the mourning Indian, and other images in Barralet's design (Anderson, p. 32). The artist may have been influenced by the oration; or, more likely, Barralet's conception had already been formulated, and Chaudron, as copublisher, was aware of the imagery employed.

The allegory of the *Apotheosis of Washington* was described in the initial advertisement:

> The subject General Washington raised from the tomb, by the spiritual and temporal Genius—assisted by Immortality. At his feet America weeping over his Armour, holding the staff surmounted by the Cap of Liberty, emblematical of his mild administration, on the opposite side, an Indian crouched in surly sorrow. In the third ground the mental virtues, Faith, Hope, and Charity. To be seen at Messrs. Shaudron's No. 12, Third Street, at J. J. Barralet's corner of 11th and Filbert-streets, where the books lie for subscriptions. (*Aurora*, December 19, 1800.)

In her analysis of this engraving, Phoebe Jacobs relates Barralet's allegorical figures to long-standing traditions in European culture (Jacobs, pp. 123–137). She compares the central theme to European apotheosis imagery; the figure of America with her pole and liberty cap to Augustin Dupré's "Libertas Americana" medal; and the Christian figures of Faith, Hope, and Charity to their standardized images in Cesare Ripa's *Iconology* (George Richardson's edition, London, 1779). Descriptions of these allegorical figures, however, could be generalized and unspecific. The recognizable figure of Father Time, with his death symbols of the scythe and hourglass, is called in one advertisement the "spiritual and temporal Genius" (Prime 2:80) and in another the "Poetical and Historical Genius" (Gottesman 3:51).

Along with the mourning figure of America trampling on a serpent (here indicating evil), the foot of the sarcophagus is strewn with symbols related specifically to the American self-image: particularly the Indian, the helmet (a favorite Barralet device to suggest military strength), and the eagle with his shield, olive branch, and "E Pluribus Unum" ribbon. The recognizable Stuart face of Washington becomes, in this context, one more symbol of America itself. In addition to national, Christian, and classical references, there are two personal emblems relating to Washington's life. Draped on ribbons on the side of the tomb are the medals of the order of Freemasons and of the Society of the Cincinnati.

More than most engravings of its time, Barralet's design had a long life in the nineteenth century. The plate was reengraved and republished several times (Davida Deutsch cites six known states, p. 329), including one issue in black and in colors by Benjamin Tanner in 1816 (Carson 942). Although numerous newspaper advertisements (Deutsch, p. 329) refer to the print as the "Apotheosis of Washington," this title was probably never engraved on the plate. It bore no title at all when it was issued in 1802 and remained that way until after 1816 when it was renamed the *Commemoration of Washington* (Stauffer 118). Barralet's image was also copied on American canvases, English transfer-printed creamware, and Chinese reverse paintings on glass (Anderson pp. 23, 32, 61; Deutsch, p. 329; Jacobs, p. 134). Finally, by a mere change of the face, it reappeared in 1865 in William Smith's memorial print of Abraham Lincoln (Taylor, p. 34).

Hart 675 // Baker 406 // Stauffer 118 // Anderson 11 // Carson 942 // *Classical Spirit* 16 // Jacobs, pp. 115–137 // Taylor, pp. 32, 34–35.

Notes

☆　　☆　　☆

INTRODUCTORY ESSAY (MILLER)

1. See [Roubaud (J. L. Audibert)], *A Compendious History of General Washington, Commander in Chief of the Americans* (London, 1777); "Particulars of the Life and Character of General Washington . . . Signed an OLD SOLDIER," in *The Gentleman's Magazine*, London, August, 1778; [Charles H. Wharton], *A Poetical Epistle to His Excellency George Washington, Esq., Commander-in-Chief of the Armies of the United States of America from an Inhabitant of the State of Maryland to which is annexed a Short Sketch* [by John Bell] *of General Washington's Life and Character* (Annapolis, 1779).

These biographies, among the first to appear following Washington's appointment as Commander in Chief of the American army, were reprinted during the following decades and became the source for the many biographies of Washington published after 1789 by such authors as Joseph Buckminster (1789), Jedidiah Morse (1789), Elhanan Winchester (1792), James Hardie (1795), Thomas Condie (1798), and John Corry (1800). After 1800, eulogists of Washington also drew from these biographies, adding information concerning Washington's later career. The image of Washington which they presented, however, continued to reflect the eighteenth-century conception of the hero and his identification with the American national purpose. See the later editions of Corry's *The Life of George Washington: Late President and Commander in Chief of the Armies of the United States of America* (Belfast: J. Smyth at the Public Printing Office, 1800); J. M. Williams, *Biographical Outline of General George Washington* (Boston: Printed for John Russell and John West, 1800); William S. Baker, *Bibliotheca Washingtoniana: A Descriptive List of the Biographies and Biographical Sketches of George Washington* (Philadelphia: Robert M. Lindsay, 1889; reprint, Detroit: Gale Research Company, 1967); Margaret Bingham Stillwell, "Washington Eulogies. A Checklist of Eulogies and Funeral Orations on the Death of George Washington," *Bulletin of the New York Public Library* (February and May 1916).

Embellishments of the Washington story began with the publication in 1800 of Mason Lock Weems' *Life and Memorable Actions of George Washington*. The book immediately became a bestseller and by 1850 had gone through fiifty-nine editions. Weems constantly changed the text; the 1806 edition, for instance, introduced the story of the cherry tree and hatchet. For discussion of the ways in which Weems created anecdotes concerning Washington and incorporated them into his biography, see Paul Leicester Ford and Emily E. Ford Skeel, *Mason Locke Weems: His Works and Ways* (New York: n.p., 1929) and Randolph G. Adams, "The Historical Illustrations in Weems's Washington," *Colophon*, Part 8 (1931).

In the mid-nineteenth century, Jared Sparks, historian and Unitarian clergyman, edited in twelve volumes *The Writings of George Washington . . . with a Life of the Author* (Boston: Tappan & Dennett, 1834–1837), a bowdlerized portrayal of Washington as the perfect symbol of the American nation. See John Spencer Bassett, *The Middle Group of American Historians* (New York: Macmillan, 1917), pp. 100–110; William Alfred Bryan, *George Washington in American Literature, 1775–1865* (New York: Columbia University Press, 1952), pp. 98–100. Washington Irving, New York storyteller and writer, based his five-volume life on Sparks' text but added to the Washington story questionable information about Washington's descent from English nobility. See Washington Irving, *Life of George Washington*, 5 vols. (New York: Putnam, 1855–1859); Dixon Wecter, *The Hero in America: A Chronicle of Hero-Worship* (Ann Arbor: University of Michigan Press, 1963), p. 141; Bryan, *Washington*, pp. 103–104.

2. *Minutes of the Supreme Executive Council of Pennsylvania*, January 18, 1779 (Harrisburg, 1852), 11: 671–672. Also published in the *Pennsylvania Packet*, January 28, 1779.

3. John Marshall, *The Life of George Washington, Commander in Chief of the American Forces, during the War which established the Independence of his Country, and First President of the United States*, 5 vols. (Philadelphia: C. P. Wayne, 1804–1807), Vol. 2, pp. 236, 527; [John Bell], "A Sketch of Mr. Washington's Life and Character," *Universal Magazine* (May 1800): 340, 343, 344; David Ramsay, *The Life of George Washington Commander in Chief of the Armies of the United States of America throughout the War which established their Independence and First President of the United States* (New York: Hopkins & Seymour, 1807), p. 319. See also Wecter, *Hero*, pp. 104–106.

4. See *Universal Magazine* (May 1800): 340. Jefferson is quoted in Wecter, *Hero*, p. 117.

5. Ramsay, *Life*, p. 328; John Adams to John Jebb, September 10, 1785; quoted in Bryan, *Washington*, p. 30.

6. Washington is quoted in James Thomas Flexner, *Washington: The Indispensable Man* (Boston and Toronto: Little, Brown, 1969), p. 26. Winchester claimed that Washington's "good destiny" along with his "consummate prudence" accounted for public confidence in his leadership despite his defeats in battle (*Short Sketch of the Life and Character of General Washington. . . .*, London, 1792, p. 65). Ramsay urged Americans to appreciate the fact that "a kind Providence in its beneficence raised him . . . to be to you an instrument of great good . . ." (*Life*, pp. 337–338).

7. Flexner, *Washington*, p. 60.

8. Joseph Campbell, *The Hero with a Thousand Faces* (New York: Pantheon, 1949), pp. 30–31. See also "A Poem

on George Washington," in *Bickerstaff's Boston Almanack*, 1790, where Washington is compared to Ulysses, Aeneas, and "Grecian Kings."

9. "American Liberty," in *Collected Poems of Philip Freneau*, ed. Fred Lewis Pattee (Princeton: Princeton University Press, 1902), Vol. 1, p. 149.

10. Winchester, *Short Sketch*, pp. 63, 64. Samuel Shaw to Rev. John Eliot, April 12, 1778; quoted in Bryan, *Washington*, p. 26; Adams to John Jebb, September 10, 1785; quoted in Bryan, *Washington*, p. 30. See also John Marshall's response in the House of Representatives on the death of Washington, quoted in Ramsay, *Life*, pp. 319–321.

11. Quoted in Bryan, *Washington*, pp. 30–31.

12. See Ramsay, *Life*, p. 1. Ramsay quotes the Senate address to the President on Washington's death, indicating that "our country mourns a father" (p. 322).

13. Winchester, *Short Sketch*, p. 67. Francis Hopkinson, *The Miscellaneous Essays . . .*, 3 vols. (Philadelphia: T. Dobson, 1792), Vol. 1, p. 120.

14. Quoted in Flexner, *Washington*, p. 123.

15. Ramsay, *Life*, p. 338; Winchester, *Short Sketch*, pp. 71–72.

16. Quoted in Ramsay, *Life*, p. 314.

17. See Arthur Holcombe, "The Role of Washington in the Framing of the Constitution," *Huntington Library Quarterly* 4 (August 1956): 317–334.

18. Quoted in Flexner, *Washington*, p. 345.

19. Quoted in Ramsay, *Life*, pp. 314–317.

20. *Ibid.*, pp. 318, 324. See also the eulogy of David Tappan in *An Address in Latin, by Joseph Willard . . . and a Discourse in English, by David Tappan . . .* ([Charlestown, Mass.], 1800).

21. Peter Gay, *The Enlightenment: The Rise of Modern Paganism* (New York: Knopf, 1966, 1976), pp. 32, 40–41. Leonard W. Labaree *et al.*, eds., *The Autobiography of Benjamin Franklin* (New Haven: Yale University Press, 1964), pp. 64, 168–169.

The libraries of such Revolutionary leaders as George Mason and Thomas Jefferson were full of Latin and Greek authors in the original—the *Iliad*, the *Odyssey*, the *Maxims and Reflections of Plato*, Ovid's *Metamorphoses*, and Cicero's *Orations*. Just as classical architecture provided Americans with the structure of their buildings, so did classical rhetoric provide them with the structure of their orations; and the constant appeal of writers and orators to "Roman principles," Marcus Aurelius, Lucretius, and Epictetus indicates how immersed Americans were in classical literature and thought. See Helen Hill Miller, *George Mason, Gentleman Revolutionary* (Chapel Hill: University of North Carolina Press, 1976), p. 31; Daniel Boorstin, *The Lost World of Thomas Jefferson* (Boston: Beacon Press, 1960), p. 219.

22. "Annuit Coeptis" = he has favored our undertaking (Virgil, *Aeneid* IX, 625), "Novus Ordo Seculorum" = a new cycle of centuries (Virgil, *Eclogues* IV, 5–7).

23. Washington to Lund Washington; quoted in Wecter, *Hero*, p. 106.

24. Quoted in Flexner, *Washington*, p. 262.

25. *Ibid.*, pp. 174, 203.

26. Described in the *Pennsylvania Packet*, November 1, 1781.

27. Winchester, *Short Sketch*, p. 67. Ramsay, *Life*, p. 330.

28. Ramsay, *Life*, p. 330.

29. John William Ward, *Andrew Jackson: Symbol for an Age* (New York: Oxford University Press, 1962), p. 10.

30. *Ibid.*, p. 8. For the Fabius image of Washington, see "Sketch of the Life and Character of Our American Fabius . . .," in *Bickerstaff's Boston Almanack*, 1790.

31. Peter Shaw, *American Patriots and the Rituals of Revolution* (Cambridge, Mass.: Harvard University Press, 1981), p. 15.

32. Quoted in Gustavus A. Eisen, *Portraits of Washington*, 3 vols. (New York: Robert Hamilton, 1932), Vol. 1, p. 312.

MAIN ESSAY (WICK)

1. Smith, p. 51. (Full publication information for all sources cited is given in the alphabetical list of references beginning on p. 173.)

2. For physical descriptions see Freeman 2:383; 3:6, 504–505; 7:383–384; and Fitzpatrick 26:321n; 35:141n.

3. Freeman 3:6.

4. Fitzpatrick 26:321.

5. Although much of the information is out of date, the two indispensable works on Washington portraiture are John Hill Morgan and Mantle Fielding, *The Life Portraits of Washington and Their Replicas* (Philadelphia: Printed for the Subscribers, 1931) and Gustavus A. Eisen, *Portraits of Washington*, 3 vols. (New York: Robert Hamilton, 1932).

6. Fitzpatrick 28:140.

7. Baker, *Washingtoniana*, p. 6.

8. Sellers, *Portraits*, p. 220.

9. Shadwell, "Hiller," pp. 240–241.

10. Sellers, *Portraits*, p. 225.

11. *Ibid.*, p. 173.

12. *Ibid.*, p. 224.

13. H. W. Sellers, p. 161.

14. Sellers, *Portraits*, p. 225.

15. H. W. Sellers, pp. 161–162. The actual number of prints distributed is open to interpretation since Peale's use of the word "ditto" could refer either to one mezzotint or to one dozen.

16. Prime 1:20.

17. *Ibid.* 1:25. In July 1778, Norman had advertised an unidentified print of Washington (*ibid.*). This could not have been Peale's mezzotint (made that October), but it does indicate that Norman's interest in Washington images had developed quite early.

18. *Ibid.* 1:29.

19. Identified in William S. Baker's manuscript supplement (now at the Historical Society of Pennsylvania) to his *Engraved Portraits of Washington*.

20. Matthews, pp. 409–453.

21. Hart, "Revere," p. 83.

22. Sellers, *Portraits*, p. 217.

23. Alexander and Godfrey, passim.

24. H. W. Sellers, pp. 165–168.

25. Sellers, *Portraits*, p. 225.

26. See p. 31.

27. E. P. Richardson, p. 169; Shadwell, "Peale," p. 133.

28. Sellers, *Portraits*, p. 237.

29. *Ibid.*, p. 239.

30. Simmons, pp. 26, 28–36.

31. An unusual mezzotint of Washington inscribed "His Excellency General Washington" and "B. Blyth Pinxt." exists in a couple of Washington collections. It is a crude mezzotint depicting a three-quarter-length figure resting one arm on a cannon at the right with other cannon firing away in the background. The face is fictitious. This image does not fit in with the Norman-Blyth-Peale image or with any other American prints of Washington. It could be an imported plate of someone else with an inscription that was changed, probably in this century.

32. *Journals of the Continental Congress 1774–1789*, p. 494.

33. Brigham, p. 83.
34. See illustration, *The Eighteenth Century*, p. 264.
35. Baker, pp. 33–34; Hart, "Frauds," p. 94; Andrews, pp. 32–33, 55–56.
36. These are the twelve subjects usually associated with the series. Portraits of Benjamin Franklin, John Paul Jones, George III, and Gen. George Augustus Eliott have also been suggested as related to or inspired by the original Shepherd-Hart-Morris series. See George 5:xv.
37. Fitzpatrick 4:298–299.
38. Hart 730; for copies see list that follows Hart 730.
39. The Washington plate in *An Impartial History* may have been based partially on an illustration in the *Hibernian Magazine* (Hart 759) published in 1776. Other engravings in the *Impartial History*, such as the portrait of David Wooster, are based directly on the Shepherd-Hart-Morris mezzotints; see reproductions in Cresswell, p. 75.
40. Hart 724 and 726.
41. Hart 729; Cresswell 207; the Shepherd-Hart-Morris mezzotints inspired a number of the illustrations in this volume.
42. Montgomery, pp. 182, 183, 185.
43. Ide, *Jay*, p. 10; *Antiques* 24 (July 1933):37; Ide, "Handkerchief."
44. The design for the Morgan medal was requested by a letter from David Humphreys to the Academy of Inscriptions and Belles-Lettres in Paris on November 25, 1785; see Loubat, pp. xvi–xvii.
45. Donnell, p. 17; see also Potts, pp. 341–375.
46. Donnell, p. 17.
47. *Ibid.*, p. 18.
48. Potts, p. 365.
49. The reason for omitting the names was not explained. In a letter dated September 12, 1782, Du Simitière wrote to Gérard: "I submit . . . to your judgement whether it would not be proper to have the names and titles engraved under each head for the easier information of the subscribers, as the motives for omitting the names in the first publication exist no more" (Donnell, p. 20).
50. The first set contained the portraits of Washington, John Jay, Henry Laurens, Horatio Gates, Samuel Huntington, and Conrad Alexandre Gérard; the second set included portraits of Baron von Steuben, Charles Thompson, Gouverneur Morris, Silas Deane, William H. Drayton, John Dickinson, Joseph Reed, and Benedict Arnold.
51. Donnell, p. 20.
52. *Ibid.*
53. *Ibid.* Du Simitière was not as enthusiastic about the engraving of the second set. He wrote Gérard that on some of the later prints, "the strokes of the tool are rather hard on the faces to do justice to the originals."
54. Fitzpatrick 28:96.
55. Donnell, p. 20.
56. *Ibid.*, pp. 17–18; Lefèvre, p. 15; Ide, *Jay*, p. 10.
57. Gardner and Feld, p. 101.
58. Hart 101.
59. Hart 85; Munn, p. 7.
60. This engraving also appeared in Charles Varlo's *Essence of Agriculture* (London, 1786).
61. Hart 94; Hart 95–100.
62. Doane, pp. xxiii.
63. The print of Esek Hopkins in the Esnauts and Rapilly series, engraved in Paris, had the same flag with the snake and motto.
64. Montgomery, pp. 279–282; Munn, p. 8; Donnell, p. 18.
65. Montgomery, pp. 279–282; Munn, p. 9.
66. Peale's notebook diary for November 9, 1776, recorded that he "began a copy of Gen. Washington for a French gentleman." In November 1777 he noted that "Le Marquis de la Fayette bespoke a whole length in miniature of the

Genl." One year later, on November 10, 1778, the *Pennsylvania Packet*, describing the Comte d'Estaing's reception for the citizens of Boston on board the *Languedoc*, noted among the decorations "a picture of General Washington at full-length, lately presented to the Count by General Hancock." See Sellers, *Portraits*, pp. 221, 223, 220. The relationship between these references is unclear. William S. Baker assumed that Peale made a miniature for Lafayette (Baker, p. 16). However, the "whole length in miniature" probably referred to a cabinet-size likeness (Sellers, *Portraits*, p. 223).
67. The replica sent to Europe may be the portrait now owned by the White House; see *Connoisseur* 160 (November 1965):192. Lafayette later acquired another Peale portrait of Washington which Charles Coleman Sellers believed was painted by James Peale (Sellers, *Portraits*, p. 7; Eisen, *Portraits*, 2:350).
68. Hart 32.
69. Hart 38; Cresswell 222.
70. Sellers, *Portraits*, p. 232.
71. The two bust portraits now owned by the Montclair Art Museum are probably the paintings Peale sent to London; *New York Times*, March 31, 1961.
72. Baker, pp. 16–17.
73. *Antiques* 101 (February 1922): 266; Beardsley, p. 144. Although Beardsley refers to a "Display" print of Jefferson, it is unknown today.
74. Kimball, "Wright, Paintings and Engravings," pp. 376–382; Kimball, "Wright, Sculpture," pp. 34–39.
75. Boyd 16:577–578.
76. Bentley 1:219.
77. *Pennsylvania Packet*, March 3, 1790.
78. Dunlap 1:188.
79. Hart, "Hiller," p. 5.
80. *Ibid.*, p. 7.
81. Hart 139 and 146.
82. Hart 170 and 168.
83. Kimball, "Wright, Paintings and Engravings," p. 382.
84. Hart 165 and 161.
85. Kimball, "Wright, Paintings and Engravings," p. 382.
86. Weitenkampf, p. 1. The painter and historian William Dunlap made an etching of Thomas Wignell in 1789.
87. Morgan and Fielding, pp. 180–181.
88. Alexander and Godfrey, pp. 32–33.
89. Stauffer 2747.
90. Hart 215.
91. Stauffer 2745.
92. Hart, "Savage," p. 7.
93. Eisen, *Portraits*, 2:462.
94. The date is recorded in Savage's letter to Washington on June 3, 1798, quoted below (see n. 96).
95. Fitzpatrick 36:188–189.
96. Hart, "Savage," pp. 9–10.
97. For statements against Savage see Dunlap, *History*, 1:321; Dunlap, *Diary*, 3:706; Dickson, "Savage," pp. 6 ff.; Dickson, *Jarvis*, pp. 35–57.
98. For statements in support of Savage as an engraver see Baker, pp. 74–75; Hart, "Savage," pp. 9–11.
99. According to one source, the nineteenth-century artist John Sartain recalled that "Savage drew outlines on copper, but Edwin did a large part of the engraving" (Fielding, *Dictionary*, p. 318).
100. Mott 1:120, 789–790.
101. *Ibid.* 1:32.
102. Kimball, "Wright, Paintings and Engravings," p. 382.
103. *Massachusetts Mercury*, January 17, 1800.
104. Fitzpatrick 35:415.
105. Hart 32.
106. Hart 33–36. There is no real evidence that Hart 33 is American as Hart suggested.
107. Although not a very accurate copy, the Ruotte engrav-

ing seems closer to Du Simitière's profile (as suggested in Baker 69) than to the Wright profile (as suggested in Hart 172), particularly in the hair. For other Du Simitière images of the 1790s see Hart 73 and 83.

108. Eisen, *Portraits*, 3:759–764.

109. Eisen suggested that Houdon designed a profile medallion to serve as a model for the medal, but this theory has not been satisfactorily proven. See Eisen 3:816–817; Eisen, "Medallion," pp. 122–125.

110. Loubat, pp. 1–7.

111. Eisen, *Portraits*, 3:817.

112. *Ibid.*, 2:453.

113. Kimball, "Wright, Sculpture," pp. 34–39.

114. Fitzpatrick 31:141.

115. Johnston, p. 49. Johnston records that this engraving was given to Gen. George B. McClellan.

116. Fitzpatrick 34:500n; Johnston, p. 49.

117. Jaffe, pp. 158–159, 315.

118. Trumbull, p. 167.

119. *Ibid.*, p. 166.

120. Gardner and Feld, pp. 103–104.

121. Sizer, p. 83. Early proofs of Cheesman's engraving are dated 1795 and June 1796. The final publication was dated August 1, 1796.

122. *Commercial Advertiser*, June 27, 1800; quoted in Gottesman 3:50–51.

123. Hart 252 and 253 (reproduced in Mitchell Catalogue, p. 40).

124. Hart 250; Anderson Gallery Auction Catalogue No. 335, November 16, 1904.

125. See Honour, passim.

126. In his two articles E. McClung Fleming traces the evolution of the allegorical representation of America from Indian princess to Greek goddess: see Fleming, "1765–1783" and "1783–1815."

127. For the evolution of the figures of Liberty and Britannia, see Sommer, "Hollis" and "Britannia."

128. For discussion of Columbia see Fleming, "1783–1815," pp. 60–66.

129. For the image of America depicted with Washington on English printed textiles, see *ibid.*, pp. 44–48.

130. Deutsch and Ring, p. 405.

131. Altick, pp. 95, 119.

132. *Gazette of the United States,* December 21, 1799; quoted in Deutsch, p. 324.

133. *True American,* December 24, 1799; quoted in Deutsch, p. 324.

134. Anderson, p. 32.

135. Jacobs, pp. 115–137.

136. Prime 2:80–81.

137. In this English translation of Lavater's work, the engraving analyzed in the section on George Washington in Volume 3, Part 2, was a derivative Peale likeness copied from the French edition. Although Lavater stated in the text that the face in the print "announces the good man, a man upright, of simple manner, sincere, firm, reflecting, and generous," he also had to express his distrust—in this case justified—in the resemblance of engraved portraits. The engraving by Thomas Holloway after Stuart's "Vaughan" portrait was bound into the book just before the Peale

likeness. According to the title page, extra portraits "from originals" were added in this translation along with the engravings copied from the French edition.

138. Hart 260, 272, 274.

139. *Commercial Advertiser,* June 27, 1800; quoted in Gottesman 3:50–51.

140. I am grateful to Davida Deutsch for references to the newspaper advertisements in these cities.

141. *Federal Gazette,* Philadelphia, February 8, 1798; quoted in Prime 2:80.

142. Fielding, p. 15.

143. Stauffer 892.

144. Sonneck, "Hail Columbia," pp. 180–189.

145. Bailey, pp. 137–138; see also Marks, passim.

146. See entry [66].

147. See entry [53].

148. See discussion of "The Presidential Profile," p. 37.

149. Elson, p. 161.

150. Adams, pp. 342–343.

151. Sonneck, *Report,* p. 46.

152. *Commercial Advertiser,* New York, January 1, 1800; quoted in Gottesman 3:48.

153. *Philadelphia Gazette,* January 1, 1800.

154. *Ibid.,* January 11, 1800.

155. *Independent Chronicle,* Boston, August 25, 1800; *Massachusetts Mercury,* September 9, 1800.

156. Deutsch, p. 331.

157. See illustration in Eisen, *Portraits,* 2:494.

158. The physiognotrace was a mechanical device invented in France for making accurate profile portraits. Saint-Mémin's original drawing on which the ring engravings were based is now lost, and there is no proof that he actually used the physiognotrace in making his Washington portrait.

159. Stauffer 1:117.

160. See illustration of what is thought to be an early replica of Rembrandt Peale's portrait in Eisen, *Portraits,* 2:412.

161. Weems 1:between 2 and 3.

162. *Ibid.* 2:126.

163. Wecter, pp. 130–138.

164. Weems 1:2–6.

165. Cooney, p. 11.

166. Only the two plates engraved in 1800 have been included here. The third, with one ten-dollar and three five-dollar banknotes, is inscribed with the date 1803.

167. See Jacobs, Schorsch, Anderson.

168. Deutsch, pp. 324–325.

169. *Philadelphia Gazette,* January 23, 1800; quoted in Deutsch, p. 325; Deutsch and Ring, pp. 406–407.

170. *Commercial Advertiser,* January 23, 1800.

171. Stauffer 1:296.

172. Scenes of these four American victories were suggested by Congress as ornamentation for the pedestal of the sculpture proposed in 1783 (see entry [17]).

173. Jacobs, p. 131; see entry [87].

174. *Mercantile Advertiser,* December 20, 1800, and *Temple of Reason,* December 10, 1800; quoted in Gottesman 3:51 and Deutsch, p. 328.

175. *Aurora;* quoted in Prime 2:80–81.

References

☆　　☆　　☆

Adams, Charles Francis, ed. *The Works of John Adams, Second President of the United States.* Vol. 9. Boston: Little, Brown, 1854.

Alexander, David and Richard T. Godfrey. *Painters and Engraving: The Reproductive Print from Hogarth to Wilkie.* New Haven: Yale Center for British Art, 1980.

Altick, Richard D. *The Shows of London.* Cambridge, Mass.: Harvard University Press, Belknap Press, 1978.

Anderson, Patricia A. *Promoted to Glory: The Apotheosis of George Washington.* Northampton, Mass.: Smith College Museum of Art, 1980.

Andrews, William Loring. *An Essay on the Portraiture of the American Revolutionary War.* New York: Printed by Gilliss Brothers for the author, 1896.

Appletons' Cyclopedia of American Biography. Edited by James Grant Wilson and John Fiske. 6 vols. New York: Appleton, 1888.

Bailey, Worth. "The Editors' Attic: Emblematical Washington. . . ." *Antiques* 55 (February 1949): 137–138.

Baker, William S. *American Engravers and Their Works.* Philadelphia: Gebbie & Barrie, 1875.
　　　　　　　　　　　　　　Baker, *Engravers*

————. *Bibliotheca Washingtoniana. A Descriptive List of the Biographies and Biographical Sketches of George Washington.* 1889. Reprint. Detroit: Gale Research Company, 1967.
　　　　　　　　　　　　Baker, *Washingtoniana*

————. *The Engraved Portraits of Washington.* Philadelphia: Lindsay and Baker, 1880.
　　　　　　　　　　　　　　　　　　　Baker

————. "The History of a Rare Washington Print." *Pennsylvania Magazine of History and Biography* 13 (October 1889): 257–264.
　　　　　　　　　　Baker, "Rare Washington Print"

————. *Medallic Portraits of Washington.* 1885. Reprint. Iota, Wisc.: Krause Publications, 1965.
　　　　　　　　　　　Baker, *Medallic Portraits*

Bartlett, John Russell. *Bibliotheca Americana. A Catalog of Books Relating to North and South America in the Library of John Carter Brown.* 2 vols. 1865–1871. Reprint. New York: Kraus Reprint, 1963.

Bates, Albert C. *An Early Connecticut Engraver and His Work.* Hartford: Case, Lockwood & Brainard, 1906.

Beardsley, William A. "An Old New Haven Engraver and His Work: Amos Doolittle." *New Haven Colony Historical Society Papers* 8 (1914): 132–150.

Bentley, William. *The Diary of William Bentley, D.D. Pastor of the East Church, Salem, Massachusetts.* 4 vols. Salem: Essex Institute, 1907.

Bowditch, Harold. "Early Water-Color Paintings of New England Coats of Arms." *Publications of the Colonial Society of Massachusetts* 35 (1951): 172–210.

Boyd, Julian P., ed. *The Papers of Thomas Jefferson.* Vol. 1—. Princeton: Princeton University Press, 1950—.

Brigham, Clarence S. *Paul Revere's Engravings.* Worcester: American Antiquarian Society, 1954.

Bristol, Roger Pattrell. *Supplement to Charles Evans' American Bibliography.* Charlottesville: University Press of Virginia for the Bibliographical Societies of America and the University of Virginia, 1970.

Burr, Frederic M. *Life and Works of Alexander Anderson, M.D., the First American Wood Engraver.* New York: Burr Brothers, 1893.

Carson, Hampton Lawrence. *The Hampton L. Carson Collection of Engraved Portraits of Gen. George Washington.* Part 1. [Philadelphia: Press of W. F. Fell Company, 1904.]

The Classical Spirit in American Portraiture. Brown University Department of Art. Providence: Brown University, 1976.

Classical Spirit

Cooney, Ralph Bolton. *Westerly's Oldest Witness.* Westerly, Rhode Island: Washington Trust Company, 1950.

Cresswell, Donald H., comp. *The American Revolution in Drawings and Prints: A Checklist of 1765–1790 Graphics in the Library of Congress.* Washington, D.C.: Library of Congress, 1975.

Crompton, Robert D. "James Trenchard of the 'Columbian' and 'Columbianum.'" *Art Quarterly* 23 (Winter 1960) : 368–397.

Deutsch, Davida Tennenbaum. "Washington Memorial Prints." *Antiques* 111 (February 1977): 324–331.

———— and Betty Ring. "Homage to Washington in Needlework and Prints." *Antiques* 119 (February 1981): 402–417.

Dickson, Harold Edward. "The Case Against Savage." *American Collector* 14 (January 1946): 6–7.

Dickson, "Savage"

————. *John Wesley Jarvis: American Painter, 1780–1840.* New York: New York Historical Society, 1949.

Dickson, *Jarvis*

Dictionary of American Biography. Edited by Allen Johnson and Dumas Malone. 10 vols. New York: Scribner's, 1927.

DAB

Doane, George Washington. *The Remains of the Rev. Charles Henry Wharton, D.D. with a Memoir of His Life.* Vol. 1. Philadelphia: William-Stavely-George Latimer; New York: Swords, Stanford, 1834.

Donnell, Edna. "Portraits of Eminent Americans after Drawings by Du Simitiere." *Antiques* 24 (July 1933): 17–21.

Drake, Milton. *Almanacs of the United States.* 2 vols. New York: Scarecrow Press, 1962.

Drepperd, Carl W. *Early American Prints.* New York: Century Co., 1930.

Dunlap, William. *Diary of William Dunlap: The Memoirs of a Dramatist, Theatrical Manager, Painter, Critic, Novelist, and Historian.* 3 vols. New York: New York Historical Society, 1931.

Dunlap, *Diary*

————. *A History of the Rise and Progress of the Arts of Design in the United States.* Edited by Rita Weiss.

2 vols. 1834. Reprint (2 vols. in 3). New York: Dover, 1969.

Dunlap, *History*

————. *A History of the Rise and Progress of the Arts of Design in the United States.* Edited, with additions, by Frank W. Bayley and Charles E. Goodspeed. 3 vols. Boston: Goodspeed, 1918.

Dunlap, *History*, 1918 ed.

The Eighteenth Century. Edited by Alfred Cobban. New York: McGraw-Hill, 1969.

Eisen, Gustavus A. "A Houdon Medallion." *Antiques* 17 (February 1930): 122–125.

Eisen, "Medallion"

————. *Portraits of Washington.* 3 vols. New York: Robert Hamilton, 1932.

Eisen, *Portraits*

Elson, Louis C. *The National Music of America and Its Sources.* Boston: Page, 1900.

Evans, Charles. *American Bibliography.* 13 vols. 1903. Reprint (13 vols. in 1). Metuchen, N.Y.: Mini-Print Corporation, 1967.

Fielding, Mantle. *American Engravers upon Copper and Steel.* Part 3. New York: Burt Franklin, 1961.

Fielding

————. *Dictionary of American Painters, Sculptors and Engravers.* 1926. Reprint. New York: James F. Carr, 1965.

Fielding, *Dictionary*

Fisher, Sydney G. "The Legendary and Myth-Making Process in Histories of the American Revolution." *Proceedings of the American Philosophical Society* 51 (Spring 1912): 55–76.

Fitzpatrick, John Clement, ed. *The Writings of George Washington from the Original Manuscript Sources, 1745–1799.* 39 vols. 1931–1944. Reprint. Westport, Conn.: Greenwood Press, 1970.

Fleming, E. McClung. "The American Image as Indian Princess, 1765–1783." *Winterthur Portfolio* 2 (1965): 65–81.

Fleming, "1765–1783"

————. "From Indian Princess to Greek Goddess: The American Image, 1783–1815." *Winterthur Portfolio* 3 (1967): 37–66.

Fleming, "1783–1815"

Flexner, James Thomas. *George Washington in the*

American Revolution (1775–1783). Boston: Little, Brown, 1968.

Ford, Worthington Chauncey. *Broadsides, Ballads, etc. Printed in Massachusetts, 1639–1800.* Boston: Massachusetts Historical Society, 1922.

Franco, Barbara. Introduction to *Masonic Symbols in American Decorative Arts,* by the Scottish Rite Masonic Museum and Library. Lexington: Scottish Rite Masonic Museum of our National Heritage, 1976.

Freeman, Douglas Southall. *George Washington: A Biography.* 6 vols. with continuation (Vol. 7) by John Alexander Carroll and Mary Wells Ashworth. New York: Scribner's, 1948–1957.

Gardner, Albert Ten Eyck and Stuart P. Feld. *American Paintings: A Catalogue of the Collection of the Metropolitan Museum of Art.* Vol. 1. New York: Metropolitan Museum of Art, 1965.

George, Mary Dorothy. *Catalogue of Political and Personal Satires Preserved in the Department of Prints and Drawings in the British Museum, 1771–1783.* Vol. 5. London: British Museum, 1935.

Goodspeed, Charles Eliot. *Yankee Bookseller.* Boston: Houghton Mifflin, Riverside Press, 1937.

Gottesman, Rita Susswein. *The Arts and Crafts in New York, 1726–1804.* 3 vols. New York: New York Historical Society, 1954–1965.

Grolier Club. *Exhibition of Engraved Portraits of Washington Commemorative of His Death.* New York: Grolier Club, 1899.
Grolier Club, *Centenary Exhibit*

Grote, Suzy Wetzel. "Engravings of George Washington in the Stanley DeForest Scott Collection." *Antiques* 112 (July 1977): 128–133.

Hamilton, Sinclair. *Early American Book Illustrators and Wood Engravers, 1670–1870.* 2 vols. Princeton: Princeton University Press, 1968.

Hart, Charles Henry. *Catalogue of the Engraved Portraits of Washington.* New York: Grolier Club, 1904.
Hart

———. "Edward Savage, Painter and Engraver, and His Unfinished Copperplate of 'The Congress Voting Independence.'" *Proceedings of the Massachusetts Historical Society* 19 (January 1905): 1–19.
Hart, "Savage"

———. "An Etched Profile Portrait of Washington by Joseph Hiller, Jr. 1794." *Historical Collections of the Essex Institute* 43 (January 1907): 1–6.
Hart, "Hiller"

———. "Frauds in Historical Portraiture, or Spurious Portraits of Historical Personages." *Annual Report of the American Historical Association* 1 (1913): 85–99.
Hart, "Frauds"

———. "Hail Columbia and Its First Publication." *Pennsylvania Magazine of History and Biography* 34 (April 1910): 162–165.
Hart, "Hail Columbia"

———. "Notice of a Portrait of Washington." *Historical Collections of the Essex Institute* 16 (July 1879): 161–165.
Hart, "Notice"

———. "Paul Revere's Portrait of Washington." *Proceedings of the Massachusetts Historical Society* 18 (December 1903): 83–85.
Hart, "Revere"

———. "Some Notes Concerning John Norman, Engraver." *Proceedings of the Massachusetts Historical Society* 18 (October 1904): 394–396.
Hart, "Norman"

Honour, Hugh. *The New Golden Land: European Images of America from the Discoveries to the Present Time.* New York: Pantheon, 1975.

Hough, Franklin B. *Washingtoniana: Or, Memorials of the Death of George Washington.* 2 vols. Roxbury, Mass.: Printed for W. E. Woodward, 1865.

Howard, John Tasker. *Our American Music.* New York: Crowell, 1965.

Ide, John Jay. "Design of Event Handkerchief Unknown to Collectors Found." *New York Sun,* April 29, 1933.
Ide, "Handkerchief"

———. *The Portraits of John Jay.* New York: New York Historical Society, 1938.
Ide, *Jay*

Jacobs, Phoebe Lloyd. "John James Barralet and the Apotheosis of George Washington." *Winterthur Portfolio* 12 (1977): 115–137.

Jaffe, Irma B. *John Trumbull: Patriot-Artist of the American Revolution.* Boston: New York Graphic Society, 1975.

Johnston, Elizabeth Bryant. *Original Portraits of Washington.* Boston: James R. Osgood, 1882.

Kelby, William, comp. *Notes on American Artists, 1754–1820: Copied from Advertisements Appearing in the Newspapers of the Day.* New York: New-York Historical Society, 1922.

Kimball, Fiske. "Joseph Wright and His Portraits of Washington: Paintings and Engravings." *Antiques* 15 (May 1929): 376–382.
Kimball, "Wright, Paintings and Engravings"

———. "Joseph Wright and His Portraits of Washington: Sculpture." *Antiques* 17 (January 1930): 34–39.

Kimball, "Wright, Sculpture"

Lane, Gladys R. "Rhode Island's Earliest Engraver." *Antiques* 7 (March 1925): 133–137.

Last Will and Testament of George Washington and Schedule of His Property. Edited by John C. Fitzpatrick. [Mount Vernon]: Mount Vernon Ladies' Association of the Union, [1960].

Lefèvre, Edwin. "Washington Historical Kerchiefs." *Antiques* 36 (July 1939): 14–17.

Leopold-Sharp, Lynne A. "The Emergence of American Identity: Words and Images on Paper." In *Treasures of Independence National Historical Park and Its Collections.* Edited by John C. Milley. New York: Mayflower Books, 1980.

Libby, Orin Grant. "Some Pseudo Histories of the American Revolution." *Transactions of the Wisconsin Academy of Sciences, Arts and Letters* 13 (1900): 419–425.

Lincoln, Natalie Sumner. "Engraved Portraits of American Patriots Made by Saint Memin in 1796–1810." *Daughters of the American Revolution Magazine* 49 (1915): 157–162.

Linton, William James. *The History of Wood-Engraving in America.* Boston: Estes and Lauriat, 1882.

Littlefield, George Emery. *Early Schools and School-Books of New England.* New York: Russell & Russell, 1965.

Loubat, Joseph Florimond. *The Medallic History of the United States of America, 1776–1876.* 1878. Reprint. New Milford, Conn.: Flayderman, 1967.

MacNeil, Neil. *The President's Medal, 1789–1977.* New York: Clarkson N. Potter, in association with the National Portrait Gallery, 1977.

Marks, Arthur S. "The Statue of King George III in New York and the Iconology of Regicide." *American Art Journal* 13 (Summer 1981): 61–82.

McCorison, Marcus A., comp. *Vermont Imprints, 1778–1820.* Worcester: American Antiquarian Society, 1963.

Mitchell, James Tyndale. *Collection of Engraved Portraits of Washington Belonging to Hon. James T. Mitchell.* [Philadelphia, 1906.]

Mitchell Catalogue

Mitchell, Stewart, ed. "New Letters of Abigail Adams, Part II, 1798–1801." *Proceedings of the American Antiquarian Society* 55 (October 1945): 299–444.

S. Mitchell

Montgomery, Florence. *Printed Textiles: English and American Cottons and Linens, 1700–1850.* New York: Viking, 1970.

Morgan, John Hill. "The Work of M. Fevret de Saint-Memin." *Brooklyn Museum Quarterly* 5 (January 1918): 5–26.

——— and Mantle Fielding. *The Life Portraits of Washington and Their Replicas.* Philadelphia: Printed for the Subscribers, 1931.

Mott, Frank Luther. *A History of American Magazines: 1741–1850.* Vol. 1. Cambridge, Mass.: Harvard University Press, Belknap Press, 1966.

Munn, Charles Allen. *Three Types of Washington Portraits.* New York: Privately printed, 1908.

Newman, Eric P. *Bicentennial Edition of the Early Paper Money of America.* Racine, Wisc.: Western Publishing Co., 1976.

Norfleet, Fillmore. *Saint-Mémin in Virginia: Portraits and Biographies.* Richmond: Dietz Press, 1942.

Ormsbee, Thomas Hamilton. "Amos Doolittle Originated Chain of States Design." *American Collector* 11 (August 1942): 5 ff.

Paltsits, Victor Hugo. *Washington's Farewell Address in Facsimile with Transliterations.* New York: New York Public Library, 1935.

Philadelphia: Three Centuries of American Art. Philadelphia: Philadelphia Museum of Art, 1976.

Piers, Harry. *Robert Field: Portrait Painter in Oils, Miniature and Water-Colours and Engraver.* New York: Frederic Fairchild Sherman, 1927.

Portrait Miniatures in Early American History: 1750–1840. Shreveport, La.: R. W. Norton Art Gallery, 1976.

Potts, William John. "Du Simitière, Artist, Antiquary, and Naturalist: Projector of the First American Museum, with Some Extracts from His Notebook." *Pennsylvania Magazine of History and Biography* 13 (October 1889): 341–375.

Prime, Alfred Coxe, comp. *The Arts and Crafts in Philadelphia, Maryland and South Carolina.* 2 parts. New York: Da Capo, 1969.

Quimby, Maureen O'Brien. "The Political Art of James Akin." *Winterthur Portfolio* 7 (1971): 59–112.

Reid, Robert William and Charles Rollinson. *William Rollinson, Engraver.* New York: Privately printed, 1931.

Reilly, Elizabeth Carroll. *A Dictionary of Colonial American Printers' Ornaments and Illustrations.* Worcester: American Antiquarian Society, 1975.

Richardson, Edgar P. "Charles Willson Peale's Engravings in the Year of National Crisis, 1787." *Winterthur Portfolio* 1 (1964): 166–181.

> E. P. Richardson

Richardson, George. *Iconology, or a Collection of Emblematical Figures.* Based on Cesare Ripa, *Iconologia* (1593). 2 vols. London: G. Scott, 1779.

> G. Richardson

Richardson, Lyon N. *A History of Early American Magazines, 1741–1789.* New York: Thomas Nelson, 1931.

> L. N. Richardson

Rosenbach, Abraham Simon Wolf. *Early American Children's Books.* 1933. Reprint. New York: Kraus Reprint, 1966.

Sabin, Joseph. *A Dictionary of Books Relating to America, from Its Discovery to the Present Time.* 29 vols. 1868. Reprint (29 vols. in 2). New York: Mini-Print, 1963–1967.

Schorsch, Anita. "Mourning Art: A Neoclassical Reflection in America." *American Art Journal* 8 (May 1976): 4–15.

> Schorsch, "Mourning Art"

———. *Mourning Becomes America: Mourning Art in the New Nation.* Clinton, N.J.: Main Street Press, 1976.

> Schorsch, *Mourning Becomes America*

Sellers, Charles Coleman. *The Artist of the Revolution: The Early Life of Charles Willson Peale.* Vol. 1. Hebron, Conn.: Feather and Good, 1939.

> Sellers

———. *Charles Willson Peale.* New York: Scribner's, 1969.

> Sellers, *Peale*

———. *Charles Willson Peale with Patron and Populace: A Supplement to "Portraits and Miniatures by Charles Willson Peale."* Transactions of the American Philosophical Society, Vol. 59, Part 3. Philadelphia: American Philosophical Society, 1969.

> Sellers, *Supplement*

———. *Portraits and Miniatures by Charles Willson Peale.* Transactions of the American Philosophical Society, Vol. 42, Part 1. 1952. Reprint. Philadelphia: American Philosophical Society, 1968.

> Sellers, *Portraits*

Shadwell, Wendy J. *American Printmaking: The First*

150 Years. Washington, D.C.: Smithsonian Institution Press for the Museum of Graphic Art, 1969.

> Shadwell, *American Printmaking*

———. "An Attribution for His Excellency and Lady Washington." *Antiques* 95 (February 1969): 240–241.

> Shadwell, "An Attribution"

———. "The Portrait Engravings of Charles Willson Peale." In *Eighteenth-Century Prints in Colonial America: To Educate and Decorate.* Edited by Joan D. Dolmetsch. Williamsburg: Colonial Williamsburg Foundation, 1979.

> Shadwell, "Peale"

Shipton, Clifford K. and James E. Mooney. *National Index of American Imprints through 1800: The Short-Title Evans.* 2 vols. Worcester: American Antiquarian Society and Barre Publishers, 1960.

Simmons, Linda Crocker. *Charles Peale Polk, 1776–1822.* Washington: Corcoran Gallery of Art, 1981.

Sizer, Theodore. *The Works of Colonel John Trumbull.* New Haven and London: Yale University Press, 1967.

Skeel, Emily Ellsworth Ford, comp. *A Bibliography of the Writings of Noah Webster.* Edited by Edwin H. Carpenter, Jr. New York: New York Public Library and Arno Press, 1958.

Smith, James Morton, ed. *George Washington: A Profile.* New York: Hill and Wang, 1969.

Sommer, Frank H. "Thomas Hollis and the Arts of Dissent." In *Prints in and of America to 1850.* Edited by John D. Morse. Charlottesville: University Press of Virginia for the Winterthur Museum, 1970.

> Sommer, "Hollis"

———. "The Metamorphosis of Britannia." In *American Art and American Culture.* Edited by Charles F. Montgomery and Patricia E. Kane. New Haven: New York Graphic Society for the Yale University Art Gallery, 1976.

> Sommer, "Britannia"

Sonneck, Oscar George Theodore. *A Bibliography of Early Secular American Music.* Revised and enlarged by William Treat Upton. 1945. Reprint. New York: Da Capo, 1964.

> Sonneck and Upton

———. "The First Edition of 'Hail Columbia.'" In *Miscellaneous Studies of the History of Music.* New York: Macmillan, 1921.

> Sonneck, "Hail Columbia"

———. *Report on "The Star-Spangled Banner," "Hail*

Columbia," "America," "Yankee Doodle." Washington, D.C.: Library of Congress, 1909.

Sonneck, Report

Sparks, Jared, ed. *The Writings of George Washington.* 12 vols. 1834–1837. New York: Harper & Brothers, 1847–1848.

Stauffer, David McNeely. *American Engravers upon Copper and Steel.* Parts 1 and 2. New York: Burt Franklin, 1961.

Stewart, Robert G. *Robert Edge Pine: A British Portrait Painter in America, 1784–1788.* Washington, D.C.: Smithsonian Institution Press for the National Portrait Gallery, 1979.

Stillwell, Margaret Bingham, comp. "Washington Eulogies: A Checklist of Eulogies and Funeral Orations on the Death of George Washington." *Bulletin of the New York Public Library* (February and May 1916).

Stokes, I. N. Phelps. *The Iconography of Manhattan Island.* 6 vols. New York: Robert H. Dodd, 1915.

———— and Daniel C. Haskell. *American Historical Prints, Early Views of American Cities, etc.* New York: New York Public Library, 1932.

Storer, Malcolm. "The Manly Washington Medal." *Proceedings of the Massachusetts Historical Society* 52 (1918–1919): 6–7.

Taylor, Joshua C. *America as Art.* Washington, D.C.: Smithsonian Institution Press for the National Collection of Fine Arts, 1976.

Thorpe, Russell Walton. "Washingtoniana." *The Antiquarian* 8 (June 1927): 27–30.

Trumbull, John. *Autobiography, Reminiscences and Letters of John Trumbull from 1756 to 1841.* New York and London: Wiley and Putnam; New Haven: B. L. Hamlen, 1841.

Waddell, Roberta. "George Washington: His Life and Times: A Selection from a Prints Division Exhibition." *Bulletin of the New York Public Library* 79 (Winter 1976): 193–202.

Warren, William L. "Richard Brunton—Itinerant Craftsman." *Art in America* 39 (April 1951): 81–94.

Watkins, Walter Kendall. "John Coles, Heraldry Painter." *Old Time New England* 21 (January 1931): 129–143.

Wecter, Dixon. *The Hero in America: A Chronicle of Hero-Worship.* Ann Arbor: University of Michigan Press, Ann Arbor Paperbacks, 1963.

Weems, Mason Locke. *Mason Locke Weems, His Works and Ways.* Edited by Emily Ellsworth Ford Skeel; 1st vol. compiled but not finished by Paul Leicester Ford. 3 vols. New York: n.p., 1929.

Weiss, Harry B. "John Norman, Engraver, Publisher, Bookseller. . . ." *Bulletin of the New York Public Library* 38 (January 1934): 3–14.

Weitenkampf, Frank. *American Graphic Art.* 1912. Reprint. Detroit: Gale Research Company, 1974.

Whelen, Henry, Jr. *The Important Collection of Engraved Portraits of Washington Belonging to the Late Henry Whelen, Jr.* [Philadelphia: Press of M. H. Power, 1909.]

Checklist of the Exhibition

☆   ☆   ☆

The catalogue number is given in brackets at the end of each entry.

1. "The Glorious Washington and Gates," c. 1775
   Unidentified artist, relief cut in Benjamin West, *Bickerstaff's Boston Almanack for . . . 1778* (Danvers, [1777])
   National Portrait Gallery [1]

2. George Washington, c. 1775
   Unidentified artist, relief cut on [Jonathan Mitchell Sewall] *Washington: A Favorite New Song in the American Camp* (Danvers, [c. 1778])
   Massachusetts Historical Society [1]

3. "Washington," 1778
   Unidentified artist, relief cut in David Rittenhouse, *Der gantz neue verbesserte nord-americanische Calender, auf das 1779ste Jahr* (Lancaster, [1778])
   National Portrait Gallery [3]

4. "His Excellency George Washington Esqr."
   Attributed to Joseph Hiller, Sr., after Charles Willson Peale, mezzotint, c. 1777
   Private Collection [2]

5. "His Excellency General Washington"
   Attributed to John Norman after Charles Willson Peale, engraving, c. 1779
   Historical Society of Pennsylvania [4]

6. "His Excellency Genl. Washington," 1779
   John Norman after Charles Willson Peale, engraving in *Philadelphia Almanack for . . . 1780* (Philadelphia, [1779])
   Special Collections Department, A. S. Alexander Library, Rutgers University [5]

7. George Washington, 1780
   Attributed to Paul Revere after Charles Willson Peale, relief cut in *The New England Primer* (Boston, [1789])
   Library of Congress [6]

8. "Farmer Washington," 1785
   Unidentified artist after Charles Willson Peale, relief cut in *The Citizen and Farmer's Almanac for 1799* (Philadelphia, [1798])
   Boston Public Library [7]

9. George Washington, 1790
   Unidentified artist after Charles Willson Peale, relief cut in *The Federal Almanack for . . . 1792* (Boston, [1791])
   National Portrait Gallery [8]

10. George Washington, 1797
    Unidentified artist after Charles Willson Peale, relief cut in Samuel Ivins' *The Columbian Almanac, for . . . 1798* (Philadelphia, [1797])
    National Portrait Gallery [10]

11. George Washington, c. 1789
    Unidentified artist after Charles Willson Peale, relief cut in *The Death of Washington: Or, Columbia in Mourning for Her Son* [c. 1800]
    Massachusetts Historical Society [9]

12. "His Excellcy George Washington, Esqr."
    John Norman after Benjamin Blyth and Charles Willson Peale, engraving, 1782
    New York Public Library [15]

13. "The True Portraiture of his Excellency George Washington Esqr." John Norman after Charles Willson Peale, engraving, c. 1783
    New York Public Library [17]

14. George Washington, 1784
    John Norman after Charles Willson Peale, engraving in *The Boston Magazine* (April 1784)
    Library of Congress [19]

15. "His Excellency Genl. Washington"
    Robert Scot after Charles Willson Peale, engraving, c. 1780
    Private Collection [12]

16. "His Excellency George Washington Esquire"
    Charles Willson Peale, mezzotint, 1780
    National Portrait Gallery [11]

17. "His Excel: G: Washington Esq:"
Charles Willson Peale, mezzotint, 1787
Private Collection [21]

18. "His Excel: G: Washington Esq."
Attributed to James Trenchard after Charles Willson Peale, engraving, 1787
Historical Society of Pennsylvania [22]

19. "Display of the United States of America" (state four, 1791)
Amos Doolittle after Joseph Wright, engraving, c. 1788–1789
Private Collection [25]

20. "G. Washington"
Joseph Wright, etching with drypoint, c. 1790
New York Public Library [26]

21. "G Washington"
James Manly after Joseph Wright, engraving, c. 1790
Historical Society of Pennsylvania [27]

22. "G. Washington"
Joseph Hiller, Jr., after Joseph Wright, etching with drypoint, 1794
New York Public Library [37]

23. "George Washington Esqr."
Edward Savage, engraving, 1792
National Portrait Gallery [31]

24. "George Washington Esqr."
Edward Savage, mezzotint, 1793
National Portrait Gallery [33]

25. "The Washington Family"
Edward Savage and David Edwin, after Edward Savage, c. 1790–1798
National Portrait Gallery [55]

26. "His Excellency Gen. Washington," 1795
Unidentified artist, relief cut in History of America, Abridged for the Use of Children (Philadelphia, 1795)
Historical Society of Pennsylvania [41]

27. "Genl. Washington," 1794
Unidentified artist after John Trumbull, relief cut in [Jedidiah Morse] The Life of General Washington (Philadelphia, 1794)
Historical Society of Pennsylvania [38]

28. "The President of the United States," 1791
Unidentified artist after Joseph Wright, engraving in The Massachusetts Magazine (March 1791)
Library of Congress [28]

29. "Genl. Washington"
Elkanah Tisdale, engraving in Charles Smith, Monthly Military Repository (New York, 1796)
New York Public Library [43]

30. "George Washington, President of the United States of America"
Samuel Hill after Edward Savage, engraving in George Washington, Official Letters to the Honorable American Congress (Boston, 1796)
Library of Congress [46]

31. "George Washington, President of the United Stataes"
Robert Field after Walter Robertson and John James Barralet, engraving, 1795
Historical Society of Pennsylvania [39]

32. "General Washington, President of the United States"
H. Houston after John James Barralet, engraving, c. 1796–1798
New York Public Library [48]

33. "General Washington's Resignation," 1799
Alexander Lawson after John James Barralet, engraving in The Philadelphia Magazine and Review (January 1799)
Library of Congress [65]

34. "George Washington Esqr."
David Edwin after Gilbert Stuart, engraving, 1798
Stanley D. Scott [56]

35. "His Excellency George Washington"
David Edwin after F. Bartoli and Gilbert Stuart, engraving, c. 1798
Stanley D. Scott [61]

36. "Washington, Sacred to Memory"
David Edwin after F. Bartoli, Gilbert Stuart, and John James Barralet, engraving, c. 1798–1800
Stanley D. Scott [61]

37. "Sacred to Patriotism"
Cornelius Tiebout after Gilbert Stuart and Charles Buxton, engraving, 1798
Mount Vernon Ladies' Association [62]

38. George Washington
John Roberts after Gilbert Stuart, mezzotint, 1799
Historical Society of Pennsylvania [66]

39. George Washington, 1797
Unidentified artist, engraving in The Nightingale of Liberty (New York, 1797)
Library of Congress [52]

40. G. Washington, 1797
Unidentified artist, after Joseph Wright, engraving in The Battle of Trenton: A Sonata (New York, Philadelphia, and Baltimore, [1797])
New York Public Library [53]

41. George Washington, 1797
Unidentified artist, after Joseph Wright, engraving in New Yankee Doodle (New York, Philadelphia, and Baltimore, [1797–1798])
Library of Congress [53]

42. George Washington, 1798
Attributed to David Edwin after Gilbert Stuart, engraving in Joseph Hopkinson, *The Favorite New Federal Song* (Philadelphia, [1798])
Library of Congress [57]

43. George Washington, 1798
Attributed to David Edwin after Gilbert Stuart, engraving on Benjamin Carr, *Dead March and Monody* [Baltimore, 1799]
National Portrait Gallery [57]

44. "George Washington"
Cornelius Tiebout after Gilbert Stuart, engraving, 1800
Historical Society of Pennsylvania [68]

45. "General George Washington"
David Edwin after Rembrandt Peale, engraving, 1800
National Portrait Gallery [86]

46. George Washington
Charles Balthazar Julien Févret de Saint-Mémin, engraved copperplate and restrike, 1800
National Portrait Gallery [74]

47. George Washington
Charles Balthazar Julien Févret de Saint-Mémin, engraving in mourning ring, 1800
Frank S. Schwarz and Son [74]

48. George Washington, 1800
Unidentified artist after Joseph Wright, relief cut in Michael Houdin's *Et Sicut Illud Statutem est Hominibus . . . A Funeral Oration on . . . Washington* (Albany, [1800])
Historical Society of Pennsylvania [97]

49. "Immortal Washington," 1800
Unidentified artist after Joseph Wright, relief cut in Mason Locke Weems, *The Life and Memorable Actions of George Washington* [Baltimore, 1800]
Historical Society of Pennsylvania [91]

50. "G. Washington," 1800
Benjamin Tanner after Gilbert Stuart, engraving in Mason Locke Weems, *A History of the Life and Death . . . of General George Washington* (Philadelphia, 1800)
Library of Congress [93]

51. "Washington," 1800
Amos Doolittle after Joseph Wright, copperplate and restrike for banknotes, 1800
Washington Trust Company, Westerly, Rhode Island [83]

52. "America Lamenting her Loss at the Tomb of General Washington"
James Akin and William Harrison, Jr., after James Sharples, engraving, 1800
Stanley D. Scott [70]

53. George Washington
Unidentified artist after Gilbert Stuart, etching, 1800
Mount Vernon Ladies' Association [72]

54. "G. Washington in his Last Illness"
Unidentified artist, etching, 1800
Mount Vernon Ladies' Association [73]

55. "Genl. George Washington"
William Hamlin after Edward Savage, mezzotint, 1800
Historical Society of Pennsylvania [77]

56. George Washington
Enoch G. Gridley after John Coles, Jr., and Edward Savage, engraving, 1800
Historical Society of Pennsylvania [81]

57. "Apotheosis of Washington"
David Edwin after Rembrandt Peale, engraving, 1800
National Portrait Gallery [87]

58. "Sacred to the Memory of Washington"
John James Barralet after Gilbert Stuart, engraving, 1800–1802
Historical Society of Pennsylvania [101]

Index

☆ ☆ ☆